Reclaiming Discipline for Education

Discipline is of profound educational importance, both inside educational institutions and outside of them in personal and social life. *Reclaiming Discipline for Education* revisits neglected philosophical ideas about discipline in education and uses these ideas to re-think practices and discourses of discipline in education today.

Chapters in this book trace the evolution of thought regarding discipline in education all the way from Kant through to Durkheim, Foucault, Peters, Dewey and Macmurray. MacAllister also critically examines the strengths and weaknesses of contemporary school discipline practices in the UK, the US and Australia, including behaviour management, zero tolerance and restorative approaches. The educational credentials of psychological constructs of grit and self-discipline are also questioned.

This book concludes by considering the current and future state of discipline in education on the basis of the different philosophical, practical and policy perspectives discussed. In particular, MacAllister examines why it is problematic to consider practices of discipline in isolation from the wider purposes of education. This book is suitable for an international audience and should be read by anyone who is interested in education and educational leadership, as well as those interested in the philosophy of education.

James MacAllister is Lecturer in Philosophy of Education at the University of Edinburgh, UK.

Reclaiming Discipline for Education

Knowledge, relationships and the birth of community

James MacAllister

LONDON AND NEW YORK

First published 2017
by Routledge
2 Park Square, Milton Park, Abingdon, Oxon OX14 4RN

and by Routledge
711 Third Avenue, New York, NY 10017

First issued in paperback 2018

Routledge is an imprint of the Taylor & Francis Group, an informa business

© 2017 J. MacAllister

The right of J. MacAllister to be identified as author of this work has been asserted by him in accordance with sections 77 and 78 of the Copyright, Designs and Patents Act 1988.

All rights reserved. No part of this book may be reprinted or reproduced or utilised in any form or by any electronic, mechanical, or other means, now known or hereafter invented, including photocopying and recording, or in any information storage or retrieval system, without permission in writing from the publishers.

Trademark notice: Product or corporate names may be trademarks or registered trademarks, and are used only for identification and explanation without intent to infringe.

British Library Cataloguing in Publication Data
A catalogue record for this book is available from the British Library

Library of Congress Cataloging in Publication Data
Names: MacAllister, James, author.
Title: Reclaiming discipline for education : knowledge, relationships and the birth of community / James MacAllister.
Description: New York, NY : Routledge, 2016. | Includes bibliographical references.
Identifiers: LCCN 2016025166 | ISBN 9781138900721 (hardback) | ISBN 9781315707099 (ebook)
Subjects: LCSH: School discipline.
Classification: LCC LB3012 .M33 2016 | DDC 371.5—dc23
LC record available at https://lccn.loc.gov/2016025166

ISBN 13: 978-1-138-60256-4 (pbk)
ISBN 13: 978-1-138-90072-1 (hbk)

Typeset in Sabon
by Apex CoVantage, LLC

For Sarah

Contents

	A note on this book and acknowledgements	viii
1	What is discipline? What should it be for in education?	1
2	Discipline in recent education policy and practice	13
3	Rules, education and moral development	32
4	Discipline and punishment in education	49
5	Disciplines of knowledge, disciplined interests and student agency	68
6	Relationships, community and personal discipline	87
7	Restorative approaches to school discipline	107
8	Discipline in education: The birth of community	125
	Bibliography	144
	Index	155

A note on this book and acknowledgements

This book aims to revisit some neglected philosophical ideas about discipline in education. However, it also seeks to use some of these philosophical ideas to think again about practices and discourses of discipline in education today. As such I hope the book might be of interest to: teachers, student teachers, education students, parents, education policy makers, teacher educators and other education scholars, philosophers, philosophers of education, scholars of Foucault, theorists of power and authority relations and perhaps, other persons besides these. It was not always easy writing for such a diverse audience. Difficult decisions needed to be made about what to include and what not to. For example, while I take discipline in education to be important in all contexts of learning, I have tended to focus on discipline in schools in this book (though I do in places consider other places of learning too, including universities and colleges). I may not always have got the balance right between a focus on philosophy or on education or on the intersection between the two either – though I hope I have in most instances. In the end I decided to write the book so that it could be read in different ways. Readers may decide they want to dip in to a particular chapter or they may decide to read the whole book. Both such readings of the book should be possible. Each chapter is intended to build upon those that precede it. I hope readers can see there is a clear narrative thread across the book and between chapters. However, each chapter does tell its own story too.

Chapter 1 provides an overview of the main arguments chapter by chapter. If readers only want to read parts of the book, this chapter may help them find their bearings about where to start. Readers most interested in education policy and practice may be particularly drawn to chapters 2 and 7 where I explore the pros and cons of behaviour management, zero tolerance and restorative approaches to school discipline. Conversely, readers most interested in the philosophies of discipline developed by Kant, Foucault and Durkheim may want to begin with chapters 3 and 4. Readers most intrigued by the concepts of discipline and education developed by Macmurray or Dewey may prefer to start with chapter 6. However, I would encourage all readers to have a look at the last chapter too. There I try to synthesise some conclusions about the current and future state of discipline in education on the basis of the different philosophical, practical and policy perspectives discussed in the book. One of my main concerns in the book is to elucidate why it is problematic to consider practices of discipline in isolation from the wider purposes of education. Indeed, I argue that students and communities stand to benefit from educators thinking more systematically about the *purposes* of school discipline. I think some of the philosophies of discipline in education explored in the book might help in this respect.

Even if readers are most interested in education policy and practice, I would nonetheless urge them to look at some of the more philosophical aspects of the book. I urge this as I think education policy and practice in respect to discipline can be improved by becoming a little more philosophical. Indeed, in the book I argue that discipline in education can help to promote community but only if many current practices are significantly altered. While it may seem a little odd to juxtapose ideas of discipline with ideas of community, there is a neglected philosophical literature (explored in the book) that does just this. In this respect, the title of the book is intended to capture the core ideas explored in the book. However, the title is also intended to be a play on Michel Foucault's influential text *Discipline and Punish: The Birth of the Prison*. Foucault's text does shine a light on some of the ways in which educational institutions use technologies of discipline to 'imprison' persons. However, it does not really offer any positive suggestions about how discipline (in education or elsewhere) may become less imprisoning. One of the main aims of this book is to provoke thought about how discipline in education may be directed towards human community rather than human imprisonment.

This book has been nearly ten years in the making. I began thinking seriously about discipline in education in 2007 when I enrolled on a PhD programme at The University of Edinburgh. Many of the ideas covered in this book were first developed during my doctoral studies. However, a number of them also emerged after I completed my doctorate in 2010 when working, first at the University of Manchester then at the University of Stirling, before finally returning to the University of Edinburgh again. Countless colleagues, students and friends have helped to refine and develop my thinking on the topic of discipline in education during the past ten years. Some have offered insight at a seminar or over a coffee, a number have suggested readings, more still have offered in depth critical comment on particular passages and sections of this book. I am grateful to everyone who has supported the evolution of this text – there are too many to mention. However, I would like to thank a few people in particular who have really gone out of their way to help me.

Quite simply this book would not have been possible without the unstinting support of Gale Macleod and David Carr. Thank you both for your time and for the knowledge you tried to pass on to me during my doctoral studies and indeed beyond. I would also like to thank Bob Davis, Morwenna Griffiths, Richard Smith, Shereen Benjamin, Robbie Nicol, Gillean McCluskey, Ed Sellman, Llinos Couch, Hilary Cremin, Anne Pirrie, Richard Pring,

x *A note on this book and acknowledgements*

Pete Allison, Malcolm Thorburn, Simon Beames, Mike Jess, John Ravenscroft, Pauline Sangster, Lindsay Paterson, Adrian Martinez, Michalis Kakos, Lesley Fox, Linda Ahlgren, Fiona O'Hanlon and Pamela Munn. Your critical feedback and encouragement was greatly appreciated at different phases of my doctoral studies. A number of persons also supported me during my time at the University of Manchester. In no particular order I would like to thank Chris Chapman, Helen Gunter, Dave Hall, Steven Courtney, Mel Ainscow, Mel West, James Duggan, Maija Salokangas, Kristján Kristjánsson, and Lynsey Halliday. There were also a number of persons who really challenged and extended my thinking during my time at the University of Stirling (again too many to mention but I am grateful to all of you!). Sincere thanks then to Ben Williamson, Shari Sabeti, Richard Edwards, Tara Fenwick, Mark Priestley, Adel Bawazeer, Fiona Copland, Gert Biesta, Julie Allan, John Field, Steven Stolz, Neal McGowan and John I'Anson. Here I would like to give special mention to Ian Munday for whose friendship, humour and insight I have been consistently grateful.

I would particularly like to thank the *Journal of Moral Education Trust* whose generous grant greatly aided the development of this book, especially the philosophical chapters and case study. I would also like to thank the publishers of *Educational Studies, Journal of Philosophy of Education* and *Educational Philosophy and Theory*. Revised sections of papers previously included in these journals feature in this book so I am grateful for the publisher permission here.[1] I am also grateful to Paul Standish, Judith Suissa, Jan Derry, Dave Aldridge, Richard Davies, Josie Booth, Michael Fielding, Mary Healy, Carrie Winstanley, Andrea English, Jen Ross, Debi Fry, Rowena Arshad, Judith Kafka and Ken Reid for helping develop my views regarding the need to reclaim the concept of discipline in education. I would also like to offer heartfelt thanks to the staff and students at Paddington Primary, all of whom went out of their way to make me feel welcome in the school. This book really benefitted from having some of your voices included. I am also thankful I have had the chance to learn from and with a number of trusted friends (again too many to mention) including Hugh Fraser, Martin Wilson, Leona Benson and Jonathan Briggs. Finally, I would like to thank all in the extended MacAllister clan (but especially my Mum & Dad, Paul, Karen and Sarah) for their time, effort, inspiration, constancy and understanding.

James MacAllister
May 2016

Note

1 These papers are MacAllister, J. (2014) Why discipline needs to be reclaimed as an educational concept, *Educational Studies*, 40 (4), 438–451; MacAllister, J. (2014) Education for personal life: John MacMurray on why learning to be human requires emotional discipline, *Journal of Philosophy of Education*, 48 (1), 118–136; MacAllister, J. (2013) School discipline, educational interest and pupil wisdom, *Educational Philosophy and Theory*, 45 (1), 20–35.

1 What is discipline? What should it be for in education?

Erin: Have you heard what *she* did in Bill's class today? She peed on some bog roll before coming to his class and then threw it at Samantha Collins. It hit her right in the face too. The other kids went nutty and they had to call the police in.

Tim: It's outrageous. She's gone too far this time – kick her out – that's what I say. A message needs to be sent out that this behaviour won't be tolerated. Once one of them thinks they can get away with something like this, then others will too.

Mary: I can see what the fuss is about but what will happen to Zoe if she's expelled? What good will punishment do *for her*? Zoe needs our care and understanding – not our judgement and punishment. She has a tough lot at home – we all know that. It's not good what Zoe did but what other school will take her if she gets expelled? Once a kid gets expelled their future prospects get pretty grim. Zoe is not all bad.

Duncan: Zoe has always been fine in my class. She has no discipline problems. I'd even say that sometimes she loves learning from poems and stories. Is part of the problem not just that she finds maths a little bit boring? And let's be honest – lots of kids act up in Bill's class. We all know his teaching is . . . well . . . a bit dull. She is acting up as we are making her take a subject she does not enjoy with a teacher who does not care about teaching kids he thinks will flunk the exam.

Mary: Zoe is not stupid. She knows the exams are coming up and she knows that she is never going to do maths again in her life. She does not need to pass the exam and that is all Bill talks about in his lessons. If it was taught differently she might not be so off the wall in his class.

Tim: Why are we blaming Bill? It was not Bill that made her do that. *She* did it. Teachers get a hard enough time as it is – it's the government that says we must get five A's for 75% of kids. . . .

Duncan: Or else we will be closed and converted into one of those awful new academies. They are like military barracks those ones – every lesson has to have five key points that are covered in the exams or else you get a telling off from the sponsors of the school. They have rules for everything, rewards and sanctions everywhere and no room for laughter, joy or individuality. At least Bill would fit in.

Tim: (exasperated) Oh stop it Duncan . . . Bill's not so bad. He is doing his best. We all are. Anyway, he is not the problem – *she* is.

Erin: I think Tim is right. Zoe needs to learn it's not all about her. She needs to learn that she just cannot treat other people like that and get away with it. She needs to learn that life is rarely about doing what we want. Why should her needs and wants be more important than the majority that are well behaved? She caused mayhem today. Besides, this is bigger than Zoe. There is a crisis of discipline in this school, in lots of schools, and it won't be solved until we get tough with kids like Zoe and show them who is boss.

Schools test students, but what is learned when students test schools?

There is a crisis of discipline in a great many schools. In this I agree with Erin, the teacher at the heart of this fictional school staffroom discussion. However, unlike Erin, I do not think the answer resides in getting 'tough' with unruly students. I actually think it is profoundly unhelpful to regard individual students as being **the cause** of incidents of indiscipline in schools. I think 'misbehaviour' in school is a symptom rather than a cause of the 'crisis'. Student indiscipline is one symptom of a much wider and more pervasive problem. The real crisis of discipline in education is not one of student misbehaviour. The real crisis concerns fundamental confusion over the purposes that school discipline serves and those it **ought** to. Discipline in education ought to serve a variety of diverse *educational* purposes. Instead it increasingly serves a narrow agenda of training, control, punishment and examination. The real crisis of discipline in education concerns the extent to which so many formal institutions of learning have confused the ends of examination and education. It should go without saying that examination and education are not the same thing. One can pass an exam and yet fail to be educated in many important senses of the term. Similarly, one can be very learned in a subject and yet never have sat, let alone passed, a formal examination in it. Most people probably know this, yet too many institutions of education today proceed as if exams are what really count when all is said and done. Might some students not have figured this out and decided learning focussed on examinations is not for them? This is what Mary in the foregoing scenario invites us to think about.

Might it not be possible that students like Zoe disengage with education and act up in schools in part because they have concluded their schooling will not help them to get on in life?[1] Note that in raising these issues I am not saying that educators like Tim and Erin are wholly mistaken. They are not. Schools do need to socialise students and prepare them for life after school. Making students aware of social norms and of others is an essential (but certainly not the only) function of schooling. Neither am I saying that exams cause student indiscipline. That would be much too simplistic an explanation for student 'misbehaviour' that would in many cases also be inaccurate. Nor I am saying that students would suddenly stop 'misbehaving' if we as a society collectively became a little less obsessed with test scores. What I am saying, however, is that schools are complex social institutions. What I am saying is that if there is a discipline issue in a complex social institution like a school, it is unlikely that only one person will be the sole cause of that issue. A range of factors will instead be at work, both personal and institutional. Yet too often individual students are punished in schools for incidents of indiscipline, while institutional practices remain unaltered. Opportunities for learning about students as *persons* are too often lost in a barrage of rules, sanctions and tests. Tests are important in educational institutions – of course they are. So are rules. Tests can help us know who knows what, and who does not. They can inform future teaching. They can help educators and prospective employers decide who might be ready to take on a particular challenge and who might not be. But in focussing on what might be learned about students through testing, have policy makers, parents, educators and educational institutions created conditions where it has become all but impossible to learn from students when *they test* the boundaries and rules in schools?

Part of growing up and becoming a person involves testing boundaries. Young people will probably always do this – inside schools and outside of them. Often this is no bad thing. Sometimes students will go too far when they test the boundaries. Yet too often this is labelled as a 'crisis'.[2] Educational institutions systematically test students, yet when students test the boundaries, too often they are punished in ways that have little to do with the ends of education. I am not saying school staff should ignore indiscipline – far from it. Instead I am saying that educators should treat discipline and indiscipline very seriously. More seriously than they often do. For me, being serious about discipline in education means recognising the complexity of persons and schools, colleges and universities. It means thinking about what discipline and education actually mean. It means thinking about whether educational institutions **should** discipline and punish students or not and why. It means thinking about what the purposes of discipline in education are and might be. It means thinking about what might be learned from incidents of indiscipline. It means eschewing easy answers like getting tough on pupils.

This book attempts to take the subject of discipline in education seriously. I do not seek to come up with easy answers to the myriad problems associated with discipline in education. I do not seek to come up with easy answers for I do not think there are any. Those of you looking for easy answers should stop reading now. If you are looking for easy answers I would suggest reading the work of Tom Bennett or Bill Rogers.[3] In this book I will instead try to think about what discipline and education mean. I will try to think about what the purposes of discipline in education are and might be. I will try to disentangle the differences between discipline and punishment. I will try to make some sense of the ways in which formal institutions of education might actually contribute to issues of indiscipline. Here I will suggest that excessively valuing examinations in education might not help many students to be disciplined. Nor too may prevalent disciplinary practices such as zero tolerance sanctions or behaviour management policies. However, rather than just critiquing some current policies and practices of discipline in education, this book also represents an attempt to consider how discipline might be reclaimed in education for the benefit of students, schools and wider society alike. Indeed, it is my argument that discipline can significantly contribute to the reclamation of education over examination. This introductory chapter will first explore different meanings of the concept of discipline in education before going on to summarise the key arguments in the book, chapter by chapter.

What does discipline mean in education?

Discipline has become something of a dirty word in education. This is both understandable and unfortunate. It is understandable as discipline in education is increasingly linked with examination on the one hand and regarded as synonymous with control and punishment on the other. It is unfortunate because (as I hope this book will show) there is more to discipline in education than examination, control and punishment. Discipline is not just about restraining, controlling, training, punishing or examining – it can also be a personal quality well worth educating. It was Foucault who in the latter half of the twentieth century first suggested that examinations can be regarded as the disciplinary technology par excellence within education systems.[4] However, discipline has had less than a favourable press with educationists since well before Foucault. Some two hundred years earlier Kant defined discipline as the essentially non-educational restraining of student unruliness.[5] These twin takes on discipline have become rather ingrained in the consciousness of many educators, students and parents, even those who have not read Foucault or Kant. I have much sympathy with Foucault here. There is too much examination, control and punishment in education. Punitive approaches to discipline have increasingly led to unfortunate educational consequences for many US high school students, as we shall see in Chapter 2. The fixation with examinations does not help many students engage with education either. However, that does not mean that *discipline, or a lack of it,* must cause or contribute to these problems. Discipline only causes or contributes to these problems if we agree with Foucault and Kant – that punishment, control and examination are about all there is to discipline. However, while discipline can mean punishment, control or examination, it can also mean much more than this.

At the level of etymology, there are at least two ways in which the term *discipline* is used: **external** discipline imposed in the army, or in schools, and the discipline *internal* to an academic subject or a musical or sporting or artistic practice. The Cambridge dictionary offers two such different definitions of discipline. Discipline as *training* and discipline as *a subject*. In respect to the former, discipline is explained as 'training that makes people more willing to obey or more able to control themselves, often in the form of rules, and punishments if these are broken, or the behaviour produced by this training'. The example given in the dictionary regarding *training*, is that the first task of every teacher is to learn how to discipline, i.e. *control* their class. However, according to the Cambridge dictionary, discipline can also be a very specific type of *academic* training – it can be more than control or self-control. Here discipline is a 'particular area of study, especially a subject studied at a college or university'.[6] Note, however, that whether discipline is conceived of as training and control, or internal to a particular academic body of knowledge, discipline is not essentially synonymous with either examination or punishment in dictionary definitions of the word. Discipline is more like control and training than punishment and examination in the dictionary definitions. Indeed, while punishment might sometimes result in a disciplinary situation gone awry, this only legitimately occurs if the rules have first been broken.

In this respect Richard Peters (1970) pointed out long ago that while **discipline** involves a pupil *observing* the rules of an activity, **punishment** is normally only justifiable when a student has *breached* the rules of such activity. Discipline and punishment are sometimes related then, but they are certainly not the same. Punishment usually only occurs after discipline has lapsed. Moreover, discipline in the sense of academic training is not the same as mere examination either. While someone might sit an examination near the end of a course of academic studies, there is no necessary connection between studying an academic discipline and sitting an examination in that discipline. Someone could spend a great deal of time being disciplined by a body of academic knowledge without ever being examined in it.[7] However, these dictionary definitions of discipline probably cannot take us that far. Discipline has taken on a variety of different meanings when related to education, some of which bear little resemblance to these dictionary definitions. To gain a deeper understanding of what discipline in education might mean, wider reflection upon the **nature and purposes** of discipline in education is needed. In this respect, there is a rich body of philosophical literature concerning the nature and purposes of discipline in education. A body of literature that has been regrettably neglected.[8] The aim of this book is to come to terms with some of this literature and to relate it to some contemporary educational challenges.

6 *What is discipline?*

The nature and purposes of discipline in education

A core purpose of educational institutions is preparing students for meaningful participation in social and economic life. Institutional disciplinary mechanisms such as examinations, school cultures and rules, play a key role in passing on ways of acting, being and knowing that are valued while discouraging types of knowing, being and acting that are not. Such institutional mechanisms may have important social and individual value and they may help to create conditions conducive for learning. However, discipline is not just something that is enacted by institutions and educators working in them. It also requires student effort. Indeed, discipline can be a valuable personal quality without which learners may lack the motivation, focus and structure to achieve the life goals to which they aspire. Discipline is then a matter of profound educational importance, both inside educational institutions (like schools, colleges and universities) and outside of them in personal and social life.

On the one hand, educational institutions do as a matter of fact discipline students for participation in social and economic life. For better and worse, institutional disciplinary mechanisms such as examinations, school cultures and rules greatly shape the school experiences of students. They also greatly shape who students might be and become. On the other hand, discipline can also be a personal quality of learners that can lead to positive change. Indeed, as we shall go on to see, without a personal sense and habit of discipline, learners may fail to make the most of their educational potential or be able to challenge social injustices when they are encountered. However, recent debate (at the levels of theory, policy and practice) marginalises opportunity for thought about *personal* discipline. Institutional, social and economic demands instead dominate discourses about discipline in education. This text therefore examines a variety of ways in which discipline has been and might be theorised and enacted in educational institutions, and it explores the wider social and personal importance of discipline in education. The argument will proceed as follows.

The order of the argument

Chapter 2 focuses on how discipline is constructed in education *policy* and *practice*. The bulk of the chapter is concerned to show how discourses of behaviour management and zero tolerance have recently dominated discipline policy and practice in the UK and the US respectively. It is claimed that behaviour management and zero tolerance approaches are both unhelpful as they 1) do not encourage students to take meaningful responsibility for their learning or behaviour in school; and 2) marginalise opportunity for the consideration of the wider educational purposes of school discipline. Such discipline policies and practices also give school staff too little incentive to care about the long-term destinations and life chances of individual students who misbehave. Here it is suggested that zero-tolerance approaches are especially worrying as they only seem to have negative long-term effects for individuals and communities, with minority youth being especially 'punished' by zero tolerance. It is concluded that zero tolerance and behavioural managerial approaches marginalise opportunity for reflection about the moral educational role of school discipline. These issues are taken up in subsequent chapters.

In chapter 3, the possible educational value of institutional rules and social norms is explored, as rules and social norms often drive processes of discipline in education. Initially, the ubiquity of rules in education is noted. It is acknowledged that rules can have great value in education. They can help students know what conduct is expected of them, both in school and in wider society. However, it is also argued that in too many instances for comfort, school rules don't work for the good of all students. In the chapter I map out three rules-based accounts of discipline in schools. Those of Kant, Durkheim and John Wilson. In different ways these scholars all held that discipline in schools: 1) is vital for moral education and development and; 2) should first and foremost initiate students into impersonal rules that apply to all, regardless of circumstance. I also argue that aspects of such thinking about discipline continues to be apparent in education policy and practice today – the best example of this being zero tolerance approaches in US schools. In this respect, though Kant thought discipline entailed a fundamentally *negative* restraining of student unruliness, he also thought education (and any discipline that is part of it) ought to aim at the future improvement of all of humanity via the cultivation of moral autonomy in persons. Zero tolerance approaches to discipline in contrast have no such noble (if naive) aspirations. I conclude the chapter by arguing that it is a conceptual error to think that impersonal rules-based approaches to discipline in education can work for the good of all. Unfortunately, this is a conceptual error that has all too often also become ingrained in educational policy and practice.

In chapter 4, I explore possible connections between discipline and punishment in education. I use the thought of Kant, Durkheim and Foucault to help me do so. I argue that Foucault's *Discipline and Punish* can be regarded as a critique of the modes of discipline and punishment advanced by Kant and especially Durkheim. Durkheim and Foucault both investigated how punishment in modern schools became less violent and more diffuse, continuous and graduated in scale. I claim that in spite of their differences, Kant, Durkheim and Foucault did agree on at least one thing. That discipline and punishment is imposed on students in schools. Discipline and punishment constrains individuals. Discipline and punishment moulds individuals into what schools and later society, needs them to be. Discipline defines individuals. I pull the chapter together by considering what Kant, Durkheim and Foucault can tell us about discipline and punishment in education today. Kant and Durkheim thought socialising students into the norms of society at school via discipline and punishment could lead to greater individual

8 *What is discipline?*

autonomy and social cohesion. In contrast, Foucault's critique helps to reveal how disciplinary mechanisms in educational institutions all too often merely normalise students and ready them to be docile productive workers. While Kant and Durkheim held rather naive beliefs that rules-based discipline could be morally educational and socially beneficial, Foucault did not. He felt that modern forms of discipline punished all students but especially those who transgressed.

Foucault suggested that the examination has become the disciplinary technology par excellence. He also suggested that disciplinary mechanisms systematically stifle resistance against the norms and (industry focused) values of society. In chapter 4, I do acknowledge that Foucault's later work on the care for the self might offer some suggestions about how the disciplinary effects of educational institutions might be opposed. However, such opposition to disciplinary power seems to be much more a matter of *care for the self than discipline*. *Disciplinary power* is generally presented in a negative light by Foucault. It classifies students according to their productive capacities – it normalises, but it does not develop their *political capacities*. I conclude by observing that Foucault's critique, despite its strengths, does not provide answers to the question of how **discipline** in educational institutions might be arranged to foster ends beyond mere socialisation and normalisation. In chapter 5, I therefore argue that there are substantial difficulties with the predominant discourses of discipline in education at the levels of theory, policy and practice.

At the level of *policy and practice*, zero tolerance and behaviour management approaches have overshadowed other possible ways of enacting discipline in US and UK schools while at the level of *theory* rules-based accounts of discipline in education have been most influential. Foucault's critique of the disciplinary technologies of modernity can certainly help to reveal inadequacies in theories and practices of discipline in education that only aim at, or have the effect of, 'normalising' students. However, what Foucault's critique does not do is provide a more positive account about how disciplinary mechanisms might become less punitive and more educational. I thus suggest there is a compelling need for discipline to be reclaimed in education for the ends of education. I therefore consider two different ways in which discipline might be reclaimed in education, for the ends of education. Following Peters and Hirst, I first suggest that it is educationally important for students to be *disciplined by knowledge*.

Unlike Kant and Foucault, both Peters and Hirst thought that discipline could be a positive part of education. According to Hirst and Peters, discipline is not just about restraining student unruliness. Instead, coming to understand educationally valuable knowledge takes significant student discipline. However, following MacIntyre, I also suggest there is an educational need for disciplines of knowledge and wider social orders to be continually questioned, and where necessary, remade. Second, I document the views of Pat Wilson and Dewey on how discipline might serve the ends of education. They agreed that students should first and foremost be disciplined by *interest* rather than traditions of knowledge. Dewey stressed that discipline is a disposition of persistence and endurance in the face of challenge and difficulty. It is a positive quality of learners because of the agency they exercise over their own learning and conduct. While Hirst, Peters, Pat Wilson and Dewey may not have agreed on the content or ways toward significant learning, all these thinkers nonetheless shared a view that discipline becomes educational for students when they *persist in the pursuit of significant learning*.

In chapter 6, I explore the importance of, and possible connections between, relationships, communication, community and discipline. I do so with reference to the educational philosophies of, first, John Dewey and then John Macmurray. Contrary to Foucault, Dewey and Macmurray both felt that discipline was needed in education if community is to be established and better social orders built. Dewey thought that disciplined communication of interests and purposes in education could help communities be and become more democratic. Dewey suggested that too often approaches to discipline in schools encourage students to take on the role of disembodied, passive spectator rather than participative, embodied agent. Dewey thought greater student agency was needed in education. He maintained that on-going disciplined communication of interests and purposes was necessary in education if community was to emerge and society become more democratic. Dewey was perhaps guilty of a certain naivety though. His seeming belief that there could with regularity develop a happy concordance of common activities from individual interests is probably unduly optimistic. However, his insistence that continuous communication about interests and purposes is needed in education stands in stark contrast to more managerial ways of thinking about disciplinary approaches in school.

Macmurray in turn emphasised the primacy of fostering disciplined relationships. Discipline should for Macmurray focus the attention of persons less upon intellectual matters, abstract ideas and the study of books and knowledge. It should instead promote the fostering of personal relationships and the overcoming of the human tendency towards egocentricity. While Kant thought discipline in education should repress feeling, Macmurray felt education needs must develop out from feeling. Unlike Kant, Macmurray held that human emotions are far from unruly passions. They are not states that need to supressed before education can begin. Rather they are the foundations upon which discipline and education must be built. I conclude that the concepts of discipline developed by Macmurray and Dewey are educationally significant but flawed. Neither philosopher valued enough the liberal idea that students might be meaningfully disciplined by traditions of knowledge pursued for their own sake.

Chapter 7 explores the strengths and weaknesses of restorative approaches to school discipline. Initially, the origins of restorative approaches in education are documented. The key features of such practices are thereafter analysed. Here it is noted that they have the significant merit of focusing on repairing relationships after a conflict has occurred rather than punishing pupils for being involved in conflict. It is argued that though restorative approaches do offer a framework for improved communication between persons in school when conflict has arisen, they cannot, by their very definition, satisfactorily account for how discipline in schools might become less punitive and more educational beyond situations of conflict. Restorative approaches to discipline have also too often been situated within wider discourses of classroom management. Such associations may limit the extent to which they can challenge existing power dynamics and structures in schools and wider society. After these reservations have been set out, the chapter culminates in the presentation of a case study from a primary school in England where the culture of discipline does seem to have benefitted from staff and pupils embracing 'restorative' principles.

Three key themes emerged from this case study. First, staff in the school thought that conventional approaches to discipline in schools may often (unintentionally) perpetuate disciplinary problems by focussing too much on rules, rewards and sanctions and not enough on relationships. Second, staff thought it both desirable and possible for school discipline to be educative and relationship-based rather than punitive and rules-based. Third, staff thought that empowering students to take responsibility for their learning and conduct through emotion education was at the heart of any successful relationship-based approach to school discipline. I acknowledge some obvious limits to this case study. However, I conclude that the case study does suggest there is an urgent need for further educational research on the nature and purposes of discipline in education. The case study also suggests that school discipline does not need to be based around rules, rewards and sanctions in order to be successful. School discipline can be done differently. When done differently, discipline can be more educational than it all too often actually is.

In the final chapter, I summarise and synthesise conclusions from the various different theories, policies, practices and perspectives on discipline in education discussed in the book. I argue that discipline in education should be employed in service of at least four goals. Disciplinary processes should first initiate students into existing community norms, rules, values and knowledge (socialisation). However, community norms, knowledge and values are not always the right ones – they could often benefit from revision. Second, I argue that discipline in education should therefore support students to learn how to question and if necessary remake the norms, rules, values and knowledge of their community (ethical development). Such updating of norms, knowledge and values will rarely be easy. It will take discipline. Moreover, discipline in education should also support students to love some aspect of learning for its own sake and preferably for the length of life. Students should not be disciplined to equate education with examination. They should be disciplined by a love of knowledge, by their interests, at least at times. Third, I claim discipline in education should contribute to the rounded epistemic development of students (epistemic development).

I finally maintain that discipline in education should also be about helping students become a little less self-absorbed. A no doubt important aspect of personal development involves learning how to set goals for oneself and see them through even in the face of challenge and difficulty. However, an equally important aspect of personal development involves learning from and with other people. Students should be supported to develop a sense of responsibility and care for others. Learning how to care for others is not easy though – it takes discipline. Fourth, I conclude that educational processes should support students to be disciplined by their own unique needs, interests and life goals as well as those of other persons (personal development). Here I stress that **personal discipline** is very different to currently faddish educational ideas like grit and self-discipline. I argue that the work of Duckworth and others on grit and self-discipline does not give sufficient regard to the inherently **reasonable** and **relational** nature of persons.

Grit places the onus on students to rather unthinkingly work harder on specific tasks (like exams) while more or less absolving educators and educational institutions of any responsibility to work towards social and educational reform. Personal discipline by way of contrast stresses that new, revised and improved social orders will only become possible when students, educators, policy makers and other community members collectively think about, value and work towards the common good. I conclude the book with some brief thoughts about how educators, students, policy makers and educational researchers may together reclaim discipline in education. Here I argue that if discipline is only used in education for the purpose of socialisation then societies will, as Foucault predicted, increasingly resemble prisons. If discipline in education is instead employed in service of a wider set of purposes including the ethical, epistemological and personal development of students, then communities might yet still be reborn for the better.

Notes

1 Noguera (2003) makes a similar point, reasoning that many students in American high schools engage in delinquent behaviour in part because they know their schooling will not help them succeed in life.
2 For example, last year *The Times* Newspaper in England reported there was a 'teaching and discipline crisis' in schools put down to a lack of authoritarian leaders (Woolcock, 2015). A report in *The Oklahoman* from the previous year suggested that discipline problems and violence in Oklahoma's largest school district constituted a 'classroom crisis' (Kemp, 2014).
3 The work of Rogers and Bennett is discussed in detail in chapter 2.

4 Foucault's (1991) writing on discipline, examinations and education will be explored in depth in chapter 4.
5 Kant's (2003) writing on discipline, punishment and education will be explored in depth in chapters 3 and 4.
6 These definitions are taken from the Cambridge Dictionary (2016).
7 While there is no doubt much more to Foucault's notion of examination than one-off exams, the point that there is more to discipline than examination still, I hope, holds.
8 Richard Smith's *Freedom and Discipline* is a notable exception that is well worth reading.

2 Discipline in recent education policy and practice

This chapter focuses on how discipline is constructed in education *policy* and *practice*. I first suggest that the rise of measurement and accountability in education means that schools are now consistently under the spotlight in respect to issues of student discipline. The bulk of the chapter is concerned to show how discourses of behaviour management and zero tolerance have recently dominated discipline policy and practice in the UK and the US respectively. I further claim that behaviour management and zero tolerance approaches are both unhelpful as they 1) do not encourage students to take meaningful responsibility for their learning or behaviour in school; and 2) marginalise opportunity for the consideration of the wider educational purposes of school discipline. Such discipline policies and practices also give school staff too little incentive to care about the long-term destinations and life chances of individual students who misbehave.

Recent education policy and practice

Official education policies shape education in practice – often considerably. They give a steer to teachers and schools as to what is expected of them. They can also make parents and (perhaps to a lesser extent) students more aware of what a given government's educational priorities are. Education policy is also often used to drive educational reform and change. For much of the twentieth century national education systems were, to a significant extent, able to determine their own agendas free from outside influence. However, education policy today is mediated less by the distinctive needs of national education systems and more by the demands of the global market economy.[1] In respect to education practice much attention has here fallen upon monitoring and (where necessary) raising pupil performance in high stakes examinations. A focus on exams is justified because getting on in life in a market society requires qualifications.

Education policies have placed growing demands on schools and teachers to collect data about what they do, and how well their students do in exams.[2] If the data collected suggests that teachers or schools are 'failing' to meet the required standards, education policies often require schools to make changes to bring about improvement.³ However, latter day education policy has also foisted new imperatives upon educational researchers. In particular there are increasing expectations that those engaged in educational research will generate evidence about 'what works' at raising standards in education.⁴ The desire to improve educational outcomes for all is to be welcomed. However, in a climate of 'what works' it has become harder for researchers to question the market orientation of much education policy and practice. Similarly, *teachers* also now face working in conditions of excessive 'managerial accountability' that have eroded opportunity for questioning the purposes of education (Biesta, 2010).

Education policies do, in short, greatly influence how students, educators' and researchers of education can and cannot think, speak and act. Here, there can be little doubt that the demands of the global market economy are today casting an ominous shadow over education policies generally, with students, parents, teachers and education researchers increasingly expected to focus much of their attention and efforts on improving attainment in high stakes assessment.⁵ It is perhaps inevitable that that the rise of measurement and accountability in education has impacted upon school discipline policy and practice. In this chapter I will consider how more recent education policy has come to influence education practice in respect to issues of school discipline.⁶ In particular, I will document how much latter day school discipline policy in the UK and US has encouraged educators (and educational researchers) to develop effective strategies for managing, controlling and punishing school students rather than educating them.⁷

Schools under the spotlight

Schools are consistently under the spotlight in respect to issues of discipline and student behaviour. Politicians, parents (and indeed teachers) understandably want all students to learn in disciplined environments that are free from excessive disruption. However, there is growing international anxiety about student behaviour in schools. In England and North America student behaviour has been identified as the most significant problem teachers face, while poor school climate has also been highlighted as a worry in Sweden, Israel and Australia (Haydn, 2014). In the face of such concerns and in a culture of educational accountability it should come as no surprise that schools are now formally inspected and graded on their capacity to effectively manage student behaviour. Indeed, behaviour is now a core element in any school inspection in England.⁸ Furthermore, the schools inspection body, OfSted, have recently detailed plans and guidelines for 'unannounced behavior inspections' in schools (Ofsted, 2015). Such developments heap further pressure on schools to present themselves in a positive light and as being able to effectively deal with student disruption at all times.

Issues of student misbehaviour often garner a high media profile too. For example, an article in The Guardian newspaper carried the headline of a 'massive rise in pupil disruption'.[9] The article detailed the results of a survey carried out by the Association of Teachers and Lecturers, which found that 90% of school staff had dealt with 'extreme behaviour' in the past year. These figures are entirely at variance with official figures from Ofsted inspections, which suggest that behaviour is 'satisfactory' or better in over 90% of schools.[10] Such disparate findings reveal how difficult it is to gauge with any certainty how significant the problems of student behaviour actually are in schools. It is probably important to remember here that different actors may bring different motives to any discussion or reporting of pupil behaviour in schools. The media may wish to sensationalise issues of student indiscipline. Indeed, they often do this unhelpfully and misleadingly.[11] A body such as the Association of Teachers and Lecturers may in turn want to highlight how difficult teaching is. In contrast, those in government may wish to accentuate the positive findings from the Ofsted inspections as these might suggest their policies on discipline are effective. Meanwhile, opposition politicians may want to heap blame on government policies by highlighting the high incidence of 'extreme behaviour' reported by teachers.[12]

The high media profile of issues of school discipline coupled with the fixation on examination scores, league tables and school inspections today make it very difficult for teachers and head teachers to be completely open about problems regarding student behaviour (Haydn, 2014). The difficulties of 'speaking up' may be especially acute at times of formal inspection when staff in schools could feel under pressure to portray their school in the best possible light. If they don't, staff could be moved on or the school could be closed or forced to merge with another. Indeed, there may be good reasons to think that official OfSted figures relating to school discipline paint too rosy a view of behaviour in schools (Haydn, 2014). After all, one in three teachers in England leaves the teaching profession within five years with half of these teachers citing poor student behaviour as the main reason.[13] It is not surprising then that English teachers often feel they have to learn to effectively manage student behaviour.

The 'Behaviour Guru'

In this respect there is a vast body of literature dedicated to the issue of how to "manage" students to help them to "behave better" in schools.[14] This managerial way of thinking and speaking about school discipline has exerted considerable influence on both education policy and practice. Indeed, the vocabulary of "behaviour management" is rather replete in UK education policy, where demands for an even greater teacher focus on managing student behaviour through systems of reward and sanction have more recently been made.[15] In England, the first key principle recommended to teachers and schools in the recent Behaviour and Discipline in Schools report is a consistent approach to behaviour management. Further principles include: classroom management, rewards and sanctions, behaviour strategies and better management of transitions.

While recent Scottish policy does endorse more relational approaches to school discipline and the encouraging of positive behaviour, precisely what constitutes "positive" behaviour is subject to little critical interrogation.[16] Furthermore, it is a mandatory expectation that all Scottish teachers will have developed a set of "positive behaviour strategies" before they can register to teach with the General Teaching Council for Scotland (GTCS, 2012). Given these practical imperatives and points of policy emphasis, it is perhaps unsurprising that the most frequently bought literature by teachers concerning school discipline is of the how to control and manage your class variety.[17] Such behaviour management literatures and discourses may well have some educational value in terms of offering practical strategies that can support teachers to get students on task and engaged in learning. However, they are also beset by problems – problems I will now explore. In the introduction to his book, *The Behaviour Guru*, Tom Bennett (whom the Department for Education in England has recently hired to improve standards of pupil behaviour in schools) asserts that good teaching will quite simply not happen without behaviour management. He states that:

> behaviour management is fundamental to good teaching. If you can't control them, you can't teach them. It's that important, in the sense that having water is fundamental to having a decent bath. It just won't happen without it.
>
> (Bennett, 2010, p xvii)

Behaviour management is, Bennett suggests, a matter of 'controlling other people'. The art of controlling people is a skill that can be learned – and the self-styled Behaviour Guru is just the man to help. Bennett professes to know behaviour management techniques 'that work' (2010, p 1) at getting pupils under control. He advises teachers' that if they don't think teaching involves getting pupils to 'do their bidding' then perhaps teaching is not for them. As he puts it: 'if you are not comfortable controlling others, then leave the room' (2010, p 9). Bennett identifies six key behaviours that he thinks teachers can quite easily and quickly assimilate and put in service of attaining 'dominance' over their students.

1 It's what you do, not what you say
2 Act tough
3 Talk like you expect to be heard
4 Think about how you move
5 It's your room
6 Don't blow your top

While Bennett does concede that these techniques are not fool proof, he nonetheless maintains they work at helping teachers dominate and control their students. Bennett believes that teachers can and should train students and 'teach' them 'how to behave'. In his view human beings are animals (2010, p 2). In so far as human beings are animals (and Bennett thinks we should assume this view 2010, p 17), they can be controlled and trained to behave in the school context. He does not think that teachers should seek to dominate students because they get a kick out of controlling others. Instead, teachers can justify controlling students if they care about them and want them to do well.

However, is 'controlling' others really the best long-term strategy for helping them to do well? Moreover, are school pupils really akin to animals that need controlling and training, as Bennett at various points suggests? While humans obviously do share various qualities with other non-human animals such as eating, sleeping and sociality, this does not in itself serve as justification for controlling school students and training them as you may animals.[18] Indeed, thinking of students as animals entirely obscures some vital differences between human and non-human animals. Some philosophers such as Aristotle (1981) and Kant (2003) maintained that *rationality* and language make humans different from other animals. In contrast to this, other philosophers including Dewey (2007) and Macmurray (1956) believed that agency is a, or even the, distinctive quality of human beings. For them being human entails living interdependently with others. Being human also demarcates a capacity to set valuable goals for individual and collective life, and a capacity to see such goals through to fruition via action. Such philosophical ideas will be explored more fully in subsequent chapters. However, before we get on to these notions, it is worth exploring how Bennett is far from alone in believing that students should be controlled and trained to behave in school in much the same way that animals like dogs can be trained.

'Positive' behaviour management

Bill Rogers is one of the most well-known advocates of teachers' learning behaviour management skills so as to overcome issues of school discipline. As he puts it: 'behaviour management is essential to the smooth running of a school' (Rogers, 2011, p 5). Rogers (2011) seems to distinguish between 'positive' discipline (positive language and possession of a global behaviour management skill set) and corrective discipline (negative language and lack of global behaviour management skill set).[19] Rogers explains that 'positive' discipline entails the adoption of positive rather than negative language – he thinks too many teachers overuse negative terms like 'don't', 'stop' or 'no'. An example of the positive language Rogers prefers is asking students to sit on the mat rather than telling them not to wander.

However, for Rogers positive discipline entails more than the adoption of positive language – 'Language alone . . . is not enough. Language is affected by the 'global set' of behaviour. Positive language is also affected by our tone of voice, how hurried or snappy our speech is, by eye contact, proximity to the student and body language... How our language is heard by the student depends greatly on our *characteristic* nonverbal behaviour' (2011, p 55). Rogers thus cites teachers' nonverbal behaviour as being as central to establishing positive discipline as their verbal utterances. Indeed, Rogers (2011, pp 56–57) identifies six key nonverbal behaviours that together make up a 'global set' of teacher skills that can augment positive language and in turn promote positive discipline. These are:

> *Tone of voice* – Don't be hostile and indecisive but instead be assertive and uplifting in use of voice
>
> *Bearing and general body posture* – Stand with confidence and move in a relaxed way – jerky movements may lead to kinaesthetic learners focussing on teacher movement rather than instruction
>
> *Postural/gestural cues* – Do we smile and show engagement and confidence in our faces with reasonable frequency?
>
> *Proximity* – Teachers should consider how physically close they are to students when they speak to them as these aspects of behaviour can evidence intent, support and care
>
> *Eye contact* – Can demonstrate attention or interest. It is important to gain initial eye contact and follow with directional language to remove ambiguity about the meaning of the eye contact
>
> *Take up time* – The use of tactical pausing can enhance expectation and be a powerful social cue

Rogers explains that these skills may not in themselves have much effect on discipline – however, taken 'globally they can convey a positive, managerial tone' (Rogers, 2011, p 58). Furthermore, Rogers exclaims that 'positive' alteration in teacher language and behaviour can positively influence the behaviour of students adding that this 'is not manipulation or mere technique' (Rogers, 2011, p 58). What should be made of these claims that teacher adoption of positive language and six key nonverbal behaviours can lead to a positive improvement in student behaviour? It is possible that such behavioural tips may have some value in terms of offering practical strategies that can support teachers to get students on task and engaged in learning. Teachers are after all often expected to be in control of their classes. The desire to seek quick fix solutions is understandable – perhaps especially so in the case of those new to the profession. However, the practical value of such managerial tricks is, for me, fairly limited in range and probably does not extend beyond student socialisation.

For example, Rogers (1998, 2011) probably makes a good point when implying that the consistent and fair application of rules and consequences in schools may help to acquaint pupils with social norms and 'reach socially responsible goals' (1998, p 11). Indeed, although it is a far from original argument (as we shall see later in this book Durkheim made much the same case for discipline to be conceived of as socialisation nearly a hundred years earlier), socialisation is an entirely valid and important purpose of education, even if it is not the only purpose of education (Biesta, 2009). However, there also appear to be both contradictory and morally questionable features in the account of positive discipline given by Rogers. To start with Rogers seems to at least partially contradict his assertion than the 'global set' of positive teacher behaviours are not mere 'technique'. He after all later states that effective behaviour management is not a matter of teacher personality – instead key nonverbal behaviours like tone of voice and body gesture are acquirable skills than can positively improve pupil discipline. Quite why Rogers classifies his list of global behaviours as 'learnable skills' but not 'technique' is left unexplained. More questionable though is Rogers' denial that the behaviour management skills he describes are manipulative.

Some problems with behaviour management approaches

In spite of Rogers' declaration that human beings are not dogs (Rogers, 2011, p 58), the six key behaviours of positive discipline that he outlines nonetheless betray some Pavlovian tendencies. Indeed, some of the key practices endorsed by Rogers seem to be underpinned by a largely behaviourist understanding of human learning. In the behaviourist model of learning made famous by Pavlov and Skinner, human behaviour is held to be straightforwardly modifiable on the basis of repeated actions and consequences (Woods, 2008). Rogers' adoption of the word 'positive' is perhaps apt then as the positive 'language' and 'nonverbal behaviour skills' he describes may well amount to no more than behaviourist strategies of 'positive reinforcement'. As Woods (2008) explains, positive reinforcement occurs when a particular desired behaviour is followed by the issue of a reward with the intention of reinforcing the future frequency of occurrence of the rewarded behaviour.

While Rogers does suggest that teachers may wish to discuss whether or not to reward pupils who display desired behaviours, he does undoubtedly seem to think that teachers can change pupil behaviour in desired directions by adopting the positivist language (accompanied no doubt by the six positive key global nonverbal behaviours) of consequences and reinforcements. In describing the importance of class routine for example he states that: 'most teachers during the establishment phase of the year develop routines for pack up, tidy up and leave the room in an orderly fashion. If they don't do these things the positive enforcement needs to include a consequence ... this is clearly not simply a punishment, it is a way of reinforcing accountability and responsibility in relation to the social good' (Rogers, 2011, p 114).

Thus, the behaviour management skills propounded by both Bennett and Rogers seem to be under the sway of behaviourist psychology. Rogers' approach to behaviour management is altogether enlivened by the language of consequences and positive reinforcements, while Bennett openly commends the consistent use of punishment in education.[20] Furthermore, Rogers holds some rather pessimistic and deterministic views of the educational potential of some pupils. He rather troublingly claims that the repertoire of behaviour management skills he pitches can help teachers 'deal with argumentative students and the more objectionable members of the human race, in our schools' (Rogers, 2011, pp 4–5). To describe pupils as 'more objectionable members of the human race' certainly underscores the impression that Rogers has fairly fixed ideas about the moral limitations and behaviour of some school pupils. A significant problem with behaviour management strategies then is that they tend towards predetermined ideas about what good or bad behaviour consists of and of how it may be brought about.[21] In Rogers' work for example positive discipline is not so much *positive for pupils* but mere *positive reinforcement*.

Little attention is given to thinking about how discipline might contribute to the wider moral education of students in the behavioural managerial view. Discipline conceived as 'management of students' increasingly comes to look like something that teachers' largely '*do*' to pupils and in a deterministic fashion rather than something that pupils can take some personal responsibility for. In this respect it may be countered that the recent English policy *The Importance of Teaching* has claimed that there is well-known academic evidence that documents how simple rules, rewards and sanctions can help pupils to improve their behaviour by taking responsibility for it. Rogers (1998), too, suggests that discipline should aim at supporting pupils to develop some personal responsibility for their conduct. However, it is a moot point whether rewards and sanctions (or more euphemistically 'consequences') actually can help pupils take personal responsibility for their conduct. Tellingly, the academic research is not named in the *Importance of Teaching* policy. This may be because there is ample evidence to suggest that rewards and sanctions actually fail to promote intrinsic motivation in pupils to engage in learning for its own sake – students are instead motivated by external factors like fear of sanction on the one hand or desire for teacher approval on the other.[22]

Advocates of behaviour management do not seem very interested in encouraging pupils to take any sort of significant responsibility for their behaviour, learning or wider moral education and development. Instead, teacher management of students is the cornerstone of discipline. Bennett is absolutely clear that teachers should set out to control pupils because 'it works'. While Rogers is less extreme and more nuanced in his views than this, he does suggest that discipline is, at base, centred round teacher action in rather predetermined managerial directions. He specifically states in fact that discipline is a 'teacher directed activity whereby we seek to lead, guide, manage or confront a student about behaviour that disrupts the rights of others, be they students or teachers' (1998, p 11). Thus, an unacknowledged effect of the behaviour management skills endorsed by Tom Bennett and Bill Rogers is a denial to students of an important degree of agency over their education and wider moral development – students are instead caught up in a web of teacher-led managerial gestures, utterances, routines, reinforcements and consequences.[23]

Indeed, in the behaviour managerial view it is arguable that students are portrayed as unruly and morally deficient and in need of management without which they could not learn, or learn to behave better. The title of another popular text on behaviour management, *Getting the buggers to behave,* certainly adds weight to the impression of students being inherently unruly and in need of teacher action (rather than student) to be 'made' better. Behaviour managerial approaches do not then generally encourage educators to think about the wider moral educational purposes of school discipline. Some behavioural managerial approaches may also encourage teachers to give up on students who don't conform to what is expected of them. For example, in a letter from a teacher worried about students who had disengaged from education Tom Bennett recommends 'showing them the door' unless they 'buck up' (Bennett, 2010, p 28). He adds that the worried teacher should 'purge the worst offenders' and put pressure on those that remain. This is strikingly glib advice. Bennett does not take this teacher's discipline problem seriously. He offers the easy answer – get tough with the students involved or exclude them. But the easy answers are often not the right ones. Might something not be learned from listening to students, from treating them as persons instead of animals to be shown the door?

Rather than take the issue of student disengagement from education seriously Bennett just advises exclusion – and on the basis of very little actual knowledge of the situation or the personal lives of the students in question.[24] For readers of Bennett's book, whether there are any legal, moral, or educational grounds for such exclusion is impossible to say due to the lack of information given. Though Bennett does advise that the remaining students should be offered support to help them believe in themselves this support would not be extended to the students who have been purged – the purged have been sacrificed for the good of those who remain. In my view policy makers such as Bennett (who is after all hired to lead the advice to the Department for Education in England on issues of student behaviour) should not advise educators to show students the door on the basis of little actual knowledge of the situation or the students in question. I am not saying exclusions can never be warranted. However, I do want to point out that exclusions have long-term consequences and usually detrimental ones, especially for those excluded. Recent approaches to discipline in US schools have also encouraged educators to all too freely exclude students for a whole manner of reasons, often minor ones. However, issues regarding school discipline have, until recently, probably also been much more concerning in the US. There the tough stance on misbehaving students in schools has arguably led to detrimental future possibilities for many excluded students.

Why zero tolerance approaches don't work

> As the name implies, "zero tolerance" discipline policies require schools and districts to show no lenience for certain kinds of student misconduct, and usually mandate suspension, expulsion and often the summoning of local law enforcement for behaviours ranging from weapon and drug possession, to fighting, smoking and even tardiness.
>
> (Kafka, 2011, p 2)

In the US, since the 1990's 'zero tolerance' approaches to discipline have become highly evident in both policy and practice.[25] Here teachers and school leaders must show zero tolerance towards students for certain types of misbehaviour. The idea that certain student behaviours in US schools necessitate punishment in every circumstance and context was enshrined in federal policy in 1994 when the then President Bill Clinton signed the Gun Free Schools Act. This act required schools to suspend any student found in possession of a weapon for one calendar year. However, a number of states and school districts significantly extended the range of student behaviours that were deemed to merit immediate zero tolerance suspension irrespective of circumstance. Indeed, many school districts also made suspension or expulsion mandatory for drug possession, any form of violence, tardiness, truancy, abusive language or general disruptive or disrespectful behaviour.[26] According to data from the US Department of Education, at least 75% of schools report having zero tolerance policies for offences such as: firearms (94%), weapons other than firearms (91%), alcohol (87%), drugs (88%), violence (79%) and tobacco (79%).[27] Sanctions for even low-level misdemeanours include corporal punishment, exclusions and criminal charges.

As part of the zero tolerance stance, thousands of schools in the US now have law enforcement officers based on site to assist with issues of student discipline and school safety. The presence of police officers in schools has often resulted in even minor infractions being dealt with by the criminal justice system when they would not have previously. The zero tolerance approach has not been received without controversy. Some incidents that bring home the flaws of the inflexible 'zero tolerance' approach have been picked up by the media and generated significant public debate. For example, the St Petersburg Times reported the case of a girl of 10 who was expelled for bringing a weapon to school. The said 'weapon' was a small knife that had in actuality been placed in the girl's lunch box by her mother for the purposes of cutting an apple. Despite the girl handing over the knife to a teacher and explaining its fruit cutting function, she was expelled. Similarly, a young male was sanctioned for breaking rules and taking a call on his mobile phone while at school. The fact that he was speaking to his mother, a soldier out in Iraq, for the first time in thirty days did not prevent the boy from being expelled.[28]

Such incidents are not isolated ones.[29] They and others like them have led to concern amongst juvenile court personnel that 'school officials may be relying on the juvenile justice system inappropriately to handle minor school misconduct' (Kim *et al.*, 2011, p 112). However, researchers have probably been the staunchest critics of zero tolerance approaches. They point to the fact that there is no reliable evidence to suggest that zero tolerance polices work.[30] While advocates of zero tolerance claim the policies deter students from misbehaving in the future, evidence suggests school suspension is actually more likely to trigger further student suspensions.[31] Similarly, while zero tolerance approaches are also defended on the grounds that removing unruly students will create a better school climate for the students that remain, the reverse has generally been found to be true. As Skiba *et al.* report in an extensive review of literature on zero tolerance: 'schools with higher rates of school suspension and expulsion appear to have less satisfactory ratings of school climate' (2008, p 854).

Especially troubling though is the evidence that disproportionally high numbers of socially disadvantaged (especially African American but also Hispanic) students are excluded from schools that adopt zero tolerance approaches.[32] In 1973, before zero tolerance approaches were as widespread, black students in the US had a suspension rate of six per cent compared with just over three per cent for white students. By 2006 however, 15% of black students were suspended and only five per cent of white students.[33] Thus, black students are three times more likely to be suspended than white students since the emergence of zero tolerance approaches to discipline. The impact of zero tolerance approaches upon minority youth is also acutely felt in the criminal justice system. Here it is claimed that zero tolerance fuels a 'school to prison pipeline' where those socially disadvantaged students excluded from school become much more likely to be incarcerated later in life.[34]

Evidence suggests that school-based arrests harm children psychologically, double the odds of them dropping out of school, lower test scores, reduce employment prospects and increase the chance of future engagement with the criminal justice system.[35] Such referrals and arrests may also have a negative long-term impact on the wider community who may grow to mistrust the heavy handed and overly punitive approaches of schools and law enforcement agencies in dealing with relatively minor infractions (Kim *et al.*, 2011). The community will also have to bear the extra economic costs associated with higher crime, unemployment and incarceration. Kafka is perhaps right to conclude that zero tolerance approaches do not seem to confer any benefits on individuals or communities (Kafka, 2011). Instead they come at a significant cost to both individuals and communities. She avers that 'zero tolerance policies represent a highly punitive form of school discipline that entails harsh consequences and disproportionately affects minority youth' (2011, p 5). But if zero tolerance approaches don't work, and penalise already socially disadvantaged students especially, how did they ever come to prominence?

How did zero tolerance approaches come to prominence?

In her book *The History of "Zero Tolerance" in American Public Schooling* Judith Kafka argues that for the bulk of American history schools and teachers dealt with matters of discipline at the local level. Although individual educators had discretion to deal with school discipline as they saw fit, there was nonetheless a high level of uniformity of disciplinary approaches in practice across schools in the US. Even without external regulations, from a historical perspective, 'behavioural expectations and disciplinary practices have been strikingly similar from classroom to classroom and district to district' (Kafka, 2011, p 6). However, until the 1950s individual teachers and school leaders did, in theory, have significant freedom of judgement in regard to issues of student discipline. This was made possible, at least in part, by the legal principle of *in loco parentis*. This doctrine holds that educators must, by law, act in the place of the parent when the child is at school. Importantly, this doctrine places responsibility upon teachers to act in the best interests of the child when teaching, including in respect to any incidents of indiscipline.

In contrast, zero tolerance approaches do not encourage educators to act for the best interests of *all* pupils under their charge. Nor are they based upon the doctrine of *in loco parentis*. According to zero tolerance approaches, educators are no longer expected to act as a parent should, with concern about the long-term well-being of the young persons under their care. Instead, zero tolerance approaches are 'explicitly intended to limit teachers' and principals' individual discretion' (Kafka, 2011, p 6). The policies were explicitly designed in fact to inhibit the tolerance of certain misbehaviours, with responsibility for discipline now being passed on to centralised education boards and officials. In deliberately situating decision-making about disciplinary issues outside of schools, zero tolerance approaches 'signal a significant shift in the implementation, regulation and general philosophy of American school discipline' (Kafka, 2011, p 7).

Kafka argues that two popular narratives have emerged to account for why the locus of decision-making about discipline moved from local teachers and schools to education boards and officials at remove from the school where the disciplinary issue occurred. The most common explanation for this shift in philosophy is that court decisions in the 1960s and 1970s granted students greater civil rights in schools, undermining the doctrine of *in loco parentis* in the process.³⁶ With teachers no longer afforded authority of discretion to discipline pupils under their care, school systems were, in effect, forced to develop official regulations and structures independent of individual teachers and classrooms so as to more fairly and effectively deal with discipline in schools. However, a second popular explanation is that rising crime, juvenile delinquency and student aggression in the 1960s and 1970s (in urban schools especially) led school districts to centralize discipline policies and begin to employ security and law enforcement staff in schools. Though there is truth in these narratives, Kafka also holds that they remain incomplete.

For one, these popular narratives 'begin too late' with many school districts centralising policies as early as the 1950s. For another, the narratives do not give due recognition of the extent to which teachers in US schools were in favour of the creation of zero tolerance type approaches that limited their own responsibilities and powers of discretion. In her book Kafka argues that the city district of Los Angeles played a leading role in shaping the change of philosophy in respect to discipline in US schools. She charts in depth how the Los Angeles school system in the 1950s to 1970s transferred control over disciplinary matters from school educators to central education officials. By the end of this period Los Angeles schools had adopted zero tolerance 'in all but name' with most city districts quickly following the example set by Los Angeles.³⁷ In Los Angeles at this time there was a rise in number of 'special' schools, and 'social adjustment rooms' in mainstream schools, for unruly and troubled students. However, teachers felt there was a need for greater investment in such provision, as schools were no longer thought to be coping with the rise of indiscipline and the growing number of students with social, emotional and behavioural needs.³⁸

Furthermore, educators in schools often did not want autonomy over matters of discipline. While the wider moral education of school pupils had historically been regarded as a core purpose of schooling in the US, by the middle of the twentieth century educators were increasingly keen to divest themselves of this responsibility.³⁹ As student unrest about racial segregation heightened and violence increased in and out of schools, there was a fear that community tensions would only be enflamed, and teacher and pupil relations further eroded, if punishments for unruly school conduct were meted out at the local level. Instead teachers and schools often beseeched the Board of Education in Los Angeles to create and enforce district level rules and sanctions that would help make issues of discipline seem less down to the arbitrary judgements of individual schools and teachers. Here there was perhaps a particular concern about the use of corporal punishment, which was still legal in Los Angeles and many other US cities, districts and states. Although complaints about corporal punishment sometimes took on a racial meaning, controversy was often less about race and more about whether or not teachers should be allowed to physically chastise *any* student. For example in one high profile incident in the 1950s the family of a white pupil pursued criminal charges against a school principal for whipping their child.⁴⁰

Even though this case was dropped, in a context of growing racial tensions, student protests, higher student aggression and increasing questioning of the doctrine of *in loco parentis,* it is entirely understandable that some teachers and teacher associations implored education officials to centralise approaches to school discipline. While teachers in Los Angeles in the middle of the twentieth century remained happy to have freedom of discretion in respect to issues of content and instruction, they were increasingly less inclined to accept responsibility for matters of discipline. Such teachers were not just weary to dole out sanctions though. They were also becoming more reluctant to be involved in the wider moral education of pupils. Here there was concern that they had neither the time nor expertise to properly support the growing body of students with significant social, emotional and behavioural needs. In this respect, it was argued that the quality of instruction would suffer if educators were also expected to act as counsellors.⁴¹ In sum, at least three factors contributed to the rise in prominence of zero tolerance approaches in US schools. First, court decisions in the 1960s and 1970s increased students' civil rights with this in turn undermining the principle of *in loco parentis*. Second, there was growing anxiety about student violence and unrest in and out of schools. Third, teachers' themselves canvassed education officials to centralise approaches to school discipline.

The death of *in loco parentis* and the purposes of schooling

The widespread adoption of zero tolerance approaches across US schools since the 1990s has had the effect of further 'distinguishing discipline from the educative purposes of schooling, and further weakening the notion of in loco parentis as a governing principle' (Kafka, 2011, p 76). This 'death' of *in locos parentis* has been welcomed by some in so far as it has contributed to the protection of students against abusive and arbitrary punishments.⁴² However, the passing of this doctrine and the widespread adoption of zero tolerance has resulted in a situation where it is now much harder for educators to morally educate students or make context-sensitive judgements about disciplinary issues based on the long-term interests of students rather than the immediate need for order and control. Arguably though, US educators need to be encouraged to think about how issues of discipline contribute to the wider moral education and long-term interests of their students, now, more than ever.⁴³

Thankfully, the growing body of evidence about the damaging long-term effects of zero tolerance approaches has not gone unnoticed at the level of federal education policy. Indeed, the most recent guidance about discipline from the US Department of Education, *Guiding Principles: A resource guide for improving school climate and discipline* can perhaps be interpreted as a very deliberate attempt to reduce zero tolerance approaches (US Department of Education, 2014). This report makes a number of recommendations for change based around three key principles. The first principle calls for educators to engage in deliberate attempts to foster *positive school climates* where young persons who are 'misbehaving' or identified as at risk, are offered tiered support according to their need. There is here also an acknowledgement that all school staff will need further training in how to support students to engage in 'positive' behaviour.[44] Such training might include de-escalation or conflict resolution techniques. Significantly, there is an expectation that school-based law enforcement officers' focus on improving school safety and reducing inappropriate referrals to the criminal justice system. The report states that schools should 'ensure that school-based law enforcement officers do not become involved in routine discipline matters' (US Department of Education, 2014, p 9). Thus, the most recent policy on discipline seeks to challenge and overturn the latter day trend of utilising law enforcement officers to deal with relatively minor school disciplinary issues.

The second principle is that schools should adopt consistent and appropriate expectations and consequences. The report suggests schools should adopt high and 'positive' expectations for students and involve all community members in school discipline policy development. Importantly, it also suggests that schools may wish to consider restorative justice style approaches to discipline as an alternative to punishment and exclusion. The idea that teachers and students should together seek to learn from conflict, and repair relationships where harm has been done, is at the core of restorative approaches to school discipline.[45] Restorative approaches are certainly less punitive and more educational than zero tolerance ones. However, as I argue in chapter 7, restorative approaches may only be apt in situations where some sort of conflict has already occurred. Indeed, as we shall see later in the book, there are a variety of other ways of thinking about discipline that may more naturally lend themselves to widespread practical use in schools. Whatever the possible limitations of restorative approaches may be though, the report undoubtedly calls for the reclamation of some teacher discretion regarding school discipline. It states that 'zero-tolerance discipline policies, which generally require a specific consequence for specific action regardless of circumstance, may prevent the flexibility necessary to choose appropriate and proportional consequences' (US Department of Education, 2014, p 13).

The third principle requires schools to continuously evaluate their discipline policies to ensure they are fair. The report cites the long-term damage that exclusion can have on pupils (especially minority youth) and suggests that schools regard exclusion as a last resort. Furthermore, the report specifically calls on schools to reduce the number of exclusions and collect and monitor data regarding all students involved in misconduct issues. Here 'school discipline teams' are recommended as one way of reducing exclusions and gathering data about how fair their discipline policies are. These teams should consist of well-trained members of staff and a diverse range of community members to ensure that students, families, teachers and other relevant stakeholders all have a say in making school disciplinary processes as equitable as possible for all students. It is too early to say if these principles will have the desired effects in practice in US schools. Further research will be needed in the years ahead to gauge how successful schools are at reducing their reliance upon zero tolerance style approaches. In this respect it is undoubtedly encouraging that all schools in the US are now being given a very clear message by the Obama administration that they need to reduce exclusions (especially in respect to minority youth), take more flexible and less zero tolerance focussed approaches to school discipline and stop relying on law enforcement agencies to deal with minor disciplinary issues. However, it is also worth remembering that many zero tolerance policies are mandated at the state and district rather than federal level. In any instances where staff in states and school districts do not want to move away from zero tolerance approaches, a federal policy like this may not have the reach to further change.

Chapter summary

There are a rich variety of ways in which educators can, and indeed do, enact discipline in schools. As we shall see in later chapters, at the levels of philosophy and practice there is much more to school discipline than either behaviour management or zero tolerance. However, in this chapter I have argued that behaviour management and zero tolerance discourses have dominated more recent policy and practice regarding discipline in the UK and the US respectively. This is not to say other practice and policy perspectives don't exist – of course they do. It is only to say that behaviour management and zero tolerance have been most influential over the last few years. In the UK behavioural managerial approaches have tended to prevail. However, such approaches are problematic, as they do not encourage: 1) students to take meaningful responsibility for their learning or behaviour in school; or 2) educators to think about the wider moral educational purposes of school discipline. Meanwhile, in the US, zero tolerance type sanctions appear to have taken hold. Such approaches are especially worrying as they only seem to have negative long-term effects for individuals and communities, with minority youth being especially 'punished' by zero tolerance.

It is worth noting here that black youth in English schools are also four times more likely to be suspended or excluded from school than any other group of students.[46] If the history of zero tolerance charted in this chapter is anything to go by though, the recent English policy of cracking down tough on misconduct in schools and allowing school staff to use 'reasonable force'

(DfE, 2014), to search students and deal with incidents of indiscipline, may not be the best way to try to overturn such troubling statistics.[47] This said, English educators generally have had considerably more freedom and authority than US-based ones to implement discipline according to the needs of the communities they are in. While there are undoubtedly differences in the policies and practices in these different contexts then, both zero tolerance and behaviour managerial approaches do nonetheless encourage educators to think most about how they can manage, control and/or punish students. In such climates school staff are given too little incentive to care about the long-term destinations and life chances of individual students who misbehave. This is perhaps especially true in America, where teachers have recently often had minimal or non-existent powers of discretion over matters of student discipline.

Punishment of errant student behaviour has too often become the name of the game in US schools. As we have seen in this chapter though, it was not always thus. Up until the 1950s teachers had substantial autonomy to deal with student indiscipline as they saw fit. Here, though, there is at least hope that the most recent federal policy in respect to discipline may lead to the reclamation of some discretionary powers and the reduction in use of zero tolerance approaches in the future. In this chapter I have also claimed that zero tolerance and behavioural managerial approaches marginalise opportunity for reflection about the moral educational role of school discipline. What might the moral and wider educational role of school discipline be though? How might discipline in education treat students like persons rather than animals? How might educators think differently about discipline? I turn to these questions in the next and subsequent chapters.

Notes

1 For an informative exploration of these themes, see both Ball (2009) and Kamens (2013).
2 For further discussion of such issues, see Ball (2003) and Biesta (2010).
3 A point made by amongst others Ball (2003) and Whitty (1997).
4 For insightful discussion of such issues, see Biesta (2010) and Whitty (2006).
5 I am far from alone in holding this view. For example, Jackson maintains that market competition is now an established feature of the English school system (2006). For different perspectives on the rise of measurement in education and the growth in influence of the market economy in education see Ball (2009), Biesta (2010), Kamens (2013) and MacIntyre and Dunne (2002).
6 In subsequent chapters I hope it will become clear that new technologies of discipline have in part driven the rise of measurement in education, at least according to Foucault.
7 It is certainly beyond the scope of this book to provide a detailed analysis of the impact of all school discipline policies globally.
8 See OfSted (2014).
9 See Townsend (2013).
10 See Haydn (2014).
11 A view I share with Haydn (2014).

12 For further discussion of precisely these issues, see Haydn (2014).
13 See Bennett (2010).
14 See for example Bennett (2010), Cowley (2010), Dupper (2010), Reid and Morgan (2012) and Rogers (2011).
15 See, for example, Department for Education (2010) and especially the Department for Education (2012a).
16 See Scottish Government (2013).
17 A point also made by Macleod *et al.* (2012).
18 These are qualities Bennett (2010) identifies.
19 Rogers elsewhere suggests that *corrective discipline* is concerned with how teacher action can 'correct disruptive, anti-social or deviant behaviour' (1998, p 10) adding that *supportive discipline* can ensure that corrective discipline is received fairly by students.
20 See especially Bennett (2010) chapter 1 and Rogers (2011) pp 39–41 and pp 100–117.
21 Rogers and Bennett are certainly not the only education researchers to suggest that teachers can acquire 'positive' managerial skills that can improve pupil behaviour. In an influential study Wheldall *et al.* (1985) for example maintained that the behaviour management training package (BATPACK) they devised can 'positively' alter teacher behaviour in predicted directions. They also claim that pupils in the classrooms of teachers who have undertaken the BATPACK training behave in measurably better ways than those pupils in classrooms where teachers have not undertaken BATPACK training. However, even if these claims are true they rest on predetermined ideas about what 'good' or 'bad' behaviour consists of.
22 See for example Kohn (1999), MacAllister (2013a), Ryan and Deci (2000) and Woods (2008).
23 Smith (1985) also speaks about the ways in which managerial approaches to discipline manipulate pupils rather than empower them. He denounces the value of behaviour management skills in fact and suggests that they can facilitate only the most trivial sorts of learning.
24 That Bennett states 'if this is sixth form' (2010, p 28) does not for me excuse his willingness to 'purge' those who don't have a life-plan. It rather suggests that he does not have any further information about the specific nature of pupil disengagement other than the correspondence from the teacher that he quotes from and this is minimal. Indeed, he does not even say that the students in question are actually misbehaving in the lessons – only that they are disengaged and don't care.
25 For discussion of how zero tolerance approaches to discipline have come to dominate policy and practice in the US, see Kafka (2011), Martinez (2009), Noguera (2003) and Skiba *et al.* (2008).
26 A point made by both Kafka (2011) and Martinez (2009).
27 These figures were generated by the National Association of School Psychologists (NASP, 2008).
28 Both these examples are discussed in Skiba *et al.* (2008).
29 Kim *et al.* (2011) for example note that in California the most common offence that led to juvenile referral was 'disturbing schools' in 2007–08 while at this time in Florida 15% of all delinquency referrals were school related. The authors also suggest that many such school-based arrests were 'improper'.
30 There is a sizeable body of research and literature that suggests zero tolerance approaches do not work (see for example Kafka (2011), Martinez (2009), Noguera (2003) and Skiba *et al.* (2008).
31 See Noguera (2003) and Skiba *et al.* (2008).
32 See for example Kafka (2011), Martinez (2009), Noguera (2003) and Skiba *et al.* (2008).

33 These figures are quoted from Kafka (2011).
34 See Kafka (2011), Kim *et al.* (2011) and Noguera (2003). In their extensive literature review Skiba *et al.* (2008) also suggest that while there is good reason to think there is a school to prison pipeline, further longitudinal research is needed to confirm this.
35 See Kim *et al.* (2011).
36 See Kafka (2011) for further discussion about protests about civil rights in US schools and the eventual 'death' of the doctrine of *in loco parentis*.
37 For further discussion of the history of school discipline in Los Angeles, see chapters 1, 4 and 5 of Kafka (2011) especially.
38 For further discussion of this point, see Kafka (2011), chapter 3 in particular.
39 For further discussion of how teachers became reluctant to morally educate students in the US, see Kafka (2011).
40 This example is taken from Kafka (2011).
41 For further discussion of how teacher concerns influenced the rise of zero tolerance, see Kafka (2011)
42 For further discussion of this, see Kafka (2011) chapter 1.
43 Goodman (2006) seems to concur with this need. She claims that current school discipline policies in the US (she focusses on Pennsylvania) are ineffective at delivering moral messages. They are poorly justified and fail to distinguish between *moral* and *conventional* school rules violations.
44 Earlier in this chapter, I was critical of behaviour management driven policies and literatures in the UK for adopting too managerial and predetermined an understanding of what 'positive' behaviour consists of and how it may be brought about. Arguably, the same charge can be levelled at the more recent calls in the US to focus on creating a positive school climate'.
45 For further discussion of restorative approaches to conflict in schools, see Sellman *et al.* (2013).
46 See DfE (2012b) for further discussion of exclusion patterns in English schools. While it is apparent that black youth are especially likely to be permanently excluded, other minority groups such as gypsy travellers are also more likely to be excluded than the norm.
47 Other less draconian measures are suggested in recent English policy on discipline too, but none as far reaching as the recent call in the US for schools to reduce the high number of minority youth penalized by school discipline practices in the US.

3 Rules, education and moral development

In this chapter the possible educational value of institutional rules and social norms will be explored, as rules and social norms often drive processes of discipline in education. Initially, the ubiquity of educational rules will be noted. The bulk of the chapter will entail mapping out three rules-based accounts of discipline in schools. In particular, it will be argued that Kant, Durkheim and John Wilson all in different ways held that discipline in schools: 1) is vital for moral education and development and; 2) should first and foremost initiate students into impersonal rules that apply to all, regardless of circumstance. I will thereafter argue that aspects of such thinking about discipline continue to be apparent in education policy and practice today – the best example of this being zero tolerance approaches in US schools. While Kant undoubtedly thought discipline should aim to curb unruliness in students, he also thought education (and any discipline that is part of it) ought to aim at the future improvement of all of humanity via the cultivation of moral autonomy in persons. Zero tolerance approaches to discipline in contrast have no such noble (if naive) aspirations. I conclude the chapter by arguing that it is a conceptual error to think that impersonal rules-based approaches to discipline in education can work for the good of all. Unfortunately, this is a conceptual error that has all too often also become ingrained in educational policy and practice.

The ubiquity of rules in education

Rules are ubiquitous in education. This is perhaps especially true in regards to matters of student discipline. It is hard to imagine a school *without* rules, in some form or other. There are rules concerning student behaviour in the corridors between lessons and there are rules for student behaviour in classrooms during lessons. One of the first things students come to grasp at school is that rules govern what is expected of them when they are there. School rules can be instructive. For example, they can help make students aware of how they should behave in a particular context, or they can inform students about the sorts of things they need to do to prepare well for a particular test. Rules can also be prohibitive. For example, students quickly learn that being violent towards others or shouting and swearing during lessons are not generally acceptable school behaviours. School rules are instructive as well as prohibitive then – they tell students what they can do as well as what they cannot. Rules are also often supported by penalties.[1] Rules would not carry the action directing force that they do in schools without students being aware of the penalties that will follow if they are broken. Whether unwritten or formally inscribed in school policy, for better and worse, it is hard to escape rules in schools.

Rules are perhaps most apparent in schools but they certainly exist in other places of learning like nurseries and universities too. In early years' settings for example there are often rules about when people can and cannot have their snacks, or play outside. While there may not be formal policies about how students are expected to behave in university seminars, often students and tutors negotiate rules between them. Students may for example agree to read a set paper each week or write a blog on a selected topic prior to a given class. While there may not be an official penalty for failing to complete such agreed university tasks, students often know that they may be rewarded for their efforts in the form of a better grade for participation in class. There is also a raft of rules and regulations governing assessment in universities, rules about what students need to do in terms of word count or referencing for example. There are rules about how student work should be marked and rules about when students might be entitled to appeal a grade. But if rules are ubiquitous in education (as I am maintaining), how did they come to be? What, moreover, might the educational justification for rules be, and how might rules and social norms be implicated (or not) in the wider education and moral development of students?

In this chapter I will address such questions. I will first chart how Durkheim (1961), Kant (2003) and John Wilson (1981) all in different ways held that a disciplined socialisation into impersonal school rules was a necessary and indeed vital part of education. Necessary and vital because such discipline was thought to contribute to the wider moral development of students. I will thereafter argue that aspects of such Kantian type thinking exist in policies and practices of school discipline today, too often negatively. Zero tolerance approaches are perhaps the best example of this. As was noted in the last chapter, one of the problems with zero tolerance approaches is that they disconnect processes of school discipline from the wider purposes of education. Kant's concept of educational discipline did not do this though. Instead, he maintained that the ultimate purpose of education would only be realisable if students first develop discipline. What though did Kant think the purpose of education should be and what part did he think discipline should play in this?

Kant on good education

> Man may be broken in, trained, and mechanically taught, or he may be really enlightened. Horses and dogs are broken in; and man, too, may be broken in. It is, however, not enough that children should be merely broken in; for it is of greater importance that they shall learn to *think*.
>
> (Kant, 2003, p 20)

The Prussian philosopher Immanuel Kant (1724–1804) argued that humans are the only beings who *need* education. In *On Education*, he insists that other animals are, from the outset, 'all they ever can be' (2003, p 3). Their natural instincts, allied to a modicum of food, warmth and shelter are all they need to go forth in the world. It is not so with humans. Human beings, unlike other animals, need education before they can fulfil their potential and become what they are meant to be. Kant stated that 'man can only become man by education. He is merely what education makes of him' (Kant, 2003, p 6). What distinguishes humans from other animals though is not so much education itself, but what education helps human beings learn to do – to reason and think for themselves. He maintained that in 'learning to think man comes to act according to fixed principles and not at random . . . a real education implies a great deal' (Kant, 2003, p 20). Whereas other animals do not need reasons for action, humans do. However, human beings are not able to work out reasons for action for themselves straightaway. Instead, others have to do this for them to start with. In time and through education though, Kant thought it possible for persons to learn how to think and act for themselves.

Kant regarded education, properly conceived, in very high esteem. He thought it necessary, indeed fundamental, to our becoming enlightened persons capable of independent thought and self-directed action. However, Kant did not just regard education as important on account of the individual enlightenment that it could bring about. Getting education right was crucial for Kant because it is the means through which all of humanity could improve itself. He stated that it 'is through good education that all the good in the world arises' (Kant, 2003, p 15). He intimated that children should not be educated for the present, but for the improvement of humankind in the future. Given these stakes, it is perhaps not surprising that he concludes that 'the greatest and most difficult problem to which man can devote himself is the problem of education' (Kant, 2003, p 11). Kant suggested that two substantial obstacles appear when thinking about how education might improve the condition of all of humanity.

On the one hand, parents' main hope is that education will attain the relatively modest end of helping their children get on in the world. They are interested in the future flourishing of their children, but not the future improvement of all of humanity. On the other hand, the rulers of the state generally only regard the next generation as tools to be used for the purposes of the state. They are interested in the future prosperity of the state, but not of the individual people that make up the state. Neither parents nor the powerful in society then care enough about how education might enable the universal good. But the universal improvement of humanity is precisely what Kant thought education should aim at, for the universal good is humanity's destiny.[2] Education is good, for Kant, when it aims at the good of all. He therefore suggested that only those with a genuine interest in, and knowledge of, the universal good should be entrusted with managing schools. A 'good education' for Kant (2003), supports young persons to not only think for themselves but, eventually, for the good of all. Crucially, Kant did not think persons could learn to think for the good of all without discipline.

Kant on discipline in education

> It is discipline, which prevents man from being turned aside by his animal impulses from humanity, his appointed end. Discipline, for instance, must restrain him from venturing wildly and rashly into danger. Discipline, thus, is merely negative, its action being to counteract man's natural unruliness. The positive part of education is instruction.
>
> (Kant, 2003, p 3)

Kant was one of the first Western thinkers to elucidate a connection between discipline in education and the long-term moral development of students. He thought that discipline helps persons resist their animal instincts. He stated that 'discipline changes animal nature into human nature' (2003, p 3). Kant held that it was the first of four parts of education (the others being culture, discretion and moral training). Though discipline is a vital part of the educational process through which persons become enlightened, Kant nonetheless thought discipline was, in and of itself, an essentially *negative* force. He defines discipline in fact as 'merely restraining unruliness' (2003, p 18). Discipline is a negative force then whose essential function is to curb the more unreasonable animal instincts of persons. Neglect of discipline he says 'is a greater evil than neglect of culture, for this last can be remedied in later life, but unruliness cannot be done away with, and a mistake in discipline can never be repaired.' (Kant, 2003, p 7)

Kant (2003) therefore thought it was crucial that discipline happened early in life. If it did not, he thought it unlikely that young people would be able to develop the ability to reason for themselves in the future. Instead they would follow their animal whims and caprice throughout life. The unruly and undisciplined are, Kant says, independent of law. Discipline is needed so that human beings can overcome their animal selves and become acquainted with the laws of mankind. He maintained that by 'discipline men are placed in subjection to the laws of mankind, and brought to feel their constraint. This, however, must be accomplished early. Children, for instance, are first sent to school, not so much with the object of their learning something, but rather that they may become used to sitting still and doing exactly as they are told' (Kant, 2003, p 3).

Kant undoubtedly regarded discipline as a vital, if largely restrictive and negative, part of education in the early years. However, he did insist that discipline should never be utterly slavish – children ought always to be conscious of their freedom, too. He remarked that 'nothing does more harm to children than to exercise a vexatious and slavish discipline over them with a view to breaking their will' (Kant, 2003, p 48). Moreover, Kant did not think that education ends with discipline. Far from it – discipline is only the beginning of education. As we have already seen, Kant thought education should enable persons to think for themselves and the good of all. For this instruction, culture, discretion and moral training are also all necessary.

Kant on instruction, rules, maxims and moral education

Kant (2003) insisted that it is through instruction that man begins to differ from other animals. While discipline is the negative part of culture and a necessary precursor for later education, instruction is the positive part of culture. He thought it important that instruction helps children acquire knowledge, the ability to distinguish between knowledge and opinion and also the capacity to put knowledge learned into practice. When the knowledge gained through instruction is of a physical and bodily nature then only discipline and exercise are needed for culture to emerge. However, when the content of learning involves the 'superior mental faculties' (Kant, 2003) it is vital that instruction encourages active pupil engagement instead of passive rule following. For Kant instruction should both cultivate the mind and improve the moral character of children. Moreover, Kant insisted that moral training must involve not discipline but *maxims*.[3] When children are disciplined, they merely follow the guidance and rules set out by their teachers. However, according to Kant, moral conduct entails acting according to maxims forged by one's self.

Kant maintained that the moral culture that children should be brought up into 'must be based upon "maxims", not upon discipline; the one prevents evil habits, the other trains the mind to think' (Kant, 2003, p 83). He thought a disciplined following of rules given to by others (often at school) could help children develop good as opposed to bad habits of conduct. However, Kant did not think that moral maturity or full human personhood consisted in habitual behaviour or the following of rules given to by others. Morality is not reducible to disciplined rule following. It requires the capacity to think and indeed act for one's self. He insisted that morality is 'so sacred and sublime that we must not degrade it by placing it in the same rank as discipline' (Kant, 2003, p 84). Instead, children need to learn to act from maxims if they are to develop mature moral character. Kant explains that maxims are a special sort of rules – they are 'subjective rules. They proceed from the understanding of man' (Kant, 2003, p 84). At first children must learn to follow 'school maxims' (Kant, 2003). These school maxims must be obeyed. Children do not, at least at first, need to appreciate why the following of these rules is good for them or others. Instead, mere obedience is essential. Obedience is especially important, Kant maintained, for school children.

Kant did not regard the education of emotions as morally important. He says that children 'ought not to be full of feeling, but they should be full of the idea of duty' (Kant, 2003, p 104). He argued that the character formation of children must be animated by rules, dutifully adhered to. Children must have set times for work, sleep and play and these times should not be altered. School children, he argued, 'must be subject to a certain law of necessity. This law, however, must be a general one . . . kept constantly in view, especially in schools' (Kant, 2003, p 86). Moreover, it is crucial that educators in schools do not show preference towards particular children. The same rules need to apply to all, 'otherwise the law would cease to be general' (Kant, 2003, p 86). He implies that once children have learned to obey school maxims they will be better prepared to learn the 'maxims of mankind'. Kant does not say much about how school children might learn the maxims of mankind in *On Education*. However, he does in other writings expand upon the idea that morally mature persons don't merely follow rules. They are rather able to author maxims that are applicable to all.

The age of discipline and the kingdom of ends

In *On Education* Kant argued that 'man's duty is to improve himself; to cultivate his mind; and, when he finds himself going astray, to bring the moral law to bear upon himself' (Kant, 2003, p 11). He expanded upon these ideas in *The Moral Law; Groundwork of the Metaphysics of Morals*. There, Kant famously set about trying to ascertain the supreme principle of morality. Kant saw the final end of morality as residing in man's capacity to formulate rational, universal, action-directing principles. The function of reason in the moral sphere, he says, is to influence action by producing a will that is good (Kant, 2007, pp 64–67). The 'will' he says is a power to choose what reason recognises to be good independent of sensory inclinations. Kant thought desires or inclinations from the world of experience often incapacitate the ability to determine the good will. However, he argued that *maxims* (self-made rules) liberate the will from the influence of such unruly inclinations.

Our fundamental moral motive, Kant says, is duty. Duty consists in reverence for, and adherence to, the moral law (Kant, 2007, pp 68–76). Kant thought that it is only dutiful application of the universal maxim (the categorical imperative) that can ensure that the will is always good. Notoriously, Kant did not consider actions motivated by beneficent feeling towards others to have any 'genuine moral worth' (Kant, 2007, p 73). Rather, an action done from duty 'has to set aside altogether the influence of inclination' (Kant, 2007, p 73). Kant claimed that there was only a single categorical imperative: 'act only on that maxim through which you can at the same time will that it should become a universal law' (Kant, 2007, p 97). What does he mean by this? Kant thought that people could only morally justify acting on maxims if such maxims could also be equally applied to all rational beings. The categorical imperative is thus an objective, universally binding moral law directed at the good of all. It must also, however, be individually created. A maxim, he says, is a 'subjective principle of volition' (Kant, 2007, p 72), a rule we have written ourselves, that we have a duty to submit to.

According to Kant (2007), each person is not merely subject to the law of maxims; he or she must also be the author of them. It is not enough to merely follow moral laws – one must also come to see the value in them for one's self. Kant also regarded mature moral personhood as residing in the capacity to treat other persons with dignity as ends in themselves. This is related to his concept of the 'kingdom of ends' (Kant, 2007, p 111). Kant describes the kingdom of ends as an ideal community, constituted of rational human beings that live, according to their own maxims, and treat all other persons there with *dignity*. The dignity of persons, he says, consists in their rational autonomy, in their ability to formulate their own maxims (Kant, 2007, pp 113–115). The kingdom of ends is so called because in this imagined community all persons treat each other with dignity, as ends in themselves, rather than as means to their own ends. However, it is notable that Kant did not think the people of his day were anywhere near capable of living in an actual kingdom of ends. He did not think all humanity had the capacity to form maxims to govern conduct for the good of all.[4]

He stated that we 'live in an age of discipline, culture and refinement, but we are still a long way off from the age of moral training. According to the present conditions of mankind, one might say that the prosperity of the state grows side by side with the misery of the people' (Kant, 2003, p 21). Here Kant seems to be suggesting that too many people in his day treated each other as means to their own ends rather than as ends in themselves. This was perhaps especially true of the powerful rulers of the state who exploited other less powerful people in the state. Though the people of his day may have followed rules, they were the rules of discipline, rules given to them by others. Unfortunately, these rules were not designed with the good of all in mind. Kant (2003) regarded his own 'age of discipline' as less desirable than his idea about the kingdom of ends. However, somewhat paradoxically, he did not think such 'an age of discipline' could be transcended without discipline. As we have seen, Kant held that it is only after children first learn to follow the rules of others through discipline that they will be ready to learn how to rule themselves.[5] As we shall go on to see, Kant's theory of discipline in education has significant flaws, but it has been profoundly influential.[6]

Durkheim on discipline in education

> This then is the true function of discipline ... It is essentially an instrument – difficult to duplicate – of moral education.
>
> (Durkheim, 1961, p 149)

Emile Durkheim (1961) further developed a number of Kant's ideas on discipline in education. Durkheim believed that education should centrally involve one generation imprinting its wisdom and customs on the next.[7] In *Moral Education; A study in the Theory & Application of the Sociology of Education*, Durkheim devoted considerable attention to the subject of disciplining schoolchildren. He identified two distinct stages of childhood: the first stage consisting of the child's life prior to attending school; the second stage commencing when children start their formal education. If, by the end of the second period of childhood, (that is the end of formal schooling) 'the foundations of morality had not been laid they never will be' (Durkheim, 1961, p 18). In the familial stage of childhood, the child becomes attached to his social group (the family) by being gently reproached in a nurturing environment. Durkheim thought that possessing a sentimental attachment toward the social group was an important step in a child's moral development. However, for Durkheim, the function of the *school* is to unite the child with larger society.

The role of the teacher is to act as an intermediary between the child and society. Just as the priest interprets the message of God to his congregation, so the teacher must establish and reinforce the values of society.[8] Durkheim (1961) insisted that schooling should mark a radical departure from a pupil's home life. It should not, he argued, foster personal attachments similar to those learned in the first stage of childhood, since 'the passions first must be limited' (Durkheim, 1972, p 176). Durkheim was insistent that formal education should remove and suppress *personal* emotion and ambition and rather develop in pupils an *impersonal* respect for societies' broader expectations. The school 'must sustain this feeling for discipline in the child. This is the task the educator must never give up' (Durkheim, 1961, pp 101–102). Durkheim held that dispassionate and objective forces should counter pupil's unruly appetites in schools. He said that it is by 'discipline we learn the control of desire without which man could not achieve happiness' (Durkheim, 1961, p 48). Durkheim (1961) believed that social cohesion depended on individual desires being limited and controlled. The constraint of desire was also a necessary condition of individual happiness as he thought that man by nature possessed passions that could never be satiated.

For Durkheim (1961) discipline was a vital part of a child's wider moral education. He speculated that there were three elements to morality: those of discipline, spirituality (which for him consisted in attachment to a social group) and self-determination or autonomy. Discipline was, in a vital sense, the fundamental element of morality that unites the others. Without discipline a person could not hope to attain the other elements of spirituality and self-determination. To lead a disciplined life, persons must have a preference for a regular existence; their aspirations must have determinate limits. Persons unable or unwilling to be disciplined would inevitably be doomed by their limitless aspirations and *anomie*.[9] Durkheim was of the view that children were especially prone to irregularity and instability and largely driven by primitive proclivities. A child's disposition is essentially volatile: he 'breaks out in anger and is mollified with the same suddenness. Tears succeed laughter, friendliness displaces hatred or vice versa' (Durkheim, 1961, p 130). He believed that childhood curiosity is similarly unstable and fleeting. Durkheim (1961) remarked that children only maintain attention on an object that attracts them for a matter of seconds. Despite, or perhaps because of this, he argued that the conduct of pupils was malleable. He thought that externally imposed habits could favourably curb and alter childish inconstancy. The function of discipline for Durkheim was to counter irregular conduct through the imposition of regular habit.

For individuals to develop discipline, Durkheim (1961) contended that they must first feel the force of authority acting on them, a force to which they must yield. Durkheim claimed that discipline was strongly dependent on authority for its success. He defined the notion of authority as a characteristic, 'with which a being, either actual or imaginary is invested through his relationship with given individuals and it is because of this alone that he is thought by the latter to be endowed with powers superior to those they find in themselves' (Durkheim, 1961, p 88). But who, or what, did he think should exercise authority over children? Durkheim contended that the authority to which individuals must yield on moral matters is the rule, the rule being written over time by the collective conscience of society. A rule is, 'essentially something that is outside a person . . . it is a way of acting that we do not feel free to alter according to taste . . . it is beyond personal preference . . . it dominates us' (Durkheim, 1961, p 28). A rule is an external command that individuals are duty bound to obey. He argued that the act of being disciplined by a rule was essentially an act of duty, duty being behaviour prescribed by rules. Here Durkheim's thinking takes on an especially Kantian aspect. However, Durkheim's thought on school discipline goes beyond Kant's.

Durkheim on school rules, morality and society

Durkheim (1961) believed that a classroom was its own society and that an undisciplined classroom was lacking in morality. The morality of the class society was, for Durkheim, determined by the resolution with which a teacher reinforces the impartial rule. When one considers the rules that a teacher is required to enforce one by one and in detail, it might be concluded that they are useless and petty vexations. However, if these rules are rather perceived as part of a larger, holistic code of conduct 'the matter takes on a different aspect' (Durkheim, 1961, p 151). In conscientiously fulfilling the disciplined obligations of the class society, the child comes to embody, 'the virtue of childhood . . . the only one that can be asked of him' (Durkheim, 1961, p 151) at that age and stage. On top of connecting the child to wider society, Durkheim suggested that the rules externally imposed by the teacher can over time become part of the pupil's internal moral constitution. Although the child does not begin life as master of his or her appetites, discipline in schools can and should enable such self-mastery to emerge.

Self-mastery of desire and attachment to the social group did not represent moral maturity for Durkheim (1961) since the capacity for self-determination was also necessary. He perceived a correlation between discipline and the capacity to establish and reach self-directed goals. However, for Durkheim discipline was not in itself indicative of this quality – it rather enabled it. A preference for regularity *prefaces* the emergence of any ability to set targets for one self.[10] However, Durkheim gives surprisingly little indication to the question of how schools should help to cultivate the final autonomous element of morality (Carr, 1991). Durkheim seems to think that teachers should help pupils to see the *value* of the rules on their own terms. Self-determination appears to consist in a sort of rational or 'enlightened assent' (Durkheim, 1961, p 120) to prevailing social standards rather than a merely habitual acceptance of them. When one considers in depth Durkheim's unusual conception of *society*, however, his theory of school discipline becomes questionable. There are, I think, at least two fundamental problems with his notion of society. He first insisted that *only* actions carried out *for the sake of* society were moral. Second, he rather implausibly posited that society was a sort of transcendent or divine being.

Durkheim emphasised that if actions only benefit individuals, they cannot be classified as moral. The term moral has *never* been employed, he says, to describe an act that has individual interest as its object (Durkheim, 1951). He maintained that moral acts are always in pursuit of impersonal ends. Behaviour 'directed exclusively towards the personal ends of the actor does not have moral value' (Durkheim, 1961, p 57). Disciplined and moral conduct must be altruistic and it must be so, *for* society. Durkheim stated that if, 'society is the end of morality it is also its producer' (Durkheim, 1961, p 86). Durkheim's moral theory was then centrally concerned with promoting the good for society. However, Durkheim had a very novel notion of society. He intimated that prior to modernity 'certain moral ideas became united with certain religious ideas to such an extent as to be indistinct from them' (Durkheim, 1961, p 8). The teacher was invested with authority and extra energy because he was, at least in part, 'speaking in the name of a superior reality' (Durkheim, 1961, p 10) of whom the symbolic expression was God. Durkheim, however, held that morality must become the sacred domain, not theology. He thought that society must strip morality of its religious symbols and replace them with rational substitutes.

The rationalisation of morality was perilous, however, as the very 'character of morality is without foundation' (Durkheim, 1961, p 10) unless it could also be bolstered by a new transcendent power. For Durkheim, the omnipresent force capable of preventing individuals from forever grasping for the infinite was society itself: 'once we rule out recourse to theological notions, there remains beyond the individual only a single, empirically observable moral being . . . society' (Durkheim, 1961, p 60). Durkheim argued that morality begins with membership of a social group.[11] Without society there could be no morality. On morality he says that it 'is a totality of definite rules; it is like so many moulds with limiting boundaries, into which we must pour our behaviour' (Durkheim, 1961, p 26). However, Durkheim believed that society possessed a special, independent quality that rendered it superior to the sum of the individuals that constitute it. 'Human groups have a way of thinking, of feeling and of living differing from that of their members when they think feel and live as isolates' (Durkheim, 1961, p 62). A society, he remarks, is qualitatively different to the individual persons that comprise it – it commands individuals because it represents the best part of them.[12]

However, to my mind, Durkheim's (1961) interesting notion of a 'divinized society', superior to the sum of individuals that constitute it, is not, as he asserts, empirically verifiable. Moreover, his idea of a divine society is more than a little bizarre. In stressing that individuals are not capable of moral action unless society benefits, I also think Durkheim needlessly undermined the range of individual actions that could be considered to be moral. When comparing Durkheim's theory of discipline in education to Kant's, it is also important to recognise that Durkheim did not think rational moral laws should be formulated and agreed upon by all persons. Instead he acknowledged that different societies have different rules. Durkheim's theory of discipline is therefore importantly different to Kant's.[13] However, Durkheim did follow Kant in trying to articulate an account of how school discipline should be connected to the wider purposes of education. Kant and Durkheim both thought that discipline was a necessary first phase of moral education. They also agreed that it was vital that educators initiate students into school rules so as to curb their otherwise limitless desires. Without first learning the norms of society through discipline in school, pupils would not be fit for further learning or later life in society. However, Kant's influence on thinking about school discipline extends beyond the work of Durkheim.

Discipline and school rules in the work of John Wilson

> If a child did not grasp and act upon the principle of discipline, of obedience to established authority, he could hardly survive at all, and a proper grasp of it is an essential enablement for the child to learn other things.
>
> (Wilson, 1981, p 44)

A philosopher of education more recently influenced by Kant was John Wilson. Like Kant, Wilson (1981) also developed a philosophy of school discipline based on submission to rules. Like Kant, Wilson also thought submission to rules was necessary for further learning and wider moral development. However, unlike Kant, Wilson reasoned that discipline is itself morally educational if it is rightly conceived (Wilson, 1981). Wilson thought that the morally formative potential of discipline lay in the child's dutiful adherence to the authority of rules, precisely because the rules are authoritative. He insisted that a disciplined person should not submit to a rule because it comes from an admired source, or even because the rule in question is a good one. The reason why rules should be observed is so that legitimate authorities can continue to influence practical action. Wilson argued that authority is a necessary foundation for any institution or society. Without it, the only recourse available for getting things done is an 'ad hoc variety of bribes or threats' (Wilson, 1981, p 39). Pupils should dutifully submit to rules in school because such rules provide necessary guidance for action.

Wilson emphasised that genuine discipline is characterised by a 'disposition to obey' (Wilson, 1981, p 38). He claimed that discipline itself has little to do with self-discipline or autonomy. Discipline ultimately requires no more or less than *obedience*. It is perhaps unsurprising then that Smith accuses Wilson of having developed a 'rather austere doctrine' (Smith, 1985, p 40) of discipline. Smith is sceptical of Wilson's tendency to compare military discipline and school discipline. He observes that whilst life and death situations might be common for the soldier on duty, the same can hardly be said of the school pupil. If the class is conceived of as a quasi-military group, then there lies a danger that the teacher might repeatedly invoke situations of crisis to justify 'compliance without consultation' (Smith, 1985, p 46) and obedience without critical thought. Smith implies that Wilson's conception of discipline borders on the authoritarian. But is this implication fair?

Wilson emphasises that it is only *legitimate authority* that should be obeyed without question and he seems to have believed that such authority should be deeply infused with rationality (1981). In Wilson's picture, discipline is essentially concerned with certain practical matters where immediate obedience is required from pupils and where *now* is probably not the appropriate time to explain the reasons why obedience is justified. However, Wilson seems to have held the view that a necessary part of moral formation involves comprehending (at the proper time) why obedience is sometimes necessary. He does after all make clear that discipline is one concept amongst others vitally connected to a pupil's broader moral education. Moreover, moral education for Wilson, centrally involves reason. Reason, he says 'requires sharing and dialogue and that has more to do with desire than obligation' (Wilson, 2000, p 274). Wilson also stresses that the actions of the morally educated person must arise from the right reasons. For Wilson, rule following alone 'is an impoverished view of moral action' (McLaughlin & Halstead, 2000, p 251). If Wilson's more expansive account of moral education is borne in mind, then his theory of discipline perhaps takes on a less authoritarian flavour.

Wilson (1981) held that family and school were the principal influences on a child's moral development. He says that the 'family and the school necessarily form the arena of the child's first encounter with the whole business of rules and authority' (Wilson, 1981, p 44). Wilson implies that parents are at least as responsible as schools for administering rules. Although he does concede that it is possible for a person to be disciplined by the rules inherent in certain activities (he cites the example of a person playing chess), he also intimates that it is not really natural to speak of a disciplined individual. Individuals, he says 'are more likely to be described as simply 'disobedient' (Wilson, 1981, p 41). Wilson insists that it is much more appropriate to adopt the term *discipline* when referring to a *group* that has a fairly specific practical task. Thus, Wilson thought discipline centrally involves being *part of* a social group. However, unlike Durkheim, Wilson did not think that discipline is essentially *for the sake of* that social group.

Wilson (1981), like Kant, attests that there is an objective morality upon which all moral rules should be based. He impresses the point that particular sets of social values have nothing to do with moral values. As he puts it, moral education, like education in science or maths, 'means the same at all times and in all places ... In particular we cannot derive our aims in moral education from 'society' (Wilson, 1981, p 40). Kant and Wilson's view, that moral education is and should be rational and cross-cultural, presents a clear demarcation between their moral thought and that of Durkheim's. There are undoubtedly differences in the accounts of discipline provided by Kant, Durkheim and Wilson then. However, they all insisted that school discipline ought to be connected to the wider purposes of schooling. In particular, they agreed that discipline in schools: 1) is vital for moral education and development and 2) should first and foremost initiate students into impersonal rules that apply to all, regardless of circumstance.

Kantian thinking on discipline in education continues to influence, but is conceptually flawed

In the preceding sections of this chapter I hope it has become clear that Kantian thinking about discipline in education has significantly influenced later theorizing about school discipline.[14] However, Kantian-type thinking about discipline in education continues to be apparent in education policy and practice today too. In the last chapter it was suggested that behaviour management and zero tolerance approaches dominate discipline policy and practice in the UK and the US respectively. Both these approaches are, in different ways, Kantian in nature, at least in part. A well-known advocate of behaviour management, Tom Bennett (2010), for example, maintains that school discipline is about training 'animal' like students to do the bidding of the teacher. It is difficult not to sense the echo of Durkheim (1961), Kant (2003) and Wilson (1981) in such a perspective.[15] Kant, Durkheim, Wilson and Bennett all think young persons in school need to be dominated by a force greater than them to curb their unruly instincts. Only when students are under the teacher's law will they be ready for further learning. However, unlike Kant, Durkheim, and Wilson, Bennett does not seem to think that school discipline is deeply implicated in the wider moral development of students.

Zero tolerance approaches are perhaps the best recent example though, of Kantian-type thinking about discipline in educational practice. Zero tolerance approaches, like Kantian thinking on discipline on education, call for rules to be enforced for all school students irrespective of context or circumstance. Zero tolerance approaches also rest on the view that it is for the good of all that impersonal rules are strictly followed in schools. While it has become increasingly clear that zero tolerance approaches do not benefit all students, as we saw in the last chapter, proponents of zero tolerance believe that they can. While Kant undoubtedly thought a rules-based approach to discipline should aim to curb unruliness in students, he also thought education (and any discipline that is part of it) ought to aim at the future improvement of humanity via the cultivation of moral autonomy in all persons. Zero tolerance approaches to discipline in contrast have no such noble (if naive) aspirations. Zero tolerance approaches, like behaviour management, also sever the connection between disciplinary practices and the wider purposes of schooling.

In the last chapter some of the historical reasons for zero tolerance approaches coming to prominence in US schools were noted. However, what the thinking of Kant, Durkheim and Wilson arguably reveals, is that the reasons for policies such as zero tolerance taking hold are not only, and perhaps not even largely, historical. Since at least the time of Kant in the nineteenth century the predominant concept of discipline in education has been a rules-based one. In such a conceptualization the task facing those who work in schools is to initiate students into impersonal rules that apply to all irrespective of circumstance. Though initially severe and negative, if accompanied by instruction, such rules will, in the fullness of time, come to serve the good of all. So Kantian-type thinking on discipline in education goes. However, what the evidence regarding zero tolerance shows is that such practices do not work for the good of all. Many students' long-term prospects seem to be undermined by the impersonal zero tolerance approach to discipline.

Moreover, a large-scale longitudinal study involving nearly 11,000 students from over 1000 US schools unearthed that student disruption was likely to be exacerbated rather than diminished by an environment of strictly enforced school rules and punishment (Way, 2011). Such studies suggest *all* students suffer when there is too much focus on enforcing school rules and meting out punishments when they are broken. The sort of impersonal rules-based thinking about discipline in education exemplified by Kant

(2003) and his followers continues to resonate in impoverished form in much education policy and practice today then. However, such Kantian-type thinking is in error. It is a conceptual, as much as a practical error, to think that an impersonal rules-based approach to discipline in education will work for the good of all. However, it is an error of thinking that has all too often become ingrained in practice. In so far as zero tolerance type approaches to discipline in education are based on errors of thinking, they are, at least in part, conceptual errors. If rules-based approaches to discipline are conceptually flawed though, how might educators come to think differently about discipline in education? I will address this question in subsequent chapters.

Chapter summary

In this chapter I have argued that rules are ubiquitous in education, perhaps especially regarding matters of school discipline. I therefore set about trying to consider the educational value of school rules. I first documented the work on discipline in education by Immanuel Kant (2003). Kant thought discipline was inherently negative. It should aim to curb unruliness in students and no more. However, he also thought discipline ought to be regarded as a vital first part of wider student education and moral development. In particular Kant thought education ought to aim at the future improvement of all of humanity via the cultivation of moral autonomy in persons. Learning to think for oneself first entails acquiring discipline and the capacity to follow rules formed by others. However, until persons learn to become authors of their own rules (maxims) and able to act for the good of all, they cannot be regarded as morally mature. In this chapter I also charted how Kant's theory of discipline in education shaped those developed by others, in particular Emile Durkheim and John Wilson.

Durkheim (1961) followed Kant in trying to articulate an account of how school discipline should be connected to the wider purposes of education. Kant and Durkheim both thought that discipline was a necessary first part of moral education. They also agreed that it was vital that educators initiate students into school rules so as to curb their otherwise limitless desires. However, unlike Kant, Durkheim did not think it helpful to regard all persons as being potentially capable of rationally forming universal moral laws. For Durkheim discipline in education was not so much for the good of all humanity but for society. We have also considered the views of John Wilson (1981) in this chapter. Wilson like Kant and Durkheim held that school discipline: 1) is vital for moral education and development and 2) should first and foremost initiate students into impersonal rules that apply to all, regardless of circumstance. I concluded the chapter by arguing that Kant and his followers erred conceptually in their thinking about discipline in education. Here, I claimed that it is mistaken to think that an impersonal rules-based approach to discipline in education will work for the good of all. I also indicated that this error of thinking has all too often become entrenched in education policy and practice.

To be clear, my argument is not that school rules have no educational value. Often they do. However, in too many instances for comfort school rules don't work for the good of *all*. The zero tolerance approaches to discipline are perhaps the best example of this. Indeed, there is a growing body of evidence that suggests zero tolerance approaches to discipline in schools do not work for the good of all.[16] While school rules are perhaps morally educational for some, it is also evident that rules have a negative impact on the long-term prospects of too many students in US schools. This is perhaps not surprising. Kant regarded discipline as fundamentally negative, and zero-tolerance approaches to discipline are also fundamentally negative. While Kant's thinking on discipline in education was flawed, he at least recognised the need for schools to support students in their moral development as well. Zero tolerance approaches by contrast do not generally contain any positive instructive element. They just discipline and punish. No wonder they are not working. In the next chapter a different theory of discipline in education will therefore be considered. One that specifically sought to bring to light how impersonal rules-based approaches to discipline in education all too often just monitor and punish. In so doing, they fail to work for the good of all.

Notes

1. As we saw in the last chapter, the consequences of breaking school rules can often be severe and far-reaching – perhaps especially in the US context.
2. For further discussion of this, see Kant (2003), chapter 1 especially.
3. See Kant (2003) chapter IV especially.
4. Kant argued that maxims could *only* be written by the self in the *intelligible world*, even though their purpose is to direct action in the *sensible* world. We must, he says, make some sort of distinction between the intelligible and sensible world (Kant, 2007, p 133). Kant thought that all rational persons have the capacity to transfer themselves to the intelligible world by willing to be free from sensuous influence. Through this process they can develop 'a greater inner worth' (Kant, 2007, p 137). The *intelligible world* he says is a rational or purely intellectual world constituted of *things-in-themselves*. By contrast, the sensible world can only provide us with knowledge of things as they *appear* to us (Kant, 2007, p 133). Kant thought that all people were capable of having an idea of the intelligible world – but only an idea, as they could have no sensory and physical acquaintance with such a world. As we shall see in later chapters, I do not agree with the metaphysics that underpins Kant's moral philosophy.
5. For further reading about Kant's ideas on moral education, see Moran (2009) who posits that there is no contradiction between Kant's theory of moral education and his wider moral philosophy.
6. For further commentary on Kant's thinking on education generally and discipline specifically, see Roth and Surprenant (2012).
7. For further discussion of this, see Dill (2007).
8. For further discussion of this point, see Dill (2007) and Durkheim (1961).
9. An acute unhappiness and loss of purpose that Durkheim thought was prevalent at the time of the industrial revolution.

10 As we shall see in chapter 5, Dewey developed a theory of discipline that is both similar and importantly different to this.
11 See for example Dill (2007) and Durkheim (1951, 1961).
12 See Durkheim (1951).
13 Indeed, Durkheim suggests that Kant's metaphysics is bound to mislead, resting as it does on the creation of a rational reality apart from the material world (1961, p 110).
14 As we shall see in subsequent chapters, Kantian thinking about discipline in education has influenced a host of other thinkers beyond Durkheim and Wilson, too.
15 I have two observations to make here. First, I want to point out that Kant adopts a view of human nature that is very different to the one articulated by Bennett and discussed in the last chapter. Whereas for Bennett humans are just one kind of animal amongst others, for Kant human beings are radically different to other animals on account of their capacity to think for themselves. Whereas for Bennett educators should 'break students in', for Kant educators should support their students to think for themselves. Second, while I am more inclined to agree with Kant than Bennett, I do want to point out that I am most sympathetic to the views of MacIntyre (1999) who holds that some animals may share a measure of reason with human beings. I will explore MacIntyre's philosophy of education in chapter 5.
16 For further discussion of why zero tolerance approaches to discipline don't work for all, see chapter 2.

4 Discipline and punishment in education

In this chapter I explore possible connections between discipline and punishment in education. I use the thought of Kant, Durkheim and Foucault to help me do so. In particular, I argue that Foucault's *Discipline and Punish* can be regarded as a critique of the modes of discipline and punishment advanced by Kant and especially Durkheim. Durkheim and Foucault both investigated how punishment in modern schools became less violent and more diffuse, continuous and graduated in scale. In spite of their differences Kant, Durkheim and Foucault did agree on at least one thing. That discipline and punishment is imposed on students in schools. Discipline and punishment constrains individuals – they mould individuals into what schools and later society, needs them to be. Discipline defines individuals. I pull the chapter together by considering what Kant, Durkheim and Foucault call tell us about discipline and punishment in education today. Kant and Durkheim thought socialising students into the norms of society at school via discipline and punishment could lead to the growth of individual autonomy and social cohesion. In contrast, Foucault's critique helps to reveal how disciplinary mechanisms in educational institutions all too often merely normalise students and ready them to be docile productive workers. Foucault suggested that disciplinary mechanisms systematically stifle resistance against the norms and (industry focussed) values of society. I conclude by observing that Foucault's critique, despite its strengths, does not provide answers to the question of how *discipline* in educational institutions might be arranged to foster ends beyond mere socialisation and normalisation.

Discipline, rules and punishment in education

In the previous chapter it was suggested that schools often employ sanctions (or the threat of sanctions) in order to reinforce school rules and school discipline. Indeed, it was claimed that school rules would often not have the action directing force that they do if they were not accompanied by sanctions. In so far as it is hard to imagine a school without rules, it is also hard to imagine a school without sanctions. But if sanctions and punishments are generally deemed to be part and parcel of school life and necessary for upholding school rules, why might this be so? What educational justification is there for the use of punishment in schools and what is the relationship between punishment and discipline? What forms of punishment *have* emerged in modern education systems? Moreover, what forms of punishment *should there be* in education, if any? This chapter charts in depth the diverse perspectives of Durkheim and Foucault on discipline and punishment in education so as to address such questions. Before we turn to these scholars though, I want to briefly consider how Kant thought punishment could be used to support the ends of discipline and education – as Kant's thinking undoubtedly influenced both Durkheim and Foucault.

In the last chapter it was noted that Kant (2003) thought school children must learn to obey the commands of the teacher. He thought discipline consisted in obeying commands given to by others. In the school context he argued that every transgression of a teacher command required punishment. For Kant school punishment could take two forms – *physical* and *moral*. Punishment is moral when teachers 'do something derogatory to the child's longing to be honoured and loved' (Kant, 2003, p 87). When children disobey a command, Kant suggested teachers should be cold and distant towards them. He thought this would be felt as a punishment by schoolchildren – a punishment because the withholding of love and esteem is painful. Kant concluded that withholding affection and praise is the best form of punishment since it carries with it moral educational potential. The moral educational potential here specifically concerns the reduction of rule breaking conduct by the student in the future. Though he thought that moral punishment was the most educationally desirable form of punishment, Kant did not preclude there being occasional need for physical punishment in education.

Physical punishment, he stressed, should merely supplement moral punishment. Kant thought physical punishment could entail either refusing a child's request, or the infliction of pain. He thought that teachers must be cautious when employing physical pain as a means of punishment in schools. If physically punished too often, or when it is not warranted, there will be no educational benefit and therefore no justification for it. Indeed, Kant thought that teachers ought to be generally very careful when employing any form of punishment in education. When punishing, the aim ought always to be the improvement of the character of the student. Teachers should not get angry when punishing students. He remarked that punishments 'inflicted with signs of anger are useless' (Kant, 2003, p 89) as children will come to regard themselves as victims of that anger instead of subjects of moral education. Any moral educational potential from the punishment would be forfeit. While Kant thought corporal punishment should be employed cautiously in schools, Durkheim (1961) did not think it should feature at all. Durkheim did, however, like Kant, think punishment often entailed withholding esteem from students so as to reinforce the value of school rules. For Durkheim, punishment so conceived is both necessary and educationally justifiable.

Durkheim on why punishment is necessary in schools

> Not without reason have sanctions always been linked to rules specifying the child's conduct . . . What, then, is the bond joining these two terms to one another? In other words why is it necessary to punish?
> (Durkheim, 1961, p 160)

In *Moral Education: A study in the theory and application of the sociology of education*, Durkheim followed up his discussion of discipline in education by focussing on the issue of school punishment.[1] Durkheim felt that rules, discipline, punishment and moral education were all intimately interrelated. As we saw in chapter 3, he thought discipline should be rules-based and regarded as the first part of a child's wider moral development. Discipline is the first step on the path to moral maturity. Discipline consists in having respect for rules. He says that in order for the 'child to subject himself to the prescription of the rule' (Durkheim, 1961, p 158) he must first feel what is in the rule that is worthy of respect. While rules ought not to be followed blindly, in the first phase of moral education (discipline) coming to respect the rules is often a matter of coming to respect the authority of the teacher. Punishment is sometimes necessary in education in order to help errant children see why the rules continue to be worthy of respect. Developing discipline is a matter of learning to respect the authority of school rules. Punishment in contrast only happens when the authority of school rules has not been respected.

Durkheim (1961) contended that at the start of the twentieth century there were two competing justifications for the use of punishment in schools, neither of which were satisfactory. On the one hand, school punishment could be justified on grounds of *deterrence*. On the other hand, punishments could be warranted when they serve to *expunge past misbehaviour* rather than deter future misconduct. In the former account 'punishment is a simple way of preventing defections from the rule. We must punish the child . . . so that he doesn't misbehave again and to prevent others from imitating him' (Durkheim, 1961, p 161). However, for Durkheim deterrence is not the primary reason for punishment in education. Although it may intimidate and prevent some students from misbehaving, punishments cannot touch the moral life of students by directing them towards the good. Deterring pupils from breaking rules is not then in itself an adequate justification for the use of punishment in schools. However, the second justification for the use of punishment in schools is not adequate either.

Durkheim (1961) took issue with the view that punishment can somehow restore order in schools after it has been broken. According to this view, punishment should inflict misery on the offender in order to counter and neutralise the effects of the offending behaviour. Here punishment 'nullifies the offence and restores things to their proper state. It turns not towards the future but towards the past . . . Some misdeed has disrupted the order;

punishment re-establishes that disrupted order' (Durkheim, 1961, p 164). However, Durkheim posits that such reasoning is based on a spurious idea of symmetry. A new pain cannot erase a past one. The essence of educational punishment does not reside in the infliction of new suffering. Nonetheless, Durkheim did maintain that punishment could, in some ways, compensate for misdeeds in school.

For Durkheim (1961) the real harm of misbehaviour in schools resides in the weakening of the authority of rules. Children submit to rules so long as they are sacred and endowed with prestige. When rules are violated, they come to appear less sacred to students. When the teacher begins to lack the authority to convince their students that school rules are sacred, discipline in schools dissipates. Punishment in school is therefore justified for Durkheim in so far as it reaffirms the disciplinary value of rules and prevents rules from losing their authority. However, it should be stressed that punishment is distinct from and subservient to school discipline in Durkheim's thought. He says that 'it is not punishment that gives discipline its authority; but it is punishment that prevents discipline from losing its authority, which infractions, if they went unpunished, they would progressively erode' (Durkheim, 1961, p 167). Punishment is necessary in schools for Durkheim so as to prevent the erosion of discipline, where discipline consists in respect for school rules. Punishment cannot 'by itself produce authority' (Garland, 1999, p 31) or respect for rules – it can only reinforce authority and respect for rules if they are already there. What form of punishment, though, did Durkheim believe capable of reinforcing in students' minds the inviolable and sacred authority of school rules?

Durkheim on the function, form and birth of school punishment

Durkheim (1961) maintained that respect for rules is an altogether different thing than fear of punishment. He felt that student fear of punishment could at best merely repress misbehaviour in school.[2] Fear of punishment could not for Durkheim remind students of the sacred and inviolable nature of rules; but this is precisely what Durkheim thought the function of school punishment should be. Durkheim followed Kant in thinking that punishment could remind students of the value of rules if esteem was withheld from offending students.[3] He says that to 'punish is to reproach, to disapprove . . . the principal form of punishment has always consisted in putting the guilty on the *index*, ostracising him . . . Since one cannot reproach anyone without treating him less well than those whom one esteems . . . all such suffering generally ends in inflicting some suffering on the delinquent' (Durkheim, 1961, pp 175–176). It is important to note here though, that the suffering of the student is an incidental effect of the punishment rather than the educational justification for it. The function of punishment is not to harm the body or soul of the student even though it may. Punishment should, according to Durkheim, affirm the value of the rule that the offence seems to deny.

Durkheim (1961) maintained that when students in school break rules a demoralising effect results, unless the teacher reinforces the authority of the rule. The function of punishment is to reaffirm and strengthen the sense of duty that offending students (and those students who witness the offence) feel towards school rules. All sanctions that fail to promote this sense of duty toward rules should be removed from schools. In this respect Durkheim was unequivocal about the need to prohibit all forms of corporal punishment in schools. For Durkheim, all discipline (and any punishment that is part of it) should be morally educational. Physical punishment of the body was not for Durkheim an effective means of morally educating. In particular corporal punishment could not instil a sense of duty towards one's fellow human beings. A fundamental aim 'of moral education is to inspire in the child a feeling for the dignity of man. Corporal punishment is a continual offense to this sentiment' (Durkheim, 1961, p 183). The beating of children is an affront to the idea that all human persons are worthy of dignity. As such physical violence had no justifiable place in schools.

Durkheim (1961) was interested in the question of why physical violence came to happen at all in some school contexts given there seemed to be no obvious educational benefit to this. He maintained that the violent flogging of children tended not to happen in a variety of different 'primitive' societies. Instead punishment and discipline in (for example) Canadian Indians and South American tribes was remarkably gentle in nature.[4] According to Durkheim, it was only with the advent of formal schooling that systematic practices of corporal punishment against children emerged. It was in Rome and especially in monastic Christian schools in the thirteenth century that the severe physical punishment of children became common practice. He notes that here the 'chief correctional procedures were slapping, kicking, striking with the fist, the rod, the lash, incarceration, fasting, the *vellicatio* (tickling), and kneeling' (Durkheim, 1961, p 186). From the thirteenth to the sixteenth century there developed an 'orgy of violence' in many European schools. The key lesson from this history for Durkheim is that violent corporal punishment against children was generally a feature of school but not of family life. Corporal punishment in education did not originate in the family to be passed to the school. Instead corporal punishment of children was born in the school – and it grew in use in the school.

In contrast to this Durkheim (1961) was against the use of corporal punishment in schools. Indeed, he was opposed to any kind of punishment that might injure child health. But if punishment ought not to be directed upon the bodies of schoolchildren, what form should it take? Durkheim suggested that the first and most important principle of punishment is that it must operate on a graduated scale. He stated that: 'but for rare exceptions, punishment should not be administered in massive doses... we must contrive to multiply the degrees and stages of the scale of punishment'

(Durkheim, 1961, p 199). Punishments ought to be very lenient to start with. A look of disapproval toward an individual might suffice. Children might be publically rather than privately reproached if a look of individual disapproval fails. They may later be deprived of their playtime or the right to participate in games or they may be asked to undertake extra schoolwork. However, the gradual increase in the severity of punishment ought to be judiciously measured in pace. This should be so as the force of non-corporal punishment is weakened each time it is used. That is why Durkheim thought it vital that schools develop ever more complex scales of punishment.[5]

To sum up, Kant and Durkheim may have differed in their views regarding the value of corporal punishment in schools. However, they both agreed that punishment in schools could only be justified if it was regarded as subservient to and ultimately in service of school discipline. Punishment for both these thinkers was clearly distinct from discipline. Punishment was not in itself educational. However, it could be implicated in education if it reinforced discipline, as discipline is a necessary first step in the moral education of the child. They also both agreed that punishments in schools must be employed with sensitivity, judgement and care. For Durkheim especially this meant employing a graduated scale of punishment. Durkheim was also interested in the historical circumstances that led to the emergence of corporal punishment in schools. He was not the only French thinker to have such an interest though. Foucault wrote much more extensively about the historical and cultural forces that gave rise to new forms of discipline and punishment in schools.[6] However, unlike Durkheim, Foucault was not in favour of the new forms of discipline that emerged in modernity and specifically the ones that punished students according to graduated scale.

Discipline and punish: The birth of the prison

Michel Foucault (1926–1984) wrote the most influential text of the twentieth century regarding discipline in education.[7] However, *Discipline and punish: The birth of the prison* is not centrally about schools or other institutions of education.[8] Arguably it is not first and foremost concerned with discipline either. The mechanisms and purposes of punishment form the beating heart of this challenging and important book.[9] The text begins with a graphic and brutal account of the public execution of Damiens, the regicide in eighteenth-century France. Foucault describes in detail the torture and killing of Damiens, not so much to shock (although his being burned, cut and pulled apart by horses is shocking), but to bring home a key idea that animates the rest of the book. Namely, that by the beginning of the nineteenth century torture and punishment as a (painful) public spectacle was dying out. Up until the nineteenth century, punishment was primarily about inflicting physical pain on the human body. However, during the Enlightenment, practices of torture were increasingly denounced as inhuman. Indeed, after this time 'the punishment-body relation is not the same . . . Physical pain, the pain of the body itself, is no longer the constituent element of the penalty (Foucault, 1991, p 11).

In place of physical pain new forms of punishment were emerging. Foucault (1991) suggested that for some eighteenth-century thinkers (such as Malby) the *soul* was to be the new site of punishment not the body. Foucault argued that from the nineteenth century onward punishment did, at least to some extent, become less about pain infliction and more about reformation of the soul. Such reformation of souls occurs in multiple contexts and ways. Sometimes it is a matter of keeping close tabs on those who transgress laws in prisons. In other instances, reformation is a matter of medical treatment – especially psychiatric treatment. Schools, too, play a part in the reformation of the soul through initiating students into social norms and by constantly examining them. In all these ways and others, punishment became for Foucault a means by which the state could define individuals. The purpose of these new forms of punishment was not pain but the neutralisation, and indeed transformation of any criminal, deviant or socially abnormal tendencies in persons. He says that:

> From being an art of unbearable sensations punishment has become an economy of suspended rights. If it is still necessary for the law to reach and manipulate the body of the convict, it will be at a distance, in the proper way, according to strict rules, and with a much "higher" aim. As a result of this new restraint, a whole army of technicians took over from the executioner . . . wardens, doctors, chaplains psychiatrists, psychologists, educationalists; by their very presence near the prisoner, they sing the praises that the law needs.
>
> (Foucault, 1991, p 11)

In the past the executioner took the life of the criminal as punishment for transgressing social norms. Torture only aimed in small part to deter future criminality – the main aim of such punishment was retribution. However, according to Foucault, in modernity, penal practices aimed at deterrence much more systematically. Modern penal practices seek to reform the offender rather than hurt them so as to render them capable of living within the law in the future. However, *individual* reformation is not the core function of penal practices. Much wider deterrence is. When deterrence is the main aim of punishment, it is not just one person (the executioner) who is responsible for reinforcing social norms through punishment. In Foucault's thinking, today maybe all of us are partly turned into executioners and prisoners via technologies of punishment and surveillance. While prisons may seek to punish and reform criminals most overtly, a whole raft of other professionals (including educators) and workers are also implicated in the definition of human souls through punishment, discipline and surveillance.

The politics and purpose of punishment

It is notable that Foucault (1991) elucidates a non-theological, historical understanding of the soul. He maintained that it 'would be wrong to say that the soul is an illusion . . . On the contrary, it exists, it has a reality, it is produced permanently . . . by the functioning of a power that is exercised on those punished – and, in a more general way, on those one supervises, trains and corrects, over madmen, children at home and at school . . . This is the historical reality of the soul, which unlike the soul represented by Christian theology, is not born in sin and subject to punishment but is rather born out of methods of punishment, supervision and constraint' (Foucault, 1991, p 29). Foucault thought punishment partly produces individuals. Punishments make people who they are, for better and worse. As such he argued that punishment ought to always be thought of as a political act. Indeed, a key intention of *Discipline and Punish* was to reveal how punishment had increasingly become a political tactic designed to deter future criminality and deviance and render individuals into docile, productive workers. As we shall see, though punishment is a political tactic, it tends to reduce the capacity of punished persons to act politically.

Unlike Durkheim, Foucault did not think that the new forms of punishment that emerged were necessarily more humane than those that preceded them. For Foucault (1991) the laws and technologies of punishment altered in the nineteenth century, not so much out of a desire for methods of punishment to become more humane, but so as to inscribe new norms onto the human soul. These new norms reflected the new social reality of transgression, where there were higher numbers of crimes against property and fewer violent crimes against persons. The purpose of punishment became less focussed on seeking retribution against the criminal and more about the prevention of future disorder amongst those who have not actually committed any crime. Here the aim is to deter the desire of persons to offend in the first place. Punishment is needed so as to reinforce social order as 'nothing so weakens the machinery of law than the hope of going unpunished' (Foucault, 1991, p 96).

Whereas the public spectacle of execution was a violent form of physical retribution aimed primarily at criminals, the new forms of punishment that emerged were less violent and more surveillance based – and they were directed towards everyone. As he puts it: 'the guilty person is only one of the targets of punishment. For punishment is directed above all at others, at all the potentially guilty' (Foucault, 1991, p 108). Foucault imagined a 'punitive city' where all citizens understand the inevitably of surveillance and punishment. There, organs of surveillance are apparent to all, at all levels of social life, complementing the machinery of justice. As a result of the complex surveillance network, people in such a city believe crime will invariably be witnessed and punished. This would have the effect of deterring future criminality. Punishments become 'a school' rather than a 'festival'. Each punishment is visible to all, including children, so as to teach the lesson that those with vices, those who infringe social norms, will with certainty be caught and punished. However, Foucault suggested that such punitive cities remain in the realm of the social imaginary. Instead, we have coercive institutions that mask and conceal the extent to which we are all being watched in an increasingly disciplinary society.[10]

Coercive institutions, constant surveillance and the disciplinary society

> The emergence of the prison marks the institutionalisation of the power to punish, or, to be more precise: will the power to punish . . . be better served by concealing itself beneath a general social function, in the "punitive city", or by investing itself in a coercive institution, in the enclosed space of a "reformatory"?
>
> (Foucault, 1991, p 130)

Foucault suggested that the school is one coercive institution amongst many. The prison is the prime example of a coercive institution. Prisons came to exist so as to reform those who have transgressed social norms. The form of this reformation was largely one of isolation, observation and, if need be, experimental medication rather than physical violence. He famously considered Bentham's Panopticon, which he dubbed a 'seeing machine'. This invention was a large tower intended for location in the middle of a prison. It was designed by Bentham in such a way as to allow prison wardens to observe prisoners in their cells at all times – at least in theory – in practice they could not actually observe all prisoners at once. However, the constant feeling that they could be watched at any time would in theory eventually neutralise any violent or deviant tendencies in individual prisoners and so reform them. If prisoners continued to transgress norms, then they could be medicated till they stop or forever kept apart from others and under surveillance. While no pure Panopticon prisons have ever actually been built, many prisons have been designed to allow prison staff to observe prisoners. He remarked that 'the Panopticon must not be understood as a dream building: it is the diagram of a mechanism of power reduced to its ideal form' (Foucault, 1991, p 205).

Foucault uses the example of the Panopticon then in a metaphorical way to try to reveal how disciplinary power works. However, he maintained that other institutions like schools, factories and hospitals have increasingly taken on prison-like features too. They start the multiple practices of isolation and surveillance that find their completion in the prison. He stated that the 'prison continues . . . a work begun elsewhere, which the whole of society pursues on each individual through innumerable mechanisms of discipline' (Foucault, 1991, pp 302–303). Thus for Foucault, increasingly we live in disciplinary societies.[11] While the Panopticon represents an ideal and extreme disciplinary mechanism, the more general growth of surveillance and 'mechanisms of discipline throughout the seventeenth and eighteenth centuries' led to the 'formation of what might be called . . . the disciplinary society (Foucault, 1991, p 209). However, Foucault implied that the birth of the disciplinary society may not have been inevitable. Other ways of reducing crime were imagined by social and legal reformers during the eighteenth century including the idea of what Foucault called the 'punitive city'. In the punitive city, the power to punish would be evenly distributed, running the length of the social network. Punishment would not be held as a power that certain individuals have over others. Signs of punishment would be visible to everyone, everywhere like an open book, eliminating crime by eliminating the idea of crime.

However, human social groups have not been able to eliminate either the idea or the actuality of crime. Instead, punishment is not deemed to be inevitable. The signs that point to the inevitability of punishment remain concealed, at least to some, as does the very nature of punishment. In reality the distribution of the power to punish is not equally held. Teachers, judges, prison wardens and psychiatrists hold a much greater power to punish than school pupils, defendants, prisoners and patients. Those who transgress social norms are perhaps especially lacking in this power. They are often the ones who are forcibly isolated upon transgressing, put somewhere else, somewhere safe – prisons. But how did such coercive, secretive and unequal powers of punishment come to emerge? Foucault maintained that the invention of new and subtle forms of punishment did not happen suddenly. For Foucault more secretive and subtle means of punishment gradually emerged in society – he called these 'disciplines'. These new forms of discipline still targeted the 'bodies' of individuals in some important ways. Discipline aims to render the body and soul docile for Foucault but not largely through means of corporal punishment. Foucault like Durkheim thought that discipline was a matter of graduated scale. However, whereas Durkheim was optimistic that the new graduated school punishments could serve educational ends and lead to greater social cohesion, Foucault was much more sceptical. He thought the proliferation of new disciplinary techniques in schools and other institutions was profoundly insidious and sinister.

Discipline, normalisation and examination

> Discipline 'makes' individuals; it is the specific technique of a power that regards individuals both as objects and as instruments of its exercise . . . it is a modest, suspicious power . . . The success of disciplinary power derives no doubt from the use of simple instruments; hierarchical observation, normalizing judgement and their combination in a procedure that is specific to it, the examination.
>
> (Foucault, 1991, p 170)

Foucault maintained that 'discipline is a political anatomy of detail' (1991, p 139) in regards to how persons are ordered in space and time. Technologies of discipline operate in multiple institutions including prisons, factories, hospitals and schools, and they do so via surveillance and control. Foucault, like Durkheim, noted negative features in disciplinary practices associated with monastic schools. However, what troubled Foucault about this was not so much the physical violence against students but the ways in which pupils were systematically observed and controlled when at school and given ranks that limited who they could be and become. He took the example of the mutual improvement school model developed by Joseph Lancaster in England to explain some of the more sinister effects of the emergent forms of discipline in schools. In mutual improvement schools, teachers supervised large numbers of older pupils, who in turn taught younger pupils basic numeracy and literacy. All this was ordered in a highly regimented fashion – the school day was very clearly demarcated and wholly predictable. The overall goal was constant and efficient pupil teaching and learning. School pupils were constantly busy and constantly watched.[12]

Foucault comments that in mutual improvement schools 'the training of schoolchildren was to be carried out in the same way: few words, no explanation, a total silence interrupted only by signals – bells, a clapping of hands, a mere glance from the teacher' (Foucault, 1991, p 166). Pupils become cogs in a machine and the school becomes a 'machine of learning'. Mutual improvement schools, like the Panopticon, may have represented an extreme and ideal manifestation of disciplinary power. However, Foucault argued that 'discipline by detail' through constant observation and regimented activity became increasingly evident in all schools in modernity, not just mutual improvement ones. Moreover, the very bodies of knowledge to be studied at school and the ways in which they were examined also carried with them an ever more damaging *normalising* power. He argued that the 'power of the Norm appears through the disciplines . . . since the eighteenth century, it has joined other powers – the Law, the Word (*Parole*) and the Text, Tradition . . . The normal is established as a principle of coercion in teaching' (Foucault, 1991, p 184).

Foucault is here suggesting that a variety of forces shape what is deemed to be normal and what is not.[13] These include social traditions and laws but also bodies of knowledge studied in places of learning as well as the new technologies of discipline by detail. However, Foucault, unlike Durkheim does not necessarily regard socialisation into such laws, traditions and bodies of knowledge as socially beneficial. Indeed, teaching becomes coercive for Foucault if it begins from the premise that there is such a thing as normal behaviour that education must seek to develop in students. Foucault thought that examinations had especially deleterious normalising effects. Examinations rank individuals as better or worse – these classifications influence where students can, or cannot, go next. He stated that the 'examination combines the techniques of an observing hierarchy and those of a normalising judgement. It is a normalising gaze, a surveillance that makes it possible to qualify, to classify and to punish' (Foucault, 1991, p 184). Part of the implication here is that some students are punished by exams in the sense that opportunities are closed off to them to study certain things in the future, or get a particular job they want, but are not qualified to do. According to Foucault, the principle of examination has become constant in education with this leading to an imbalance in power between teacher and student.[14]

Whereas traditional power consisted in the powerful being seen, in disciplinary mechanisms power is invisible. In disciplinary power it is not the powerful who are visible – instead one's visibility means that power can be exercised over one. For Foucault (1991) the examination is the technique par excellence through which teachers and schools come to exercise power over students. It is examinations that turn students into objects of knowledge. Examinations make the abilities of students, or lack of ability, abundantly visible to all. Examinations place students 'in a field of surveillance' and so hold a power over students by making them visible, by classifying their capacities. Foucault thus concludes that in a 'system of discipline, the child is more individualized than the adult' (1991, p 193). However, it is not just examinations or coercive teachers and schools that normalise others. Rather, the 'judges of normality are present everywhere. We are in the society of the teacher-judge, the doctor-judge, the educator-judge, the "social-worker-judge"; it is on them that the universal reign of the normative is based; and each individual, wherever he may find himself, subjects to it his body, his gestures, his behaviour, his aptitudes, his achievements' (Foucault, 1991, p 304).

The power of, and limits in, Foucault's "critique"

Foucault's *Discipline and Punish* can be regarded as a critique of the modes of discipline and punishment advanced by Kant and especially Durkheim.[15] While Foucault is most routinely associated with Nietzsche, it has been suggested that *Discipline and Punish* is a delayed continuation of Durkheim's thinking.[16] Although it is true that Foucault only most fleetingly mentions Durkheim in *Discipline and Punish,* I think the preceding analysis shows that Foucault did, in some respects at least, pick up where Durkheim left off. Durkheim and Foucault both, after all, investigated how punishment in modern schools became less violent and more diffuse, continuous and graduated in scale. However, Foucault criticised Durkheim for failing to see that the new forms of discipline and punishment in schools formed only part of a larger fabric of punishment and discipline in wider society.[17] Moreover, this wider fabric of interconnected disciplinary mechanisms had only questionable educational credentials for Foucault. The new 'disciplines' often merely normalised individuals, objectifying rather than educating. Whereas Durkheim sung the praises of graduated scales of discipline and punishment in schools and regarded them as necessary aspects of education and socialisation, Foucault largely lamented this trend – in both schools and wider society.

Gephart puts it like so: 'Durkheim's solution to the problem of moral disorder in modern society, namely, a firmly constructed realm of normativity, is precisely the problem for Foucault' (1999, p 69).[18] It is probably fair to say, as Ramp (1999) does, that Durkheim is an apologist for the very technologies of disciplinary power critiqued by Foucault. Foucault's critique of the modern forms of discipline and punishment has certainly provoked thought about the extent to which places of learning like schools and universities *normalise* rather than *educate* through disciplinary devices of heightened surveillance, exclusions, examinations and league tables. Indeed, perhaps the great strength of Foucault's critique lies in its prescience. Foucault saw, well before most others, that education practices were becoming increasingly focused around examinations, surveillance and measurement. While educators and educational researchers today routinely bemoan the fixation with measurement in education, Foucault was one of the first to unmask the troubling impact that the proliferation of examination practices was having in education. Foucault also recognized well before most others just how problematic the normalising tendencies in education systems were, especially for students deemed abnormal.

While Kant and Durkheim thought that initiating students into social norms at school could lead to social enlightenment in the end, Foucault concludes *Discipline and Punish* by warning that social norms may not be so innocent. Rather the social norms of society may more than anything serve the ends of commerce and industry. Foucault thus suggested that discipline and punishment in education do not in practice have particularly noble aims or effects. Disciplinary mechanisms rather systematically stifle resistance against the norms and ends of society. The insane are hospitalised, the criminals imprisoned, the misbehaving marginalised and/or medicated. It would, though, be misleading to say that Foucault thought power is inherently harmful and negative – power also produces.[19] In this respect while *disciplinary power* heightens the *productive capacity* of individuals, it weakens the *political capacity* of individuals. Foucault remarked that 'discipline increases the power of the body (in economic terms of utility) and diminishes these same forces (in political terms of obedience)' (1991, p 138). Disciplinary power also only benefits the economic utility of *some* individuals, while constraining others. After all, the ultimate disciplinary tool, the examination, qualifies some individuals to participate in the world of commerce and industry while disqualifying (the less normal) others. While there are great strengths in Foucault's critique of discipline and punishment in education then, there are also at least two significant limitations. The prime limitation of Foucault's critique lies in his reticence to suggest how the new disciplinary mechanisms in schools and society might be challenged or overcome.[20]

Foucault thought that disciplinary power fosters political obedience in persons. In spite of this, *Discipline and Punish* contains very little, if any, discussion of how persons working or learning in educational institutions might seek to subvert normalisation. However, this silence seems to have been quite deliberate. Foucault did not think it was his responsibility as an academic to suggest solutions to social problems. In an interview he reasoned that 'my role – and that is too emphatic a word – is to show that people are much freer than they feel . . . to change something in the minds of people – that's the role of an intellectual' (Foucault, quoted in Ball, 1990, pp 1–2). Foucault thought it was enough that he unmasked the effects of, and ways in which, power was not wielded openly or fairly in society. Indeed, he seems to think that critique is valuable even if it changes nobody's mind. In *"What is Critique?"* he defends the value of critiquing social norms, institutions, powers and practices as meaningful in and of itself. As Ransom puts it: 'Foucault separates critical thought from positive visions of social worlds that will replace today's reality' (Ransom, 1997, p 2).[21] Foucault has understandably been criticised by some for his reluctance to form answers to the question of how societies might become less disciplinary. However, others such as Gert Biesta (2008) have suggested that his thought can, despite appearances, provide a framework for action and change as well as critique.[22]

Ransom (1997) argues that *Discipline and Punish* needs to be read in the context of Foucault's other works if it is to be properly understood. This is undoubtedly true. In this respect, I am not claiming that Foucault had nothing to say about how individuals may actively oppose technologies of discipline. While Foucault was largely silent about such issues in *Discipline and Punish*, in his later work he did suggest that individuals can learn to care for themselves.[23] However, it is my argument that Foucault thought *disciplinary power* in itself tended to inhibit the political power of persons via constant surveillance and normalisation. It is activity concerning care for the self, more than technologies of discipline, which enables individuals to question dominant power relations and become more political. While Foucault does in his later work suggest that power relations can be productive in emancipating ways, in *Discipline and Punish* the productions that arise from *disciplinary power* are generally portrayed in a negative light – especially for those who transgress. Indeed, disciplinary power is not something that disciplined individuals have much control over. As Ransom remarks: for Foucault 'disciplines do not function through consent' (1997, p 16). There is though a second problem with his account of discipline and punishment.

Discipline and punishment in education today

Foucault may not have provided explicit answers to the question of how educational institutions might help societies become less disciplinary, at least in *Discipline and Punish*. However, important lessons can still be gleaned from this work. There Foucault shows that the new forms of discipline and punishment that emerged in modernity are myriad in form and widely diffused. Foucault brought to light how discipline and punishment were not just imposed in schools. Disciplinary mechanisms can be found in a host of other institutions too. Discipline starts in the home and the school but it ends, and finds its most complete expression in the prison. Systems of discipline and punishment in education are still thoroughly connected to disciplinary networks in wider society, probably more so than when *Discipline and Punish* was first published in 1975. One need only consider the emergence of the school to prison pipeline (discussed in chapter 2) to realise that Foucault's dystopian take on discipline and punishment is all too real, at least in some parts of the world. While corporal punishment has largely receded from Western education systems, it still exists in some parts of the US.[24] However, if Foucault's critiques of discipline and punishment show anything, it is that corporal punishment is often not the most sinister side of discipline.[25]

Though corporal punishment may generally be rare, there are now a variety of other ways in which pupils are punished by graduated scale in schools today – many of which were unmasked by Foucault. They include, but are not limited to: mild rebukes and reproaches from the teacher, withdrawal of playing time, detention, exclusion, medical treatment for ADHD, expulsion, criminal prosecution, incarceration, highly structured timetabling, regimented activity and, of course, examination.[26] Foucault sought to unmask how the power to punish is not equally held in educational institutions. Teachers hold a power to punish over pupils, with those who transgress being especially punished. However, Foucault also suggested that we are all increasingly being punished by new technologies of discipline. Though Foucault felt that schoolchildren were the ones most punished by examinations, increasingly teachers are also becoming objectified by examinations and inspections too.[27]

In spite of all their differences Kant, Durkheim and Foucault did agree on at least one thing. That discipline and punishment is imposed on students in schools. Discipline and punishment constrains individuals – they mould individuals into what schools, and later society, needs them to be. Discipline defines individuals and in preordained directions. Whereas Kant and Durkheim thought this constraining, moulding and defining was good for education and good for society, Foucault, in general, did not. Kant and Durkheim held that pupil socialisation into school rules was a vital part of wider moral development and the eventual emergence of the educational ideal of autonomy. However, Foucault's work brings into question whether the disciplinary norms and mechanisms that animate institutions of education actually educate for autonomy or if they merely normalise young persons for participation in capitalist societies. What neither perspective brings out, however, is that discipline might be something that students themselves take responsibility for. For Kant, Durkheim and Foucault, discipline is imposed on students by institutions (and persons working in them) – it is not something that students themselves do.

Indeed, a second fundamental problem with Foucault's account is the blurring of boundaries between discipline and punishment. Kant and Durkheim were clear that discipline and punishment were quite distinct. Foucault, in contrast, uses the term discipline or 'disciplines' to specifically describe new and subtle forms of punishment. In blurring the boundaries between discipline and punishment Foucault masks from view the variety of possible ways in which discipline might be and become educational. This was probably not his intention, but it has been an effect of his conceptual blurring of discipline and punishment.[28] Discipline and punishment are not the same things though. Moreover, discipline and punishment need not just be imposed upon students by institutions and educators working in them. Instead, discipline might be something that students in educational institutions can take significant responsibility for. As we shall see, discipline can be a valuable personal quality without which learners may lack the motivation, focus and structure to achieve the life goals they aspire to. Discipline need not, in short, just define individuals – discipline can also help persons to define themselves.

Chapter summary

In this chapter I have documented the links between discipline and punishment in schools and wider society. I have used the thought of Kant, Durkheim and Foucault to help me do so. What I hope has emerged in this chapter is that punishment in education takes many forms. Some forms are obvious – such as corporal punishment. Others are more subtle. But just because they are subtle does not mean they engender no damaging or far reaching effects. Far from it! Durkheim and Foucault helped to reveal how new forms of punishment emerged in modernity – ones of graduated scale and detail. These new punishments disciplined students through a combination of regimented activity, rules, surveillance, examination, and in the case of misbehaviour – often exclusion, isolation, medication and incarceration. While Durkheim held rather naive beliefs that such discipline could be morally educational and socially beneficial, Foucault did not.

Foucault felt that the new forms of discipline punished all students but those who transgressed especially. His critique may have helped to reveal how disciplinary mechanisms in educational institutions all too often merely socialise students into the norms of society – readying them to be docile productive workers. What it did not do was provide answers to the question of how *discipline* in educational institutions might be arranged to foster ends beyond mere socialisation and normalisation. I am not claiming that Foucault had nothing to say about how individuals may actively oppose the technologies of discipline that he explicated in *Discipline and Punish*. Indeed, in his later work Foucault did suggest that individuals can learn to care for themselves. However, it is my argument that Foucault thought *disciplinary power* in itself tended to inhibit the political power of persons via constant surveillance and normalisation. In subsequent chapters I hope to show that discipline in education can be conceived of and enacted differently. There I claim that discipline in education need not just be about heightening the productive power of individuals while inhibiting the political. Discipline in education can help persons and communities grow and change for the better.

Notes

1 Durkheim (1961) devotes chapters 2, 3, 4, 9 & 10 of this text to the issue of discipline in schools and chapters 11, 12 & 13 to the issue of punishment in schools.
2 As Pickering puts it, 'Durkheim distinguished respect for rule and authority, which is held to be good, from the fear of punishment, which is bad' (Pickering, 1999, p 53).
3 While Durkheim does not cite Kant's thought on punishment here, it is difficult not to see alignment in their views. Both thinkers held that punishment could and should reinforce the value of school rules via the withholding of esteem. Both also thought the withholding of esteem would be felt as a form of suffering by misbehaving students.
4 It is important to note here that there are well-known problems with Durkheim's 'history' of punishment (Garland, 1999). It has been suggested that he: 1) misunderstood the normative frameworks to be found in primitive societies and 2) that his 'historical periodization is crude' (Garland, 1999, p 25). Nonetheless, I am inclined to agree with Garland – that his analysis is functional rather than historical. While his analysis of punishment may lack a 'genuine historical consciousness' (Garland, 1999, p 26), this does not destabilize his main argument – to connect punishment with the goal of social solidarity.
5 For further discussion of Durkheim's account on the form and function of punishment, see Pickering (1999). Pickering endorses the interpretation that punishment should for Durkheim deprive children of pleasures like games playing while operating on a graduated scale that starts leniently and gradually becomes more severe.
6 Cladis (1999) suggests that Durkheim and Foucault both explored the social and historical conditions that shape human understanding of themselves, including issues such as discipline and punishment. Both Durkheim and Foucault also display interest in the religious roots of secular phenomena (Ramp, 1999). However, as Ramp (1999) points out, Foucault is very dismissive of Durkheim – in spite of the fact that his treatise *Discipline and Punish* owes a largely unmentioned debt to Durkheim.
7 Foucault has inspired a multitude of works regarding discipline and punishment in education. See for example Ball (1990, 2013), Biesta (2008), Cladis (1999), Edwards (2008), Fejes and Nicol (2008), Hunter (1994), Marshall (1990), Millei *et al.* (2010) and Zembylas (2005).
8 This text was first published in French in 1975.
9 In his own inimitable way Foucault acknowledges that the function of punishment in modern society is the idea at the core of *Discipline and Punish*. He states that: 'This book is intended as a correlative history of the modern soul and of the new power to judge; a genealogy of the present scientifico-legal complex from which the power to punish derives its basis, justification and rules, from which it

extends its effects and by which it masks its exorbitant singularity' (Foucault, 1991, p 23).
10 Foucault does not suggest that such a social imaginary would necessarily be a good thing. Indeed, he was, as we shall see, notoriously reluctant to make judgements about how social institutions *should be* arranged.
11 Ransom (1997) agrees with this reading of Foucault.
12 For a more thorough account and explanation of mutual improvement schools, see Hassard and Rowlinson (2002).
13 According to Ransom (1997), we should not see the idea of normalization in an automatically negative light. The norm is merely 'a standard of some kind that a multiplicity of individuals must reach and maintain to perform certain tasks' (1997, p 47).
14 For an excellent discussion of how Foucault's concept of examination figures in his other writings, see Hoskin (1990). Hoskin maintains that the examination is not just a core idea in *Discipline and Punish* – it also features prominently in Foucault's later work on the care of the self. However, Hoskin also claims that Foucault is mistaken in suggesting systematic examination was an invention of the eighteenth century – the practice rather emerged in the twelfth century for Hoskin. Despite failing to be historically accurate, Hoskin nonetheless praises Foucault's capacity to 'sense the significant' and render the 'familiar strange'.
15 Biesta (2006a) and Marshall (1990) both for example claim that Foucault explicitly criticizes Kant's philosophy.
16 Ramp makes this very point (1999). To claim that Foucault's thinking owes a debt to Durkheim is not to deny Foucault was indebted and influenced by Nietzsche too. He clearly was.
17 He says that by 'studying only the general social forms, as Durkheim did, one runs the risk of positing as a principle of greater leniency in punishment processes of individualization that are rather one of the effects of the new tactics of power, among which are to be included the new penal mechanisms' (Foucault, 1991, p 23).
18 Gephart is not alone in holding such a view. Cladis says that what 'Durkheim celebrates, namely social bonds, Foucault dreads. Durkheim . . . champions normative social constraints, whereas Foucault . . . finds them intrinsically problematic (1999, p 6).
19 He says that 'we must cease once and for all to describe the effects of power in negative terms: it "excludes", it "represses", it "censors", it "abstracts", it "masks", it "conceals". In fact power produces' (Foucault, 1991, p 194). I therefore see substance in Edwards's view – that in Foucault's scheme discipline does not just turn people in to docile, passive subjects. Rather, 'discipline as a form through which power is exercised cannot work unless subjects are capable of action' (2008, p 23). Here action does not entail an escape from power – rather persons 'are empowered in particular ways through becoming the subject of, and subjected to, power (2008, p 24). While sympathetic to Edwards point, I am also inclined to think that disciplinary power in itself generally acts on persons, it normalises them. It is activity concerning care for the self, more than technologies of discipline that enable individuals to fashion themselves.
20 Ball (1990) and Ransom (1997) also both agree that Foucault was reluctant to offer blueprints for social improvement.
21 Elsewhere, Foucault similarly states that 'critique doesn't have to be the premise of a deduction which concludes: this then is what needs to be done . . . It isn't a stage of programming. It is a challenge directed to what is' (Foucault quoted from Biesta, 2008, p 200).
22 Similarly, Ball (2013) suggests that while Foucault may not himself have volunteered prescriptions about what should be done, he nonetheless hoped to inspire others to write books about these challenges.

23 See especially *The ethic of care of the self as a practice of freedom* by Foucault (1987). For further discussion of how Foucault's later work might inform interpretation of *Discipline and Punish*, see Ransom (1997).
24 While corporal punishment is legally prohibited in the UK, Canada and much of Europe, some 19 states in the US have yet to take this step.
25 I am not, of course, endorsing corporal punishment here – it should not in my view be carried out anywhere.
26 For insightful discussions of the growing phenomenon of the medicalization of disruptive behaviour in schools, see Allan and Harwood (2013) and Tait (2010).
27 A point I expanded upon at the start of chapter 2.
28 This may partly be an issue of vocabulary being lost in translation. The title of *Discipline and Punishment* in its original French is *Surveiller et Punir*. However, as the translator for this text points out (1991), there is no adequate English term for *surveiller*. The English word surveillance has a narrower and more specific meaning and does not capture the nuance of *surveiller*. However, 'discipline' is probably not ideal either despite being chosen by Foucault.

5 Disciplines of knowledge, disciplined interests and student agency

In this chapter I initially argue that discipline needs to be reclaimed *for education*, as recently dominant discourses of discipline are problematic at the levels of theory, policy and practice. I thereafter consider two different ways in which discipline might be reclaimed in education, for the ends of education. Following Peters and Hirst I first suggest that it is educationally important for students to be *disciplined by knowledge*. Unlike Kant and Foucault, both Peters and Hirst thought that discipline could be a positive part of education. According to Hirst and Peters, discipline is not just about restraining student unruliness. Instead, coming to understand educationally valuable knowledge takes significant student discipline. However, following MacIntyre, I also suggest there is an educational need for disciplines of knowledge and wider social orders to be continually questioned, and where necessary, remade. Second, I document the views of Pat Wilson and Dewey on how discipline might serve the ends of education. They agreed that students should first and foremost be disciplined by *interest* rather than traditions of knowledge. Dewey stressed that discipline is a disposition of persistence and endurance in the face of challenge and difficulty. It is a positive quality of learners because of the agency they exercise over their learning and conduct.

Reclaiming discipline *in* and *for* education

There are a variety of possible ways of *thinking about discipline* in education. There also exists a diverse range of ways in which *discipline might be enacted* in educational institutions. However, I hope it has now become apparent that certain discourses of discipline have dominated education policy, practice and theory in more recent times – all too often to the exclusion of other, different perspectives. As we saw in chapter 2, at the level of *policy and practice*, zero tolerance and behaviour management approaches have overshadowed other possible ways of enacting discipline in US and UK schools. At the level of *theory*, rules-based accounts of discipline in education have been most influential.[1] As was shown in chapters 3 and 4, Durkheim (1961), Foucault (1991), Kant (2003) and John Wilson (1981) all in different ways locate pupil obedience to rules, norms and teacher authority as being central to school discipline, with all (apart from Foucault) concluding that rules-based programmes of discipline can be morally educational if judiciously implemented. Kant, Wilson and Durkheim all held that pupil socialisation into school rules was a vital part of wider moral development and the eventual emergence of the educational ideal of autonomy.

However, Foucault's work brings into question whether the disciplinary norms and mechanisms that animate institutions of education actually educate for autonomy or if they merely normalise young persons for participation in capitalist societies. In this respect, I tend to agree with Foucault on one important point at least. That discipline in educational institutions (including schools, colleges and universities) too often serves the ends of the current economic order without containing spaces for learners to question existing social and economic orders. However, important questions remain about how discipline in education might be arranged in less 'punitive' ways. Foucault's critique of the disciplinary technologies of modernity can certainly help to reveal inadequacies in theories and practices of discipline in education that only aim at, or have the effect of, 'normalising' students into the rules and norms of society. However, what Foucault's critique does not do is provide a more positive account about how *disciplinary mechanisms* might become less punitive and more educational. But consideration of such issues is exactly what is needed if discipline in educational institutions is to become less punitive. Given there are profound difficulties with the predominant discourses of discipline at the levels of theory, policy and practice, I think there is a compelling need for discipline to be reclaimed in education for the ends of education.[2]

In this respect, there is a diverse, if largely neglected range of philosophical texts that explore how discipline might engender distinctively educational ends. In this chapter, I will begin to unpack some of these neglected philosophical literatures by exploring two very different ways of thinking about the relationship between discipline and education. I will first document the views of Peters, Hirst and MacIntyre. These thinkers all regarded education to be impossible without *disciplines of knowledge*. Here, it will be noted that the disciplined pursuit of what a community deems to be valued knowledge has remained a key purpose of education since the times of Aristotle at least. However, following Pat Wilson and Dewey, it will thereafter be argued that students should be encouraged to pursue their *interests* in educational settings too. Here discipline is conceived of as a positive quality of learners because of the agency they exercise over their own learning and conduct. Dewey stressed that discipline is a disposition of persistence and endurance in the face of challenge and difficulty. Let us consider then these two different perspectives on how discipline might be reclaimed for the ends of education.

Liberal education and objective knowledge

In third-century Athens Aristotle maintained that meaningful learning was difficult. In Books VII and VIII of his *Politics* (1981) he suggested that all Athenians should be qualified for a share of rule after they had participated in a liberal education. He implied that in so far as *schole* (the leisurely pursuit of wisdom free from the demands of work) is the best end of a community, citizens ought to be prepared, through their education, with this liberal end of leisure in mind. However, Aristotle emphasised that leisured learning is not play (1981, pp 34–50). Meaningful learning is very different from play on account of the hard work required and the nature of the knowledge involved. Following Plato, Aristotle thought that the most valuable forms of knowledge were eternal and unchanging in form. Moreover, he also thought that some types of eternal knowledge were teachable – particularly *episteme*, which he more or less defined as eternal, teachable knowledge.[3] In the twentieth century, the Platonic and Aristotelian idea that some forms of knowledge are objectively true and difficult to obtain, but nonetheless worth pursuing for their own sake, was taken up by liberal educationists such as Richard Peters and Paul Hirst.

In *Education as Initiation* Peters argued that 'Plato's image of education as turning the eye of the soul outwards towards the light . . . emphasised, quite rightly . . . the necessity for objective standards being written into the content of education' (1968, p 97).[4] Hirst (1968), too, argued that the Greek notion of a liberal education hinged on the idea that the good life is spent freeing the mind from error and searching for knowledge. He averred that it is from these Greek doctrines that 'there emerged the idea of liberal education as a process concerned simply and directly with the pursuit of knowledge' (Hirst, 1968, p 114). Peters, like Kant, believed that children could not fulfil their potential if left to their own devices. He maintained that education is not just a process of natural maturation. Instead, the 'teacher has to choose what is worth-while encouraging children in' (Peters, 1968, p 95). Education becomes worthwhile when it involves initiation into objective forms of knowledge (Peters, 1968).

However, Peters criticised Kant for focusing his theory of mind on the private individual and for failing to appreciate the extent to which cognitive development is only enabled through initiation into public traditions of knowledge. The impersonal content of knowledge by which experience is structured, is, for Peters and Hirst, enshrined in *public traditions* that have taken mankind millennia to refine. In his essay *Liberal Education and the Nature of Knowledge* (1968) Hirst argued that it 'is a necessary feature of knowledge as such that there be public criteria whereby the true is distinguishable from the false, the good from the bad, the right from the wrong. It is the existence of these criteria which gives objectivity to knowledge' (Hirst, 1968, p 127). For both Peters and Hirst a liberal education entails the development of the mind through engagement with objective forms of knowledge.[5]

Educated persons, community values and teacher knowledge

> 'Education' . . . suggests passing on the ultimate values of a community, so that the individual can make them his own. 'Education' suggests not only that what develops in someone is valuable but also that it involves the development of knowledge and understanding.
>
> (Peters, 1972, p 3)

In *Education and the Educated Man* (1972), Peters suggested that educated persons are in an important sense defined by their ability to understand knowledge valued by one's community. Peters explained that the modern concept of the liberally educated person arose in the nineteenth century and differentiated those who had been trained in some specialist skill or knowledge from those who had been broadly educated. He stated that 'we distinguish educating people from training them because for us education is no longer compatible with any narrowly conceived enterprise' (Peters, 1972, p 10). Liberal educationists such as Hirst and Peters placed significant emphasis on the value of learning for its own sake. As such their views stand in contrast to the increasingly conventional view (at least amongst policy makers and the OECD) that education is more than anything about getting qualifications and getting ready for the world of work. A liberal education is about more than socialisation or getting qualifications. The liberally 'educated' have come to appreciate the value of pursuing knowledge for its own sake, as opposed to for what it can help one get.

For Peters, liberal education involves the idea of a community passing on objective knowledge that has more than instrumental value. Both teacher knowledge *and* student effort are required here. Peters argued that teachers are put in positions of 'provisional authority' for school-based learning, because they have 'qualified' as authorities in their subjects. While teachers *begin* the teaching process as knowledgeable authorities in their subjects, their purpose is to guide those they are teaching to a similar position of knowledgeable authority. This is what makes the teacher's authority only provisional. The role of the teacher is manifestly not 'to stuff the minds of the ignorant with bodies of knowledge' (Peters, 1973, p 47). Instead, Peters specified that education can only occur if students also become committed to pursuing what is worthwhile – namely knowledge and understanding. Education, he stated, 'must involve knowledge and understanding and some kind of cognitive perspective, which are not inert' (Peters, 1970, p 45).[6] Peters suggested that educational activities do not involve pupils passively receiving knowledge. Pupils must rather be supported to voluntarily engage with and think about valuable knowledge so as to develop their understanding of it. According to Hirst and Peters, coming to understand valuable knowledge takes significant student discipline.

Disciplines of knowledge

Like Kant (2003), Peters indicated that the essence of discipline lies in submission to rules. However, unlike Kant, Peters maintained that discipline is also a positive quality of students – positive on account of it being necessary for the pursuit of valuable knowledge. He stated that 'discipline, etymologically speaking, is rooted in a learning situation; it conveys the notion of submission to rules or some kind of order' (Peters, 1970, p 267). The rules to which pupils should submit can have a wide variety of purposes and involve a range of different activities. Peters' rules can probably be grouped into two categories though: those that *directly involve the pursuit of knowledge* and those that *clear the way for the pursuit of knowledge*. He argued that rules pertain to *what* is to be learned or they may be necessary to ensure that something *can be* learned. In the former case discipline involves grasping the rules that govern a particular worthwhile activity or aspect of knowledge. Discipline is here intimately related to the specific thing to be learned (Hirst & Peters, 1975). Hirst and Peters speculated that there is a reason why traditional school subjects are sometimes referred to as 'disciplines'.

> Presumably they are so called because the learner submits himself to the rules implicit in them.
>
> (Hirst & Peters, 1975, p 127)

However, discipline can also involve pupils submitting to more practical and procedural rules that ensure the order necessary for learning to occur. There must, Peters argued, be minimum conditions of classroom order 'sufficient to let a large number of children work in a small space' (Peters, 1970, p 193). Importantly, rules can be self-imposed or imposed by someone in authority (Hirst & Peters, 1975 & Peters, 1970). However, there are limits to the forms of learning that can be imposed on pupils. Peters specified that 'education . . . rules out some procedures of transmission, on the grounds that they lack wittingness and voluntariness on the part of the learner' (Peters, 1970, p 45). Indeed, despite their belief that teachers should where appropriate enforce rules in class, Peters and Hirst indicate a preference for self-discipline (Hirst & Peters, 1975). All school rules must have a point; they must be intimately related to what is worthwhile and desirable. If restriction is imposed on pupils, 'it must promote what is good' (Peters, 1970, p 195). For liberal educationists the pursuit of objective forms of knowledge, for its own sake, constitutes the highest educational good.

The notion that discipline can be connected to an education for 'good' is very reminiscent of Kant's views on discipline in education explored in chapter 3. However, Peters and Hirst also moved beyond Kant's account. For Kant discipline is an essentially negative restraining of student unruliness. It is no more than this. It prepares the way for intellectual development but it is not in itself part of intellectual development. In contrast, Peters and Hirst thought student discipline was necessary if valuable knowledge is to be grasped and the mind developed. Students need to work hard and *be disciplined by knowledge* if they are to come to understand that knowledge. Contrary to Kant, for liberal educationists, discipline is not just something that happens prior to the most valuable learning – it is part and parcel of the most valuable learning.[7] Alasdair MacIntyre has also developed the notion that education should entail initiation into disciplines of knowledge. However, MacIntyre calls into question whether education can or should be founded upon *objective* traditions of knowledge.

Education as initiation into conflicting disciplines of knowledge

MacIntyre suggests that teachers are practitioners of the discipline or disciplines of knowledge that they teach.[8] He also suggests that education should involve student initiation into disciplines of knowledge. However, he does not think that disciplines of knowledge should be presented to students as being objectively true or complete in themselves. For MacIntyre, disciplines of knowledge in good working order should always be regarded as contestable. They should be subject to on-going critical questioning and debate. Educators should not initiate students into knowledge disciplines with the mind-set that knowledge is unproblematic and beyond questioning. Knowledge in education should not be presented to students as being objectively true. Instead, educators should help make students aware that all disciplines of knowledge have histories. Histories that are embodied by continuities of conflict, of disagreements over content and different interpretations of the same knowledge content (MacIntyre, 1984). Students in turn need to take up what they have been taught and question it. They need to make it their own. For MacIntyre, the task of the teacher is to 'induct a pupil into the tradition of the discipline, allowing the pupil, should they pursue the practice long enough, to escape dependence on teacher testimony' (Fordham, 2015, p 11). Thus, for MacIntyre discipline is not something that teachers hold over and against students. Instead *disciplines* are bodies of knowledge that teachers can help students get to know, critically interrogate and if need be, remake.

Students are not passive in the disciplinary process. The more they get to know a discipline of knowledge, the more they can question and remake it. However, MacIntyre does not think this active student questioning of disciplines of knowledge happens often enough in education. Indeed, MacIntyre is critical of contemporary educational practice. He does not think that schools and universities today generally do enable students to question the disciplines of knowledge into which they are initiated. As such, he calls for change. He maintains that contemporary universities need to be reconceived as places of 'constrained disagreement, of imposed participation in conflict in which a central responsibility of higher education would be to initiate students into conflict' (MacIntyre, 1990, p 231). Staff and students in universities of this nature would have the dual task of advancing inquiry from within a particular point of view while also entering into conflict with other, rival points of view. Here, reading texts from more than one perspective becomes crucial. He maintains for example, that if one wants to gain a balanced understanding of the Enlightenment philosophical tradition, then it is necessary to read texts that critique this tradition. According to MacIntyre, texts need to be read against each other if they are not to be misread (MacIntyre, 1990). Moreover, in reading from different traditions and disciplines, persons should deliberately seek to evaluate the merit of the key claims in a tradition or discipline against the strongest possible objections to them. Indeed, the purpose of initiating students into conflicting and rival points of view is to reveal why some disciplines of knowledge need to be reformed and in what ways. MacIntyre indicates that a further benefit of such an education is that it will help students learn how to think for themselves.

While much of MacIntyre's writing on education focuses on universities, there is reason to think he believes schools should initiate students into rival traditions and disciplines of knowledge too. MacIntyre suggests that Western educators have three key purposes. They need to support students: 1) to be fit for future social roles; 2) to become able to think for themselves; 3) to act for the common good. He says that the first purpose of educators 'is among the purposes of almost all education almost everywhere: it is to shape the young person so that he or she may fit into some social role or function ... The second purpose is ... the purpose of teaching young persons to think for themselves' (1987, p 16). On the face of it, MacIntyre seems to defend a Kantian view of education aimed at promoting rational autonomy in students. However, while MacIntyre cites Kant in his lecture on the educated public, he is not a Kantian thinker. Nor does he think education only ought to aim at student socialisation and the development of the capacity for independent thought. Education should also support students to become able to question dominant social orders and act for the common good. The first thing to note about MacIntyre's defence of the idea that educators ought to encourage students to think for themselves is that he regards this as a necessarily communal process. He states that 'it is a familiar truth that one can only think for oneself if one does not think by oneself' (1987, p 24).

MacIntyre seems to suggest there are at least two ways in which we can learn to *think for ourselves with others*. On the one hand, persons can think with others via rational debate about matters concerning the common public good (MacIntyre, 1987, 1990; MacIntyre & Dunne, 2002). This might mean more explicitly helping students to learn how to ask hard questions about why meeting the (often unjust) needs of the market economy is generally deemed more important than meeting the needs of the poor and/or vulnerable in society. On the other hand, persons can also learn to think with others by reading and then debating canonical texts from different traditions of inquiry. The two varieties of thinking with others are not mutually exclusive. They rather overlap and interrelate. MacIntyre for example argues that close reading and debating of common texts in university seminars can help provide persons with shared frames of reference that can inform debate about the common good. If debate about the common good is to be based on reason rather than rhetoric, then shared frames of reference and standards of appeal by which arguments can be judged as better or worse are needed (MacIntyre & Dunne, 2002). Reading canonical texts with others in the context of educational institutions like schools and universities can help to provide such standards and frames of reference (MacIntyre, 1987, 1990; MacIntyre & Dunne, 2002). MacIntyre maintains that educational institutions must initiate young persons into their community's stock of stories, their disciplines of knowledge and their valued practices but in ways that are open to evolution.

Universities should, he says, found their curriculum on a core of 'great books' including the likes of Homer, Plato, 'two Shakespeare plays', Descartes, Voltaire and Huckleberry Finn (MacIntyre, 1990). In relation to the school curriculum he similarly identifies texts from a variety of different cultures, saying that: 'there are some things that every child should be taught . . . Mathematics . . . English language and English literature . . . but also including at least one Icelandic saga . . . and a good deal of history together with . . . civic studies' (MacIntyre & Dunne, 2002, p 14). Overall, MacIntyre seems to think some disciplines of knowledge must be studied because they have goods internal to them that are worth pursuing for their own sake (MacIntyre, 1999; MacIntyre & Dunne, 2002). The particular texts and traditions of knowledge MacIntyre identifies for school and university curricula may seem somewhat arbitrary or culturally relative. However, for MacIntyre texts, stories, traditions and disciplines of knowledge are not merely to be passed on and passively assimilated but openly contested and made new, in line with communal interest and need. Indeed, the presence of open and rational scrutiny of the knowledge and values of a given community and those of others is a central indicator that a community is a genuinely educated one.[9]

The problem with educational measurement and the value of knowledge

MacIntyre stresses that engagement with canonical texts from different subject disciplines and from different cultures can support students to think for themselves because the process will help them see issues from multiple perspectives (2009). MacIntyre's philosophy of education is, in one sense then, a liberal one. He says that towards the end of formal education, educators need to be able to help students pursue practices like historical, scientific or literary inquiry with an eye on the goods internal to the discipline rather than for external reward. He states that 'part of what such students need to learn is to value, for example, the activities and outcomes of scientific enquiry for their own sake and not just for the technologies that result from such enquiry. Students who ask about their academic disciplines "But what use are they to us after we leave school?" should be taught that the mark of someone who is ready to leave school is that they no longer ask that question' (MacIntyre & Dunne, 2002, p 5). MacIntyre is clear then that the pursuit of different disciplines of knowledge ought to be regarded as intrinsically worthwhile, at least at times, in educational institutions.

MacIntyre is also sceptical of valuing educational institutions according to their efficiency and productivity and their capacity to support students to attain high grades in important examinations. MacIntyre dubs a fixation with measurement and student examination as an input/output model of education. What is 'wrong with this model is that it loses sight of the end of education, the development of its students' powers, and substitutes for this end that of success by the standard of some test or examination. Yet what examinations principally test is how good one is at passing examinations' (MacIntyre & Dunne, 2002, p 4). MacIntyre is not entirely opposed to examinations – he just thinks that they are currently over-valued in education. Indeed, if I am reading MacIntyre correctly, important exams and qualifications can be regarded as *external educational goods*. Goods that can be used to get other more valued goods, like a job or place at university – things that persons very often need in order to flourish in later life. For without external goods, persons cannot access richer *internal goods* (1999), goods that are worthwhile in their own right rather than for later reward.

MacIntyre maintains that engaging with disciplines of knowledge is not just worthwhile on account of the goods that such engagement might foster in individual persons though. Rather persons best develop individual goods through debate with others and where the focus is also placed on learning to reason *and* act for the common good. MacIntyre thought student engagement with different disciplines of knowledge is needed if communities are to be made more just. Indeed, he argues that a vital aspect of thinking for oneself entails asking questions of currently dominant social and economic orders (MacIntyre & Dunne, 2002). For educators in Western culture this means supporting students to ask questions about why Western society is so geared toward the accumulation of individual wealth and the growth of the market economy rather than on the more even distribution of wealth for the overall common good. It may also mean encouraging students to ask questions about the massive debt burden being thrust upon an unprecedented number of persons today (MacIntyre, 2013).

MacIntyre suggests that educational institutions should not just focus on helping students to *rationally question* injustices where they exist. Educational institutions should also support students to actually combat injustice *and* support vulnerable others (MacIntyre, 1999). He suggests that a person is ethical in so far as they are committed to the pursuit of the common good as well as their own. Such commitment may entail questioning the market orientation of many dominant institutions. It might also involve the capacity to actively respond to others in need. MacIntyre claims that the young, the old, the infirm and the disabled are examples of others that may especially need help. The support persons' need may often be immediate and material – it may involve the need for food and shelter. However, all persons also have a need for participative recognition in community life too. Educators should help vulnerable others to have a voice. According to MacIntyre, educational institutions should not just socialise– they should also help students learn how to think for themselves and act for the common good.[10]

There are some similarities between the views of Peters, Hirst and MacIntyre. All these thinkers thought that education should be founded on a disciplined engagement with different traditions of knowledge.[11] However, MacIntyre stresses the importance of regarding disciplines of knowledge as necessarily contestable, more consistently than Peters and Hirst did.[12] He thought it educationally vital that students come to appreciate that all disciplines of knowledge should be subject to ongoing contest and questioning. Indeed, MacIntyre felt that educational engagement with different disciplines of knowledge could and should support students to develop the capacity to ask questions of dominant social orders too. MacIntyre's stresses more than Hirst and Peters did, that disciplines of knowledge are most educationally valuable when they support students and communities to become more socially just.[13] Furthermore, unlike Foucault, MacIntyre considers how *disciplinary arrangements* in educational institutions might become less 'punitive'. In indicating that the preoccupation with examinations in education needs to be scaled back and replaced with a focus on encouraging students to think for themselves and ask questions of dominant social orders, MacIntyre at least gives suggestions as to how such important educational challenges might be faced.[14] Foucault remained all too silent about such matters.[15] However, the liberal idea that students should be disciplined by traditions of knowledge has also been subject to criticism.

Education and student interests

Like Hirst, Peters and MacIntyre, Pat Wilson thought that education should be about much more than socialisation and readying pupils for the world of work. However, he did not think that initiating students into disciplines of knowledge was the best way to overcome such instrumental thinking in education. Indeed, he was extremely critical of the liberal view of education. Instead, pupil interest should form the cornerstone of the curriculum. Wilson reasoned that children's *interests* provide a substantially better justification for education than individual or social need or for that matter, disciplines of knowledge. Wilson had a very specific conception of interest in mind here. Children's interests are often assumed to be essential to education by progressively minded teachers. However, he thought that the notion of interest should not be employed as a caveat by teachers to generate higher motivation for pupil inquiry into 'something otherwise dull' (Wilson, 1971, p 38). The term interest, Wilson implied, had become over-used but under-conceptualized by proponents of progressive education in the 1960s and 1970s. Contrary to this, he argued that the identification of a child's genuine interest is an extremely elusive and complex business. Simply asking children to state verbally the subjects they are drawn to is unlikely to make manifest their interest. Nor, for that matter, is observation of a child's behaviour a reliable indicator of interest.

He states that 'implicit in a child's interest is all that is most personal and unique about him' (Wilson, 1971, p 53). As such, in crowded classrooms discovering each student's unique interests takes a great deal of time. But how exactly did Wilson think that a child's interest could be revealed, if at all? His statements about this are not entirely clear, but it seems to have revolved around grasping what students become more habitually interested in. Moreover, I think that interest is for Wilson not just any disposition but a *particular sort of disposition*. Interest is not a disposition to pay half-hearted attention to any passing whim. Interests in themselves could be a 'perfect rag bag of the trivial' (Wilson, 1971, p 37) that are not actually in that child's or anyone else's interests. Interest is significantly more than spontaneous and indiscriminate fancy. It involves the observation and scrutiny of an object of experience in a sustained and serious way. Interest entails persistence in the task of understanding why something one is attracted to is worthy of attention. To develop an interest is to become progressively able to relate to an object of experience in such a way as to locate its intrinsic point. Moreover, teaching should be about sustaining interest. It should not be a matter of influencing children to 'take' a subject.

> [The] only way of engendering interest in anything is through helping the child to see something of its significance ... unless there is something of intelligible interest in what the teacher is doing nothing of interest is likely to develop. The most that a teacher can do, I think, is try to communicate his view of what is interesting in an intelligible way.
> (Wilson, 1971, p 60)

Some of the spirit of this seems very sensible. Meaningful educational experiences often involve a student or students coming to appreciate (often with the support of the teacher) the intrinsic value of something. However, according to Wilson, the teacher's perspective of worth is, and can only be, based upon a prior interest of the child. Interest and any value in it must start with the child. A child's interest is always a good reason for engaging in an activity. Indeed, the sole educational function of teachers is to aid pupils' in their pursuit of interests. There is always value in pursuing student interests, even if what is valued turns out to be 'utterly worthless' and 'positively detrimental to the achievement of other valued goals' (Wilson, 1971, p 66).

Wilson went as far as to argue that there is nothing apart from a child's interest that can be educated. The philosophy of education that emerges in Wilson's treatise on education is thus radically child-centred. It should come as no surprise that his philosophy of discipline in schools is too.

Disciplined interests and control and compulsion in schooling

Pat Wilson thought traditional forms of discipline in schools were morally problematic because of the forms of control and compulsion involved. Wilson reasoned that moral compulsion entails doing what one should because one knows that one must. Wilson endorsed a theory of moral duty in regard to discipline in schools, albeit a rather unique and peculiar one. He stated that the compelling force of a moral imperative originates in the 'interest which one finds in trying to live according to it, rather than anyone's pleasure, happiness or any other "good"' to which it may contingently prove conducive' (Wilson, 1971, p 74). Proper discipline in schools does not entail the following of a code of conduct written by someone else, nor does it involve any relation to the wider happiness and flourishing of self or other. The morally compelling feature of discipline in schools is rather the pupil's own interest.

> In schools, then, the children's discipline must derive ultimately not from empirical considerations or calculations (by the children or anyone else) of the ways in which to obtain or produce goods, but from the moral compulsion implicit in their own interests in the school activities themselves.
>
> (Wilson, 1971, p 74)

Wilson contrasted discipline and control. He stated that both are forms of order that necessitate compulsion. However, the compulsion particular to each is quite different. Control is a way of ordering things to get something done. Here the compulsion involved can be physical and/or psychological. The compulsion involved in discipline, by comparison, is both logical and moral. Discipline should be based on student interest. An interest could not in fact be a genuine interest if it were not susceptible to discipline. Issues of non-moral compulsion only arise when the interests of children are lost from view. Wilson implied that it is incumbent on teachers to help discipline the interests of children when lost, to refocus them, to educate them and to help them find new ones. Where teachers themselves lose sight of the interests of children, compulsion can only take on a more sinister form of manipulation. It can only be instrumental: 'a kind of motivational leverage brought to bear upon the child in order to control his behaviour in desirable ways of whose intrinsic value he has no inkling himself' (Wilson, 1971, p 75)'. When the discipline of children in schools is external to a child's interest the order is not educational but controlling and should not be called, or thought to be, discipline.

He stated that when 'we exercise control over people . . . we are not disciplining them' (Wilson, 1971, p 78). Discipline does not arise when a person or persons are subject to the will and control of others. Discipline comes from immersion in the 'work itself' (Smith, 1985, p 60). Pupil interest is, for Wilson, the educative order that is most worth pursuing. Control is a merely non-educative order. A child subject to control is perhaps being schooled, but they are not being educated. Although discipline is not something that teachers can exercise over their pupils, Wilson did believe that teacher and pupil alike could enter into a disciplined relationship. He speculated that a 'disciplined relationship is one in which both parties to the relationship (the teacher as well as the class) submit to the educative order of the task in hand. The discipline is not something which one party to the relationship possesses over or manages to impose on the other (Wilson, 1971, p 79). There is something quite appealing about this aspect of Wilson's concept of discipline in education. Indeed, in the next chapter we will explore the importance of developing disciplined relationships in education as opposed to merely imposing discipline on students. However, there are significant problems with Wilson's account of discipline in education. Problems we will now consider.

Two problems with Pat Wilson's interest-based theory of educational discipline

There are at least two problems with Pat Wilson's account of discipline in education. They are epistemological and moral. In terms of the epistemological problem, it is notable that *Interest and discipline in education* has next to nothing to say about knowledge and how it might be related to all important pupil interest. Wilson arguably recognized this gap in his theory as he attempted to trace the links between interest and knowledge in a later paper (Wilson, 1974). Knowledge of educational value, Wilson argued, is precisely and only that knowledge which interests the pupil (Wilson, 1974).[16] Wilson contrasted his view on what is educationally worthwhile with the liberal educational view. He took issue with Peters' (1968) famous implication that children are barbarians at the gates of knowledge. He also took issue with the liberal educational idea that discipline and punishment should be employed where necessary to ensure that certain inherently valuable subjects can be studied by schoolchildren. He insisted that the content of knowledge shared between teacher and pupil should come not from the teacher's tradition and culture, but from each pupil's:

> The pupil's thinking, too, has a tradition, and, unless the teacher begins his instructive communication with the pupil in a language and in relation to experiences and activities which already the pupil understands

something of the point of, then no conceptual development and no development of interest will result directly from the encounter.
(Wilson, 1971, p 90)

I agree with Wilson's general assertion that it is important to connect school knowledge to knowledge and experiences already familiar to students. However, his insistence that students have their own culture and tradition upon which teaching should be based is rather odd. It seems to me that traditions and cultures are to an important degree external to particular individuals, at least at first. Traditions of knowledge may not be objective or permanent. They may need to be subject to ongoing questioning – but nor are they entirely personal. Indeed, I think there is considerable confusion in the idea that education should almost exclusively entail children developing interests in their own personal traditions. Children are not barbarians at the gates of knowledge, but nor are they fully mature and independent inquirers capable of generating their own knowledge and traditions from within.

Wilson's conception of discipline as an educative order ultimately rests on too romantic and utopian a conception of the child. In this regard, Wilson's educational theory is very reminiscent of Rousseau's (1993). The latter, however, was only concerned to describe the education of an individual boy who had a tutor entirely to himself.[17] Few, if any, schools today have the luxury of being able to match every child to his or her own teacher. Wilson did not give nearly enough thought to how the competing demands of individuals may often clash in a class of pupils. Any education and discipline arranged *solely* around personal interest concedes far too much freedom to individual students in their immediate contexts. Teachers can and should take a continuing and active concern over their students' interests. They should, moreover, be committed to forging disciplined personal relationships with their students. However, a teacher who is convinced that individual student interest should determine the entire content of the curriculum and procedures of class discipline seems to be in the grip of an extremely romantic view of education. It is a view that misconstrues the necessarily social nature of school life and learning, and it is a view that does not pay enough attention to public disciplines of knowledge.

The second problem with Wilson's philosophy of discipline is that it rests on a decidedly limited and individualistic view of moral agency. Wilson's argument is, after all, that interests are the only things that can or should be educated or disciplined. All attempts to control ill-disciplined behaviour by means external to student interest are, for Wilson, morally misguided. Instead, the moral benefits of education lie *only* in the child's own interest. The sole intervention a teacher is justified in making in their students' moral formation is the refocusing of their interests, whatever those interests may be. Wilson's vision of the educated person is, I think, decidedly one-dimensional; the only moral quality he thinks worth pursuing is personal curiosity. Wilson's philosophy of discipline is ultimately undermined by his radical wider philosophy of education. However, John Dewey articulated a much more plausible argument about how discipline in education might be meaningfully developed from student interests, well before Wilson attempted to do so.[18]

Dewey on interest, discipline and student agency in education

> A person who is trained to consider his actions, to undertake them deliberately, is in so far forth disciplined. Add to this ability a power to endure in an intelligently chosen course in face of distraction, confusion, and difficulty, and you have the essence of discipline.
>
> (Dewey, 2007, p 156)

John Dewey was one of the first philosophers to raise awareness of the potential pitfalls of teachers being overly directive of students in their efforts to establish a climate of school discipline. Dewey was critical of the view that society should *only* discipline by transmitting and communicating habits of doing, thinking and feeling from the older generation to the younger. His famous work *Democracy and Education* contains some pertinent observations on the nature of discipline, particularly in the tenth chapter, which bears the title *Interest and Discipline*. There, he first explicates the concept of interest. The interested person, he maintained, is simultaneously lost and found in some matter or other of experience. The term interest indicates the 'engrossment of the self in an object' (Dewey, 2007, p 153). Dewey argued that, etymologically speaking, interest is that which provides a link between otherwise disparate things. This aspect of interest has important educational ramifications.

He stated that guiding someone to perceive the connection that exists between the agent of learning and any material to be learned is 'simply good sense; to make it interesting by extraneous and artificial inducements deserves all the bad names which have been applied to the doctrine of interest in education' (Dewey, 2007, p 155). However, interest does not terminate when a person comes to understand an object. Interest is the 'moving force' (Dewey, 2007, p 156) in a process of broader developing events whose fruition is reached in action. To be interested in something necessarily involves having wider aims and purposes. A link between student interests and wider purposes is in fact a crucial feature of Dewey's concept of discipline. Discipline was, for Dewey, a disposition of persistence and endurance in the face of challenge and difficulty.

The disciplined person has the important executive ability to set goals based on their interests as well as the wherewithal to think about what actions are necessary to achieve these goals. The merely obstinate, by way of comparison, carries an action through just because they have started down that road. Their stubborn activity need not bear any relation to their wider ambitions. Indeed, they need not have any conscious purposes. Discipline however, is a positive quality because of the agency persons take over their own action and conduct. Discipline is not something that happens to students but something that students do. Only when student action is self-directed and consciously chosen does it makes sense to describe it as displaying agency.

The idea that discipline involves a disposition to actively and consciously take responsibility for one's own learning and development, even in the face of obstacle, is very different to the notion of discipline advanced in the behaviour management or zero tolerances literatures. It is also very different from the rules-based accounts of discipline variously developed by Kant, Durkheim and John Wilson. Although the Deweyian view of discipline as something that pupils do through their own agency has been largely neglected in recent discourses of discipline in education, I think discipline needs to be reconceived and reclaimed in education along something like these lines.[19] Indeed, this possibility will be considered in the chapters that follow. There we will see that Dewey's interest-based account of school discipline does not fall prey to the same problems of Pat Wilson's concept. Dewey stressed that education and any discipline that is part of it must be about more than the *individual interests* of students. Instead, discipline and education are necessarily social and must be geared toward promoting greater democracy.

Chapter summary

In this chapter I have claimed that recent discourses of discipline in education are problematic at the levels of theory, policy and practice. At the level of *policy and practice*, zero tolerance and behaviour management approaches have overshadowed other possible ways of enacting discipline in US and UK schools. At the level of *theory* rules-based accounts of discipline in education have been most influential. Foucault's critique of the disciplinary technologies of modernity can certainly help to reveal inadequacies in theories and practices of discipline in education that only aim at, or have the effect of, 'normalising' students. However, what Foucault's critique does not do is provide a more positive account about how disciplinary mechanisms might become less punitive and more educational. In consequence I have argued that discipline needs to be reclaimed in education, for the ends of education. I have presented two different ways of thinking about how discipline might promote educational rather than punitive ends.

Following Peters and Hirst, I first suggested it is educationally important for students to be *disciplined by knowledge*. Unlike Kant, both Peters and Hirst thought that discipline could be a positive part of education. According to Hirst and Peters, discipline is not just about restraining student unruliness.

Instead, coming to understand educationally valuable knowledge requires substantial student discipline. Following Macintyre, I have also suggested there is an educational need for disciplines of knowledge and wider social orders to be continually questioned, and where necessary, remade. MacIntyre stresses much more than Hirst and Peters did, that disciplines of knowledge are most educationally valuable when they support students and communities to become more socially just. Furthermore, unlike Foucault, MacIntyre considers how **disciplinary arrangements** in educational institutions like universities and schools might become less 'punitive'. In suggesting that the preoccupation with examinations in education needs to be scaled back and replaced with a focus on encouraging students to think for themselves and ask questions of unjust dominant social orders, MacIntyre at least gives suggestions as to how such important educational challenges might be faced. This is more than Foucault did.

Second, I charted the views of Pat Wilson and Dewey on how discipline might serve the ends of education. They held that students should first and foremost be disciplined by *interest*, rather than traditions of knowledge. Wilson was especially critical of the liberal educational idea that students should be initiated into disciplines of knowledge. Instead, their interests should form the cornerstone of the curriculum. Wilson and Dewey show that discipline need not be thought about as either the imposition of rules or knowledge into students. While Hirst, Peters, Pat Wilson and Dewey may not have agreed on the content or ways toward significant learning, all these thinkers nonetheless shared a view that discipline becomes educational for students when they *persist in the pursuit of significant learning*. Wilson and Dewey make especially clear that discipline entails a capacity to work toward valuable goals and overcome obstacles in the process. For them discipline is a positive quality of learners because of the agency they exercise over their learning and conduct. However, Pat Wilson's interest-based account of discipline is too individualistic and is beset by both epistemic and moral problems as a consequence. The possibility that fostering disciplined relationships in education might promote greater democracy and community will therefore be considered in the next chapter.

Notes

1. I am *not* here claiming that rules-based theories of discipline are the *only* ones that exist. Clearly, other ways of theorising discipline in education do exist. Indeed, it is my claim that other ways of theorising discipline in education need to be brought into the fold of debate about discipline in education so that they can challenge the dominant rules-based explanations.
2. Indeed, I have elsewhere argued that discipline needs to be reclaimed as an educational concept (MacAllister, 2014a). Kafka also argues that discipline needs to be reclaimed for education (Kafka, 2011).
3. For further discussion of Aristotle's account of episteme, see MacAllister (2012). For further discussion of his views on education, see Curren (2000) and Kristjánsson (2007).

4 Plato (1987) argued that there are two worlds of possible human acquaintance: 1) the *intelligible* world of ideas and ideal forms and 2) the *visible* world of appearances (Republic, 507a). Plato insisted that the forms were permanent and true representations of reality, only *intelligible* to the mind through intellectual reflection. In the simile of the cave (514–521b) Plato said that it is through education, that one can be mentally guided to appreciate such immutable, ideal forms. For further discussion of Plato's views on education, see Barrow (2007) and Curren (2000).
5 See especially Hirst (1968, 1973) and Peters (1968, 1970).
6 Peters is undoubtedly following Whitehead (1967) here. It was Whitehead who first argued that education should avoid the transmission of 'inert ideas'. For discussion of Whithead's views on discipline and education, see MacAllister (2013a).
7 For further discussion of the idea that discipline can be part of (rather than merely being prior to) important learning, see MacAllister (2013a). For further discussion of Peters's view on discipline in education, see MacAllister (2014a, 2014b).
8 He makes this claim in conversation with Dunne (MacIntyre & Dunne, 2002). Much ink has been spilled over whether MacIntyre thinks teaching is a practice or not. I don't intend to revisit this debate here, though I have commented on it elsewhere (MacAllister, 2015, MacAllister, 2016). However, I do want to point out that I am inclined to agree with Fordham (2015) – that teachers don't have to generate new knowledge in their discipline in order to be regarded as practitioners of that discipline.
9 See MacIntyre, (1987, 1990 and in debate with Dunne (MacIntyre & Dunne, 2002) especially.
10 For further discussion of this point and of MacIntyre's philosophy of education more generally, see MacAllister (2015).
11 They are certainly not the only educational thinkers to posit this either. Nussbaum (1997) for example has suggested that more recently emergent knowledge disciplines such as women studies and the study of human sexuality can add value to the traditional knowledge base of more conservative instantiations of liberal education. She also suggested that the study of non-Western traditions of thought could also greatly help to cultivate the humanity of Western students.
12 It should be noted here that that the later educational thought of Hirst (1997) and Peters (1981) took a turn toward the direction of MacIntyre. Hirst renounced his view that knowledge is objective and instead conceded that knowledge embodies social practices and traditions that are subject to change and alteration. Hirst suggested in a footnote to this text that MacIntyre partly helped to change his mind on this issue. Similarly, though Peters indicates that there is and should be an objective content to education, he does elsewhere suggest that students need to make traditions of knowledge their own. Moreover, though Peters is perhaps best known for his argument that education should initiate students into worthwhile forms of knowledge (1970), in *Essays on Educators* he concedes that 'though this is *an* aim of education, it is surely a very narrow one' (1981, p 35). Peters therefore set out a range of other possible aims of education including flourishing, a concern for truth and others, emotional and moral development and preparation for working life as well as the fostering of democratic values. Here Peters stresses that democracy requires widespread participation in public life as well as rational questioning and discussion of public policy (1981, p 37).
13 Michael Young and colleagues somewhat similarly maintain that in depth engagement with disciplines of knowledge in education is a matter of social justice. Here

it is argued that denying young persons' access to *powerful knowledge* (knowledge of subject disciplines) might be detrimental to their life chances (Young & Muller, 2010). Detailed specialist subject knowledge 'ought' to be an entitlement of all school pupils as powerful knowledge helps those who have it access future opportunities (Young et al., 2014). However, Young's (2009) insistence that powerful knowledge is 'context independent' and more valuable than context dependent knowledge is less than convincing. MacIntyre's view that traditions of knowledge are constructed by communities and no less weak for being context dependent is for me much more persuasive.

14 For further discussion of MacIntyre's philosophy of education, see MacAllister (2015, 2016).
15 In chapter 4 I acknowledge that Foucault's later work may offer clues as to how Foucault thought disciplinary technologies might be opposed. However, I also suggest that *disciplinary power* in itself generally normalises individuals and inhibits their political capacities.
16 Wilson also perplexingly insisted that all actions are instrumental and that all knowledge has the instrumental function of enabling the discovery of further knowledge. The educational value of knowledge depends on its capacity to generate more knowledge. His attempt to explain the worth of knowledge founded on interest is, I think, less than satisfactory. I do not appear to be alone in reaching this conclusion, as this paper 'was dismissed with less than philosophical decorum' (Pring, 2007, p 77) at a dramatic meeting of the Philosophy of Education Society for Great Britain.
17 A view I take from (Plamenatz, 1972).
18 Dewey (2007) undoubtedly influenced Pat Wilson (1971). In fact, he takes Dewey's ideas of interest in education as the starting point for his discussion on interest in discipline in education. For further discussion of Wilson's account of discipline in schools, see Clark (1998) and MacAllister (2013a).
19 Fenstermacher (2006) also suggests that the notion of student agency is central to Dewey's philosophy of education. He adds that education research, policy and practice today all too often ignore the importance of student agency in education – with detrimental educational consequences.

6 Relationships, community and personal discipline

This chapter explores the importance of, and possible connections between, relationships, communication, community and discipline. It does so with reference to the educational philosophies of, first, John Dewey and then John Macmurray. Contrary to Foucault, Dewey and Macmurray both felt that discipline was needed in education if community is to be established and better social orders built. Dewey thought that disciplined communication of interests and purposes in education could help communities be and become more democratic. While perhaps unduly optimistic about the democratic potential of discipline, Dewey's notion nonetheless stands in stark contrast to more managerial ways of thinking about disciplinary approaches in school. Macmurray in turn emphasised the primacy of fostering disciplined relationships. Unlike Kant, Macmurray held that human emotions are far from unruly passions. They are not states that need to supressed before education can begin. Rather they are the foundations upon which discipline and education must be built. While sympathetic to the concepts of discipline developed by Macmurray and Dewey, neither philosopher valued enough the liberal idea that students might be meaningfully disciplined by traditions of knowledge pursued for their own sake.

Relationships, communication and school discipline

Relationships and communication are at the core of discipline in schools. When school discipline supports and enables meaningful learning, it is almost certain that relationships and communication will have contributed to this in some way or other. Conversely, when school discipline is not able to support or enable meaningful learning, it is equally likely that there will have been a breakdown in communication and/or relationships of some kind. In fact, given the necessarily social and interpersonal nature of schools, it is nigh on impossible to make sense of discipline issues unless serious attention is given to how they are shaped by, and in turn shape, wider relationships and patterns of communication in school. Latter day research and policy regarding school discipline often stresses the importance of positive relationships and communication.[1] However, when it does so, it is important to ask positive *for what*, and *for whom*? What exactly does it mean for there to be 'positive' relationships and communication in schools? What sorts of relationships and patterns of communication should teachers and schools try to promote and why? How might relationships and patterns of communication enhance school discipline and school community? How might they diminish it?

This chapter considers such questions and issues with reference to the educational philosophies of, first, John Dewey and then John Macmurray. As we saw in the last chapter, Dewey endorsed an interest-based account of discipline that places an onus on schools to foster student agency. Here schools do not merely impose rules, knowledge and wider social norms on to students. Instead, students also need to be supported to take substantial responsibility for their learning, conduct and development. Whereas in a behaviour managerial model teachers' discipline positively when they are able to manage their students effectively (or in the case of Tom Bennett – get students to do their bidding!), in Dewey's account teachers discipline positively when they are able to support their students to take some sort of authority over their own education and conduct.[2] Dewey did not ignore the societal need for educational processes to make students familiar with prevailing cultural rules and norms. He just thought that education should *improve* rather than *reproduce* society. In this respect he championed the need for constant communication between teachers and students.[3] Here it is vital to recognise that he endorsed communication of a very particular sort, with a very particular end.

Dewey on communication and community

> There is more than a verbal tie between the words, common, community and communication. Men live in a community in virtue of things which they have in common; and communication is the way in which they come to possess things in common.
>
> (Dewey, 2007, p 8)

Dewey (2007) maintained that communities maintain themselves through processes of transmission, participation and communication. He suggested that unless the older generation systematically transmitted valued ways of thinking, acting and feeling to the younger generation, then most civilised groups would degenerate into savagery. Schools have an important role to play here, as they are institutions whose function is to formally and deliberately educate the young. Dewey's philosophy of education is similar to that of Kant's then in that it acknowledges a social need (to prevent a descent into barbarism) for cultural norms to be transmitted to the young.[4] However, unlike Kant (2003), whose views were explored in earlier chapters, Dewey did not think that discipline was only a matter of imposing rules and valued ways of thinking and acting into schoolchildren. Instead student and teacher alike need to engage in on-going communication. For Dewey it is communication rather than rule following that enables common understandings, expectations and purposes to emerge.

While communication should in part help to ensure that persons come to have 'things in common', Dewey (2007) did not think that communication in school (or elsewhere) should aim at conformity. Instead, he insisted that communication is only educative when the attitudes and dispositions of all participants in communication are altered as a result of the communication. Communication is educational when it is fully participative and consensual. He reasoned that community is not essentially about physical proximity – it is about open and on-going communication. Community emerges when it becomes apparent (through communication) that individuals share interests and common ends. Common ends are not enough for community – the common ends need to be established by communication. For without communication of interests and purposes between all involved the ends might not, in point of fact, be common. Without communication ends might be enforced upon a person or group, without their consent.[5]

Dewey (2007) argued that it many social groups this sort of on-going communication about interests and ends did not occur. He stated that a large proportion of human relationships exist on a 'machine like plane'. Here individual persons use 'one another to get desired results, without reference to the emotional and intellectual disposition and consent of those used' (Dewey, 2007, p 9). Moreover, when such 'machine like' relations occur in the school context they are not, according to Dewey, educative. He maintained that when parents, pupils, teachers and school governors and governed merely 'give and take orders', without sharing wider purposes and communicating interests then relationships will remain machine like rather than educational. The continuous communication of interests and purposes between teachers and students (and for that matter students and students) is utterly central to Dewey's philosophy of education then, as well as his concept of discipline in education.

Dewey on individualism, social control and democracy

In stressing the centrality of communication to all educational experiences Dewey avoided the pitfalls of defending narrowly individualistic educational goals on the one hand or narrowly socialising educational priorities on the other. Dewey (2007) was critical of Rousseau's idea that children will naturally fulfil their potential if left to their own devices, suggesting that it is too individualistic a view of education.[6] However, he was also critical of the alternative Kantian idea that children must first be socially controlled and disciplined if they are to eventually grow to a state of mature perfection. Indeed, Dewey did not believe that human nature could be perfected, with or without, formal educational intervention. Instead, he thought education should aim at the continuous reconstruction of human experience rather than the perfection of human experience. In particular he felt educational experiences should foster the growth of individuals and the democratic renewal of society.[7]

> It is the aim of progressive education to take part in correcting unfair privilege and unfair deprivation, not to perpetuate them. Wherever social control means subordination of individual activities to class authority, there is a danger that industrial education will be dominated by acceptance of the status quo.
>
> (Dewey, 2007, p 92)

Dewey (2007) believed that if there was constant communication of interests and purposes in education, individual growth and democratic renewal could become intertwined. More than anything, *communication* is what makes individual growth and democratic renewal possible. He maintained that educators should not subordinate the interests of one social class of students to another. If they do this there will be no hope of progressively improving the current condition of society. However, he conceded that education all too often merely resulted in the social control of students and the reproduction of society rather than the democratic renewal of society.[8] Dewey thought that the flaws in society at least in part reflect the flaws in education. To challenge social inequity, it is necessary to change practices in education and make sure they are more focussed upon democratic processes and ends. Indeed, he contended that educational processes needed to be and become more democratic if society was to be and become more democratic. However, he articulated a famously unconventional understanding of democracy.

For Dewey (2007), democracy was not primarily about voting in one's preferred candidate for government once every few years. Democracy does not involve irregularly deciding who will regularly make one's decisions for them. Instead, democracy requires that persons routinely exercise agency over their own affairs in regular dialogue with others. As such, democracy should happen all the time instead of once every three or four years. Democracy is not, according to Dewey, a rare occurrence but rather a shared way of living. A way of living that has constant communication at its heart. He stated that 'democracy is more than a form of government; it is primarily a mode of associated living, of conjoint communicated experience' (Dewey, 2007, p 68).

Importantly, democratic processes should increase the number of persons who participate together in shared interests and activities. Democratic processes should also serve to ensure that each person considers the impact of their actions on others with the contrary standpoint that the actions of others will give point and purpose to one's own. Dewey believed that such sustained sharing of interests and purposes both constitutes and further enables conditions of democracy. He believed that associated living through constant communication is 'equivalent to the breaking down of those barriers of class, race, and national territory which kept men from perceiving the full import of their activity' (Dewey, 2007, p 68). As we shall now see, Dewey thought that on-going disciplined communication of interests and purposes was necessary in education if community was to emerge and society become more democratic.

Dewey on spectatorship, student agency and formal discipline

In the last chapter it was suggested that Dewey thought discipline in education should foster significant student agency. Having considered Dewey's wider philosophy of education, in this chapter we are now beginning to see that he thought that discipline should encourage a *particular kind* of student agency. According to Dewey, agency should be founded in action and communication and directed toward individual growth and social democratic renewal. Dewey contrasted two modes of student activity, those of spectator and agent. Whereas *spectators* are like prisoners, watching events outside their cell window, unable to alter them and indifferent to them, *agents* 'are bound up with what is going on' (Dewey, 2007, p 96). Agents are *participants in* rather than *spectators of* events and activities. Agents do not stand aloof from present events. Instead, they participate in the present with concern for the future. Spectators merely let events take their natural course whereas agents act to ensure the best possible consequences. However, Dewey suggested that too often approaches to discipline in schools encourage students to take on the role of spectator rather than agent. He was especially critical of the doctrine of 'formal discipline' here.

Dewey argued that the doctrine of formal discipline was very popular in the early part of the twentieth century. Here discipline entailed repeated training and exercise so as to furnish students with the particular mental powers that it is the task of education to inculcate. Dewey remarked that the 'forms of power in question are such things as the faculties of seeing, perceiving, retaining, recalling, associating, attending, willing, feeling, imagining, thinking' (Dewey, 2007, p 50). The focus of education should be on sustained exercise and disciplined practice of these faculties of mind. Dewey provided the example of a spelling exercise. In the theory of 'formal discipline' the student who repeatedly practices their spelling will not only acquire the ability to spell the particular words in question, they will also increase their general powers of observation, recollection and attention and be able to draw upon these powers whenever they are needed. However, Dewey was very critical of the doctrine of formal discipline and its reliance upon specific knowledge and subject matter being passively received by students.

What is wrong with this theory of discipline is its dualism and its 'separation of activities and capacities from subject matter' (Dewey, 2007, p 52). He maintained that there is no such thing as a *general power* of attention or seeing – there is only a power to see or attend to a *particular object of experience*. Dewey did not think that the solution to such dualism lay in initiating students into specific disciplines of knowledge. Indeed, he remarked that the 'remedy for the evils attending the doctrine of formal discipline ... is not to be found by substituting a doctrine of specialised disciplines' (Dewey, 2007, pp 101–102). Dewey did not think that the knowledge and subject matter of education should be regarded as complete in itself – it should be revised where needed. Moreover, Dewey thought education must do more than just remake traditions of knowledge where needed. Instead, educators needed to stop thinking that the human mind is better than and set apart from the human body. Educators needed to reform their very notions of mind, body and discipline in education.

> The chief source of the "problem of discipline" in schools is that the teacher has often to spend the larger part of the time in suppressing the bodily activities which take the mind away from its present material. A premium is put on physical quietude, on silence, on rigidity of posture and movement ... The teachers' business is to hold the pupils up to these requirements and to punish the inevitable deviations which occur.
> (Dewey, 2007, p 108)

Dewey felt that education too routinely valorised the idea that mind is superior to, and independent of, the world of material things. He felt that in schools the bodily activity of students was too often suppressed into conformity, with sense perceptions divorced from mind and action. According to Dewey, however, 'mind is not a name for something complete by itself; it is a name for a course of action in so far as that it is intelligently directed' (Dewey, 2007, p 101). Dewey believed it takes discipline to develop the mind so conceived (as that which gives embodied action intelligent direction) – just not *formal discipline*. Dewey maintained that in the doctrine of formal discipline educators should silence and still students and then present subject knowledge to them to be passively received. However, Dewey suggested this view is dualistic as students are cast in the role of disembodied spectators of education rather than active participants in education. Educational instruction should not present students with abstract knowledge divorced from immediate experience. It should rather engage students in activities that have aims and purposes of obvious experiential interest to them. However, unlike Pat Wilson (1971), Dewey is clear that there is a need for individual interests to be disciplined by the interests and purposes of others too via constant communication.[9]

Dewey on discipline for democracy

> The school cannot immediately escape from the ideals set by prior social conditions. But it should contribute through the type of intellectual and emotional disposition which it forms to the improvement of those conditions. And just here the true conception of interest and discipline are full of significance.
>
> (Dewey, 2007, p 105)

For Dewey 'true' discipline in education requires constant communication of interests and purposes – it needs must be communal. If discipline is not interest-based and communal, it will not be able to transcend mind and body dualisms or further conditions of social democratic renewal. Dewey suggested that twentieth-century education was still unhelpfully influenced by the old ideal of liberal education. He commented that in industrial societies so long as educational provision is arranged by class division, the intelligence of the majority of working persons will become unduly practical, while the intelligence of those in control of industry will become 'devoted to the manipulation of other men for ends that are non-human in so far as they are exclusive' (Dewey, 2007, p 104). According to Dewey though, the best way of preventing social exclusion and the reproduction of social inequity was through encouraging students to discipline their interests in intelligent directions in ongoing communication with others. This is an appealing idea if one is inclined to think (as I am) that discipline might be able to reduce social exclusion and encourage students to take some meaningful responsibility for their learning and conduct. However, there are no doubt problems with Dewey's philosophy of discipline in education.

Dewey is perhaps guilty of a certain naivety. His apparent belief that there could with regularity develop a happy concordance of common activities from individual interests is probably unduly optimistic. Even if every effort is made to foster open communication, it is hard to imagine groups of students routinely sharing the same interests and purposes without some students imposing their will on others in some small ways at least. His notion of mind as that which gives action intelligent direction is also unduly narrow. The mind might well give action intelligent direction on occasion or often, but surely it can engage in other forms of thought such as disinterested contemplation too? Dewey's definition of mind suggests otherwise.[10] Similarly, in spite of his protestations against liberal and vocational dualism, he tended to value knowledge traditions in so far as they facilitated action to improve present conditions. He after all remarked that 'knowledge of the past and its heritage is of great significance when it enters into the present, but not otherwise' (Dewey, 2007, p 60). For Dewey, knowledgeable persons seek connections between past and present in order to solve present problems.[11] Educational processes should not focus on the transfer of knowledge but on helping young people learn how to use knowledge to solve present problems.

While partly sympathetic to such a view, the pragmatic valuing of knowledge may well preclude the liberal idea that there is educational merit in pursuing knowledge for its own sake. Indeed, Dewey remarks that while it is legitimate to be satisfied with the possession of knowledge (rather than the application of knowledge to present problems), he rather oddly regards such satisfaction as aesthetic rather than intellectual (2007, p 249). However, his insistence that on-going communication of interests and purposes is needed in education stands in stark contrast to more managerial ways of thinking about relationships and disciplinary approaches in school.[12] His belief that *discipline* is necessary in education for the democratic renewal of society also radically deviates from Foucault's notion of *discipline*, which suggests the opposite. For Foucault discipline is more a *cause of than cure for* social exclusion and the reproduction of social injustices.[13] Dewey's discussion of the problems with disciplining bodies into a state of subjection in education does bring Foucault's later work to mind. However, Dewey offers criticism of society *and* guidance for its improvement with his concept of discipline in education where Foucault only provides critique.[14] Dewey was not the only person to suggest that discipline is needed in education if communities are to be improved though. His work greatly influenced John Macmurray.

Macmurray on learning to be human in community with others

> Going to school is itself a stage in the process by which we learn to live in community . . . we learn to live in community only by living in a community. It is a necessary part of the school's business to absorb new children every year and . . . integrate them into the community.
>
> (Macmurray, 2012, pp 670–671)

There has been a recent resurgence in interest in the (too long neglected) views on education of the Scottish philosopher John Macmurray (1891–1976).[15] Macmurray appears to have been significantly inspired and influenced by Dewey. Like Dewey, Macmurray felt that education should help persons to live together in community with others. He explained that it is the task of schools to accommodate young children into the community beyond their own family and household. He remarked that young persons 'pass from the small, cosy and intimate community of the family to a wider, more demanding, more complicated community' (Macmurray, 2012, pp 670–671). According to Macmurray, learning to live in community with others entails at least four things: 1) being and becoming *human* rather than a merely productive or efficient worker; 2) thinking and feeling from the standpoint of humankind rather than that of British or European, Indian or American; 3) being creative and emotionally alive; 4) disciplining one's emotions in relation with others.

Macmurray suggested that the technical and functional task of preparing pupils for the world of work so dominated the education of his day (the middle of the twentieth century) that the wider priority of learning to be human in community with others was being neglected. He stated that the 'special training for the world of work by which an individual will earn his living in the social economy . . . is not the whole of education . . . it is not even the most important part. It is rather the minimum that an industrial society must demand for efficiency's sake' (Macmurray, 2012, pp 672–673). However, a merely efficient society is not a humane and personal one. Macmurray did not think that education should pit nation-states (and persons in them) in competition with one another. Instead education should support persons to live together. Education should help persons learn how to think and feel from the standpoint of humankind rather than from a nationalistic perspective. For example, Macmurray thought that British persons were first and foremost *human* rather than British, European or Western. Macmurray also suggested that being and becoming human involves leading a creative yet disciplined life in community with others.[16]

He declared that to 'learn to be human is to learn to be creative. The imaginativeness of children is their birthright: it requires the discipline of the objective world for its training . . . And the discipline of the imagination cannot be intellectual; it must be rooted . . . in the life of the senses (Macmurray, 2012, p 672). Unlike Kant, Macmurray held that human emotions are far from unruly self-centred passions. They are not states that need to be supressed before education can begin. Rather, they are the foundations upon which discipline and education must be built. He stated that 'the first priority in education – if by education we mean learning to be human – is learning to live in personal relation to other people. Let us call it learning to live in community' (Macmurray, 2012, p 670). Two more practical principles seem to underpin Macmurray's account of learning to be human in community with others. Namely that: 1) education must support persons to become less egocentric by 2) attending more to sense experiences and education of the emotions.

In terms of the first principle Macmurray explained that the essential human condition into which all are born is one of total dependence – at the beginning of life young infants can only survive by being cared for by others (Macmurray, 2012, 1961b). Although persons commence life in a *dependent state*, Macmurray thought they could and should strive beyond this towards *interdependence*. According to Macmurray, it is by trying to get past the state of dependence and into one of mutuality and interdependence that a person learns to be human. As he puts it, for the young child 'dependence on others is his life – yet to be human he must reach beyond it, not to independence, but to an interdependence in which he can give as well as receive. Thus his humanity consists in learning to be human' (Macmurray, 2012, p 667). Whereas Kant thought persons become human when they are able to reason independently, Macmurray thought humanity consists in mutually interdependent communal living.[17]

Macmurray on being and becoming a person through education

Macmurray (1956, 1961a, 1961b, 2012) suggested that people first live as *individuals* rather than as *persons*. Individuals are characterized by their dependence on others and by their egocentricity. In contrast, persons are characterized by their capacity to live in interdependent relation with others. Persons have learned how to transcend the human capacity to egocentricity. Young infants are the paradigmatic example of individualistic existence given by Macmurray, but he appears to have thought that the majority of adults are prone to egocentricity too. However, according to Macmurray egocentricity constitutes a certain perversion of, and failure in, human relations. That is why he thought all persons should experience an education that encouraged them to look beyond their own interests and emotions and outwards towards others. He indicated that education should seek to challenge human self-centredness by promoting *personal relations* – relations that are characterized by a focus on other persons rather than the self.

Fostering personal relationships should be the primary task of education for Macmurray because it is through such friendship-type relations that persons can successfully overcome the human predilection to egocentricity. Macmurray felt that education fails when persons take their own feelings and interests to be more important than those of others. He posits not only that educational success is the gradual conquering of egocentricity, but also that emotion education holds the key to educational success and to the transcending of the human tendency towards dependence and egocentricity. Thus, an enhanced concentration on the education of sensibility and emotions is the second educational priority specified by Macmurray (2012, p 671). He suggested that a person only fully exists as a *person* when they relate to what is other than and different from them. Our personhood depends upon our learning to relate with other persons. Moreover, he thought personal life requires that persons discipline their senses in relation with others. For when persons discipline their emotions, they learn about the world outside of themselves, and in learning about what is other than them they reveal their full humanity.

Macmurray maintained that there are two different ways in which sense experience can be integrated into human life. On the one hand, human senses can be used as instruments to provide facts about the world, which can in turn be used to solve practical and instrumental problems. Here our senses are used in a *functional* way. On the other hand, persons can *live* in their senses, by construing their sensory experiences not as a means to practical ends and problem resolution, but rather as ends in themselves. Here our senses are not so much used but *creatively and personally* felt. Though people generally use their senses for functional reasons, the real value of sense experience is rather to be found within personal rather than functional life. It must be stressed that Macmurray was not advocating a self-absorbed dwelling in, and focus on, one's own feelings. Human sense experiences only become intrinsically valuable when they are *contemplative;* and contemplative sense experiences are both directed at objects or persons other than the self and concerned to apprehend more fully the value of what is other than the self.

He stated that 'contemplation when it is genuine centres our attention and interest upon something outside of us, and so is a powerful counteraction to the egocentricity which keeps us juvenile and adolescent. It centres our emotional capacities upon the object in a search for *its* uniqueness and reality; and so provides an emotional objectivity for the apprehension of *its* value. So contemplation is a powerful agent for the education of the emotions' (Macmurray, 2012, p 672). Macmurray added that if contemplative sense experiences are not cultivated in education, then 'our emotional nature remains ... crude and childish' (Macmurray, 2012, p 672). Emotion education is therefore important because it is the means by which persons can learn about the world outside of their own ambitions.[18] In learning about the world beyond themselves persons mature and become more human. However, it takes discipline to experience genuinely contemplative (other directed) emotions (Macmurray, 1961a, 2012). It therefore seems important to further explore Macmurray's conception of discipline that is educational and discipline that is not.

Macmurray on emotional reason, discipline and emotion education

Though Macmurray spoke about the human need for contemplative emotions in his lecture on learning to be human, his most extensive treatment of the subject of discipline and emotion education is to be found in *Reason and Emotion*.[19] There his main argument was that reason and emotion were too often and unhelpfully perceived as antagonists, with reason allotted the role of overseeing and suppressing the irrational and unruly emotions. Macmurray, however, wanted to draw a different comparison – between *intellect* and emotion rather than *reason* and emotion. He believed that reason could be operative in both intellectual and emotional life.[20] Macmurray argued that if we want to understand how human emotions can be imbued with reason, then we must first understand the nature of reason in general.

For Macmurray reason is not a detached state of mind that is in some way set apart from and impervious to sense experience. Reason is rather the ability to be *objective in regard to reality*. In particular, it is the ability to appreciate and respond to the essential character of objects (including persons) that are other than the self. Macmurray stated that 'reason is the capacity to behave consciously in terms of the nature of what is not ourselves ... reason is the capacity to behave in terms of the nature of the object, that is to say, to behave objectively. Reason is thus our capacity for objectivity' (Macmurray, 1961a, p 19). Notably reason is not just a matter of *comprehending* the real nature of an object but also a matter of *acting* objectively (rather than selfishly) in relation to that object.

Macmurray felt that all human beings are inclined to construe the world in an illusory and egocentric way – illusory and egocentric because a bias is placed upon one's own subjective interests. Reason is vital in human life, however, precisely because it the means by which persons can perceive the world as it really is, rather than in a fantastical and self-absorbed manner.[21] He declared that we 'all like to feel that we are the central figure in the picture ... We feel that life should make an exception in our favour. The development of reason in us means overcoming all this. Our real nature as persons is to be reasonable ... It is to acquire greater and greater capacity to act objectively and not in terms of our own subjective constitution' (Macmurray, 1961a, pp 22–23). Macmurray stressed that being able to judge the real and objective value of a thing is *always* first and foremost a matter of emotional reason rather than intellectual reflection.[22] Emotional reason is the most important species of reason for Macmurray. Indeed, he specified that 'the development of human nature ... is, in fact, the development of emotional reason' (Macmurray, 1961a, p 50).

He clarified that the 'real problem of the development of emotional reason is to shift the centre of feeling from the self to the world outside. We can only begin to grow into rationality when we begin to see our own emotional life not as the centre of things but as part of the development of humanity' (Macmurray, 1961a, p 30). The notion of *emotional reason* that Macmurray developed in *Reason and Emotion* thus tightly reflected his idea of *contemplative emotions* in his lecture on *learning to be human*.[23] The person with well-developed emotional reason/contemplative emotions is able to both focus their attention upon what is distinct from them and in such a way that they can discern the real (as opposed to illusory) value of the object or person that is distinct from them. Importantly, it is precisely because persons are apt to misconstrue their feelings 'that we should recognise that our emotional life really does need educating' (Macmurray, 1961a, p 34). How though did Macmurray think our emotional life should be educated?

He argued that the first step in emotion education must be to reverse the (dominant) view that our sense experiences are shameful and in need of suppression. Instead, emotion education should cultivate 'a direct sensitiveness to the reality of the world outside of us' (Macmurray, 1961a, p 46). Macmurray held that our senses are the gateway to the world outside of us – they are the primary source of all knowledge. The knowledge provided by the senses can be both real and unreal. Knowledge provided by senses is unreal when persons too highly value their own ends and purposes to the exclusion of others. Knowledge from emotions is objective and real when persons don't put a premium on their own goals and wishes. As McIntosh puts it in 'contrast to objective reason, an unreasonable emotion is subjective and unreal . . . (it) has an inward rather than an outward focus of reference; thus producing self-centred as opposed to other-centred behaviour' (2002, p 134).[24] Importantly, an emotion education that is open and responsive to the reality of the external world and other persons in it is not one that can be imposed from without – it must rather develop a person's capacity to feel reality for themselves. And the development of such capacity requires discipline.

Macmurray on traditional and personal discipline

> The important question concerns what is meant by discipline. The first distinction we have to draw is between discipline imposed by authority, and that discipline which is discovered in experience. These are fundamentally different in kind.
>
> (Macmurray, 1961a, p 68)

The need for a new understanding of discipline is the first thing that Macmurray mentioned in his lecture on *Education of the Emotions*.[25] He contrasted a traditional and repressive form of discipline that imposes the world upon the child with a personal form of discipline that invites the child to engage with the world. Discipline on the traditional view can be conceived as the imposition into the child, of the knowledge and values of a given community where this imposition is justified because it is thought to be of benefit (now and/or later) to the child and to wider society. On this view discipline inducts the child into the community but the community is unlikely to be altered as a result. Discipline in Macmurray's more radical and personal view is of an entirely different order – it requires that children be free to work out for themselves what is valuable in experience. Here, the child is not to be initiated into the external knowledge and values of a community. Instead, the disciplined and personal valuations that children themselves give to objects must drive education and learning and in the process renew the wider community.

Macmurray (1961a) explained that the distinction between discipline that is imposed by authority, and discipline that is discovered in experience is most easily understood by considering the notion of intellectual rather than emotional authority. He argued that in medieval times thought was disciplined by authority – students were expected to think in strict subservience to intellectual authority and if they did not, their thinking was 'bad thinking'. However, he stated that 'such a discipline of thought . . . is a repression of thought. It succeeds in securing conformity it all thinkers . . . But it does so by destroying the very springs of real thinking' (Macmurray, 1961a, p 68). Modern scientific thought in contrast is free from dogmatic authority and free to be disciplined by the reality of the objects under consideration. Macmurray felt that the next generation should be free from the dogma of authority, however, in both their intellectual and emotional lives. Indeed, as he puts it: 'emotional education should be . . . a considered effort to teach children to feel for themselves; in the same sense that their intellectual training should be an effort to teach them to think for themselves' (Macmurray, 1961a, pp 69–70).

He explained that there is an identical difference of disciplinary types at play in the emotional as well as the intellectual fields – between dogmatic intellectual authority and free intellectual inquiry on the one hand and dogmatic emotional authority and free emotional experience on the other. The discipline of emotional authority 'aims at securing the repression of types of emotion that are considered improper and fostering tendencies that are laudable and good . . . It makes for conformity . . . for the maintaining of tradition. But it succeeds only by destroying the free spontaneity of emotional life. Against this dogmatic authority we must set our faith in the freedom of the individual to feel for himself . . . That this involves discipline is certain; but it is discipline of a very different kind. It is the discipline which comes through the continuous effort to discover the real value in life for oneself' (Macmurray, 1961a, p 69). He believed it was good that practices of emotional discipline by repressive imposition of values into the child were receding. However, he thought that educators should not abdicate their responsibility towards the discipline of children altogether. Teachers rather have the new responsibility of helping children to learn to feel not only for themselves but also for the sake of others. He acknowledged the immensity and significance of this task.

> In a world which is changing so rapidly and so fundamentally . . . the task of the teacher, particularly in the field of discipline, is exceedingly difficult. He has to train his pupils for life in a society of which he knows nothing because it does not yet exist. He has to train them, not to take their places in a familiar and stable social order, but to be the creators of a new social order . . . Only a disciplined generation will be able to build it. Discipline is perhaps of greater importance than it has ever been.
> (Macmurray, 1961a, p 82)

Macmurray (1961a) thought it possible to exploit, repress and manipulate the emotions of the young through traditional disciplinary measures and so gain a degree of control over their thinking and behaviour. However, this was for him a false discipline – real discipline involves the integration of personality rather than the repression of personality. According to Macmurray, 'real discipline' is vital because it is the means by which personal integration can be achieved and new and better social orders built. In keeping with his wider philosophy, Macmurray stressed that integrated personality can only be developed by disciplined persons acting together – discipline is thus not something that can be done in isolation, rather 'all discipline is communal' (Macmurray, 1961a, p 90). Furthermore, children must not be conceived as 'material to be moulded' but instead as 'potential creators of society' (Macmurray, 1961a, p 90). What should be made of all this? How distinctive and educationally significant is Macmurray's account of discipline and emotion education?

Macmurray was certainly not the first or only scholar to suggest that the discipline of the young might be something that is best discovered in experience rather than imposed by a community. Even if Macmurray's notion of repressive disciplinary control predates the influential work of Foucault (1991), Whitehead (1967), Dewey (2007) and P.S. Wilson (1971) all also advanced accounts of discipline through experience and based on pupil interest. Indeed, there can be little doubt that Deweyan and Macmurryian ideas bore particular similarity to each other given that they both stressed that discipline should be relational, founded in experience and able to advance communal progress.[26] Nor was Macmurray's call for enhanced concentration on emotion education without precedent. As Dixon notes as early as 1820, the infant school movement 'pioneered a form of education based on love and affection' (2012, p 482). However, Dixon adds that the 'importance of the emotions to education continued to be endlessly forgotten and remembered again throughout the twentieth century' (2012, p 483). Indeed, many writers have explored similar themes to Macmurray in more recent times.[27]

Nonetheless, I think the notion of *personal discipline* of *sense experience* for the wider purpose of learning to be human provides Macmurray's thought on discipline with distinctive and original aspects. For one, it can provide an alternative vision of how discipline in education can enlarge the humanity of persons. Liberal educationists such as Oakeshott (1972) and Peters (1970) stressed that the disciplined pursuit of knowledge and understanding was the main way in which persons could be supported to develop their humanity. As we saw earlier in the book, Peters maintained that bodies of knowledge that can illuminate the human condition are called 'disciplines' because coming to understand them is a tough demanding business that requires much effort (1970).[28] Oakeshott perhaps explained even more clearly than Peters how a disciplined liberal education can help to humanise the next generation. He said that:

> Education . . . is the transaction between the generations in which newcomers to the scene are initiated into the world in which they are to inhabit. This is a world of understandings . . . and . . . states of mind . . . To be initiated into this world is learning to become human . . . Thus, an educational engagement is at once a discipline and a release . . . It is a difficult engagement of learning by study . . . Its reward is an emancipation from the mere 'fact of living', from the immediate contingencies of place and time of birth, from the tyranny of the moment and from the servitude of a merely current condition.
> (Oakeshott, 1972, pp 47–48)

In contrast to the idea that education should help persons to escape the present moment, Macmurray (1961a) instead emphasised that we can only learn to become fully human by disciplining our current emotions but in ways where the interests and desires of other persons are given as much credence and value as our own. Thus, for Macmurray, learning to be human is not a matter of being initiated into valuable knowledge and working hard to understand that knowledge (the liberal view) – it is instead a matter of working hard to become ever better at relating with other persons and in a spirit of other-centred friendship rather than self-serving functionality. Disciplined effort and attention in education should be given to fostering the well-being of others rather than to the accumulation of knowledge and understanding in the self. For Macmurray the sensory experiences and emotional responses of pupils (rather than wider community values and knowledge) are the foundation upon which discipline must be built and from which valuable learning follows. Indeed, learning to be human would be impossible without discipline because sensitive apperception of the reality of the other requires discipline. However, Macmurray's theory of discipline in education is also flawed.[29]

Macmurray's anti-intellectual philosophy of education

In his lecture on learning to be human Macmurray maintained that the idea that knowledge should be an end in itself is fictitious, pious and the cause of an unhelpful divide between theory and practice (2012, pp 672–673). Similarly, in *Reason and Emotion* Macmurray maintained not only that the emotions are at the heart of human life, but that the intellect grows out from them and is subordinate to them. He declared that 'the intellect is essentially instrumental. Thinking is not living. At its worst it is a substitute for living' (Macmurray, 1961a, p 75). While the intellect at its best can help persons to live better, it cannot in general contribute to the development of integrated personality and personal relations because the intellect 'must divide and it must abstract' (Macmurray, 1961a, p 77). The belief that intellectual life is derivative from and inferior to emotional and practical life is one that Macmurray articulated again and again in his work.

In both the *Self as Agent* (1956) and *Persons in Relation* (1961b) Macmurray subverted the influential ancient Greek philosophical view that the best human life was spent in disinterested theoretical speculation. He argued that the 'I think' must be replaced by 'I do' in human affairs because the essential human self exists first and foremost in the practical life of action, relation and sense experience rather than the abstracted life of the intellect. Macmurray was keen to resist any dualism between thinking and action when making his case for the self to be conceived of as agent (1956). He maintained that the self that thinks and the self that acts is the same self. However, he did make quite clear his belief that contemplative thought is and can only ever be a negative and derivative aspect of human agency. Macmurray felt that anything that excludes the possibility of action and embodied living could only ever be of secondary importance in human life (1956). The act of reflective thinking is secondary then precisely because it excludes the possibility of embodied action.

However, I find Macmurray's view that *all* speculative thought is instrumental in nature to be highly questionable. In deeming all disinterested contemplation to be egocentric, I think Macmurray effectively excluded the possibility of a person having a positive motivation for more theoretical contemplation. Indeed, the notion of a love for knowledge, of pursuing knowledge *for its own sake*, would seem to be ruled out by Macmurray altogether for he famously stated that 'all meaningful knowledge is for the sake of action and all meaningful action is for the sake of friendship' (1956, p 15). Macmurray did to be sure state that knowledge can become an end in itself – however, he added that this is 'irrational and meaningless' (1956, p 183). For me, Macmurray's view that the free play of ideas characteristic of intellectual contemplation is always meaningless amounts to anti-intellectualism.[30]

The limitations of Macmurray's philosophy of education also become apparent upon consideration of his view that there is no educational value in discipline based upon the judgements of other people in positions of authority. He states that there can be 'no hope of educating our emotions unless we are prepared to stop relying on other people for our judgments of value' (Macmurray, 1961a, p 37). However, a rejection of discipline by the authority of others (and this is what Macmurray appears to calls for here) effectively renders as obsolete all sources of knowledge and values that are in any way independent from the immediate sense experience of school pupils. Macmurray's philosophy of education thus reveals itself to be anti-intellectual and anti-authoritarian, at least in so far as it allots no educational value to the intellectual and emotional authority of the teacher.

Chapter summary

In this chapter the concepts of discipline developed by Dewey and Macmurray have been explored. Dewey appears to have greatly influenced Macmurray. Both thought that learning to live in community with others is a hard and exacting process that cannot be done alone. Contrary to Foucault, Dewey and Macmurray maintained that ***discipline*** was needed in education if community is to be established and better social orders built. Dewey suggested that too often approaches to discipline in schools encourage students to take on the role of disembodied, passive spectator rather than participative, embodied agent. Dewey thought greater student agency was needed in education. He maintained that on-going disciplined communication of interests and purposes was necessary in education if community was to emerge and society become more democratic. Dewey was perhaps guilty of a certain naivety though. His seeming belief that there could with regularity develop a happy concordance of common activities from individual interests is probably unduly optimistic. However, his insistence that on-going communication about interests and purposes is needed in education stands in stark contrast to more managerial ways of thinking about relationships and disciplinary approaches in school.

Macmurray in turn emphasised the primacy of fostering disciplined relationships. Discipline should for Macmurray focus the attention of persons less upon intellectual matters, abstract ideas and the study of books and knowledge. It should instead promote the fostering of personal relationships and the overcoming of the human tendency towards egocentricity. While Kant thought discipline in education should repress feeling, Macmurray felt education needs must develop out from feeling. Macmurray held that human emotions are far from unruly self-centred passions. They are not states that need to be supressed before education can begin. Rather, they are the foundations upon which discipline and education must be built. While I do think that learning to live in community with others requires discipline along the lines advanced by Macmurray and Dewey, as we shall see in subsequent chapters, I do not agree that this is the only form of discipline that has educational value. Neither Dewey nor Macmurray valued enough the liberal idea that students might be meaningfully disciplined by traditions of knowledge pursued for their own sake. In spite of this weakness, their thought can nonetheless provide insight into the question of how contemporary practices of school discipline might become less rules-based and punitive, and more relational and educative. In subsequent chapters we will revisit these themes. Indeed, in the next chapter I examine restorative approaches to issues of school discipline. Restorative approaches are becoming more popular. It has been claimed they can challenge conservative school structures.

Notes

1 As we saw in chapter 2, the well-known proponent of managerial skills, Bill Rogers (2011), endorses 'positive' communication and non-verbal skills in schools while the Scottish Government (2013) also stresses the importance of positive relationships and communication.
2 For further discussion of the differences between agentic and managerial understandings of school discipline, see MacAllister (2014a).
3 As Gert Biesta succinctly puts it: 'Dewey's philosophy of education is . . . not a child-centred approach but a thoroughly *communication centred* philosophy' (Biesta, 2006b, p 33).
4 As Hansen (2006) points out, Dewey retained a lifelong respect for Kant's philosophy.
5 For further discussion of the role of communication in Dewey's philosophy, see Biesta (2006b).
6 There are indeed significant problems with Rousseau's philosophy of education. For further discussion of these, see especially Darling (1986, 1993) and Mintz (2012). Darling suggested Rousseau's educational ideas might be regarded as sexist today.

7 Dewey suggested that growth should be without fixed ends, the end of growth (and for that matter education) should be further growth. Dewey's idea of education for growth without end has been much criticized and is no doubt problematic, perhaps especially today where growth can all too easily be assimilated to growth of competitive power in a market economy (Saito, 2006). However, I am inclined to agree with Saito who draws upon Emerson and Cavell to claim that his idea of growth is closely aligned to his idea of democracy. Individuals need others to grow. Processes of individual growth can and should for Dewey reinforce rather than inhibit conditions of democracy.
8 For an excellent further discussion of Dewey's work on social control and social efficiency, see Hickman (2006). Hickman explains that while ideas of social control are today generally regarded as Orwellian and sinister, in Dewey's lexicon social control could help in the progressive reconstruction of persons and institutions. Whereas social control in education can result in the subordination of student interests to state purposes, it need not. Moreover, genuine social efficiency entails constant communication of interests.
9 For further discussion of Pat Wilson's views on discipline, see the last chapter.
10 Hansen also suggests that Dewey's writing on 'mind' is 'often opaque and elliptical. This fact reveals Dewey's own struggle to understand the words that emerged on the typewriter page before him. 'Just as Orpheus's lyre grew into his shoulder . . . Dewey's typewriter grew into his arms, given the man's phenomenal published output' (2006, p 3)
11 Hansen comments that for Dewey 'knowledge describes an ability to act effectively in the world' (2006, p 13).
12 See chapter 2 for further discussion of managerial approaches to school discipline.
13 In chapter 4, I acknowledge that Foucault's later work may offer clues as to how he thought disciplinary technologies might be opposed. However, I also suggest that **disciplinary power** in itself generally normalises individuals and inhibits their political capacities.
14 In chapter 4, I acknowledge that it may be possible that Foucault's later work on the care for the self might offer some suggestions about how the disciplinary effects of educational institutions might be opposed. *Discipline and Punish* is all too silent about such issues though. There *disciplinary power* is presented in a generally negative light. It classifies students according to their **productive capacities** – it normalises, but it does not develop their **political capacities**.
15 Michael Fielding (2006, 2007a, 2007b, 2012) has been at the centre of this resurgence, helping Macmurray's seminal Moray House lecture on education as *Learning to be Human* (delivered in 1958) to be published for the first time in a special issue of the Oxford Review of Education (2012), an issue itself devoted to exploring Macmurray's views on education. There are a range of insightful perspectives taken on Macmurray's views on education here, including papers by Pring, Facer, Stern, Cunningham, Noddings, Gaita and Fielding (all 2012).
16 For further analysis of Macmurray's views on creativity and emotion education, see McIntosh (2015)
17 For further discussion of Macmurray's ideas on community and education, see Fielding (1999)
18 For an excellent analysis of Macmurray's views on emotion education, see Dunlop (1984)
19 This is a text based around a series of lectures he delivered in the 1930s.
20 A number of other philosophers have conceived of the emotions in something like this way – for example Aristotle (2004), Goldie (2000) and Pugmire (1998).

21 Fergusson similarly notes that 'Macmurray's philosophy is unashamedly realist. Thought must be determined by the nature of a reality which exists prior to and independently of the knowing mind. The task of thought is therefore to bring itself in to conformity with this reality' (2002, p 36). I would add though that for Macmurray it is feeling more than thought that has this task.
22 See Macmurray (1956, 1961a, 2012) in particular here.
23 Macmurray also spoke about how the 'emotional mode of reflection' can help provide 'knowledge of things in themselves' in *The Self as Agent* (1956, p 194)
24 Given that McIntosh agrees that a Macmurryian emotion education entails learning how to pay attention to the other rather than the self, I find her aligning of Macmurryian thought on emotion education to Goleman's (1996) to be rather surprising. Macmurray's theory of emotion education is considerably more nuanced than that of Goleman's. Macmurray calls for persons to attend to sense experience in all its richness and variety, whereas Goleman seems to want to merely regulate and manage sense experience.
25 This lecture is included as the fourth chapter in *Reason and Emotion* (1961)
26 Cunningham (2012) and Pring (2012) both note the similarity between the work of Dewey and Macmurray too.
27 For example, Bartky (1996) has (like Macmurray) suggested that shame is an educationally destructive emotion, especially for women. Boler (1997) and Zembylas (2005) have also drawn upon feminist and poststructuralist literature to suggest that discourses of power are missing in respect to emotion education and teacher identity. In the absence of such discourse they suggest the role of schools is not generally a *positive* challenge of social norms and inequity but *rather* a negative disciplining of teacher and pupil emotions so that pupils become adapted to existing norms and social structures.
28 For further discussion of Peters' views on discipline in education, see MacAllister (2013a).
29 For further analysis of Macmurray's philosophy of discipline in education, see MacAllister (2014b)
30 While I take on board Fergusson's suggestion (2002) that there is not a hint of anti-intellectualism in Macmurray's philosophy, I am nonetheless inclined to disagree. As we have seen, according to Macmurray, the pursuit of knowledge is without meaning unless it promotes personal relations. I personally think that this line of thought amounts to more than a re-orientation of the value of theoretical knowledge (as Fergusson has it). Macmurray for me adopts an essentialist, pro practical and anti-intellectual stance here.

7 Restorative approaches to school discipline

This chapter explores the strengths and weaknesses of restorative approaches to school discipline. Initially, the origins of restorative approaches in education are documented. The key features of such practices are thereafter analysed. Here it is noted that they have the significant merit of focussing on repairing relationships after a conflict has occurred rather than punishing pupils for being involved in conflict. It is argued that though restorative approaches do offer a framework for improved communication between persons in school when conflict has arisen, they cannot, by their very definition, satisfactorily account for how discipline in schools might become less punitive and more educational beyond situations of conflict. Restorative approaches to discipline have also too often been situated within wider discourses of classroom management. Such associations may limit the extent to which they can challenge existing power dynamics and structures in schools and wider society. After these reservations have been set out, the chapter culminates in the presentation of a case study from a school in England where the culture of discipline does seem to have benefitted from staff and pupils embracing 'restorative' principles. Staff in this school felt that a focus on relationships and getting to know pupils as persons is the most effective long-term way of establishing educational discipline in schools. It is concluded that if discipline in education is to become significantly less rules, rewards and sanction focussed, then educators will need to reflect not only upon how to restore relationships when they have broken down, but also upon how to foster open, respectful, caring and communicative relationships in the first place.

The rising prominence of restorative approaches to school discipline

Restorative approaches to issues of school discipline are growing in popularity and prominence. Since the 1990s schools in a host of countries including New Zealand, Australia, the US, South Africa, the UK and Canada have been increasingly turning to restorative approaches.[1] National education policies on school discipline and pupil behaviour are also endorsing restorative approaches more and more.[2] There are good reasons to be cheerful about this restorative turn, as it encourages educators to foster respectful, transparent and nurturing relationships in schools rather than the mere punishment and management of bad behaviour. For as we saw in chapters 1 and 2, school staff in the US and the UK have all too often been put under pressure to either punish pupils in zero tolerance fashion or manage them in such ways that they are not given enough opportunity to take meaningful responsibility for their learning and behaviour. Restorative approaches are to be welcomed then precisely because they seek to challenge cultures of excessive punishment, management and normalisation in education.

However, in this chapter I argue that though restorative approaches do offer a framework for improved communication, care and respect between persons in school when conflict has arisen, they nonetheless cannot, by their very definition, satisfactorily account for how discipline in schools might become less punitive and more educational beyond situations of conflict.[3] Here I suggest that claims that restorative practices can positively transform relationships and cultures are paradoxical. Restorations, by their very nature return things to how they were before – they don't remake and transform them into something new. In this chapter I first document the origins of restorative approaches to school discipline before analysing some of the strengths and weaknesses of such practices. I here claim that restorative approaches to discipline have too often been situated within wider discourses of classroom management. It is suggested that such associations may limit the extent to which restorative approaches to discipline can challenge existing power dynamics and structures in schools and wider society.

Second, after these reservations have been set out, I present a case study from a school in England where the culture of discipline does seem to have benefitted from staff and pupils embracing 'restorative' approaches. Three key themes emerged about discipline in this school. First, it was felt that conventional approaches to discipline in schools often inadvertently perpetuated disciplinary problems by excessive focus on rules, rewards and sanctions and not enough on relationships. Second, staff thought it both desirable and possible for school discipline to be educative and relationship-based rather than punitive and rules-based. Third, staff thought that empowering pupils to take responsibility for their learning and conduct through emotion education was at the heart of any successful relationship-based approach to school discipline. Although claims that restorative approaches to school discipline can 'transform' relationships and cultures probably exaggerate the possible impact and influence of this method of working, I conclude the chapter by suggesting that the desire to develop discipline differently (with more focus on relationships in schools and less on rules and punishment) should nonetheless be welcomed. I suggest that if discipline in education is to become significantly less rules, rewards and sanction focussed, then educators will need to reflect not only upon how to restore relationships when they have broken down, but also upon how to foster open, respectful, caring and communicative relationships in the first place. Here school staff might especially need to think about how they can support the development of *personal discipline* and *school community*.

The origins of restorative approaches in education

The principles underpinning restorative approaches to conflict in schools are in no small part derived from the criminal justice system.[4] *Restorative approaches in education (RA)* are closely related to *restorative justice (RJ)* practices in the courts (Sellman *et al.*, 2013). Restorative justice processes focus most on redressing harm caused to victims and the community rather than merely punishing perpetrators of crime.[5] Offenders continue to be held accountable for their actions but rather than being punished for their offence in a traditional manner, they are instead expected to make good on the harm their actions have caused, both to individuals and the wider community of which they are part. Sia explains that a 'key feature of restorative justice is that the response to criminal behaviour focuses not only on the offender and the offence. Peace-making, dispute resolution, and rebuilding relationships are viewed as the primary method for achieving justice and supporting the victim, the offender and the interests of the community' (2013, p 14). Many different 'restorative' programmes for use with youth in conflict with the law have been developed, including peer mediation, peace-making circles and community conferencing. Amongst other things, the *UN Handbook on Restorative Justice Programmes* delineates that Restorative Justice Programmes should:

- Respond to crime by repairing harm caused to the victim as much as possible
- Ensure offenders accept responsibility for their actions and come to understand their conduct is not acceptable
- Provide victims with opportunity to express their views on the best way for the offender to make reparation
- Foster new values and skills in offenders – as such these approaches may be especially apt for juvenile offenders

However, several competing ideas about restorative justice have emerged.[6] Johnstone and Van Ness (2007) and Van Ness (2013) have suggested there are at least three different versions of restorative justice: encounter, reparative and transformative. In the *encounter* notion, the focus is placed upon those involved in a crime (the offender and victim in particular) meeting and making a collective judgement about the best way to respond to the crime. In the *reparative* version of restorative justice, the emphasis is placed upon the offender repairing the harm caused by the commission of that crime. It is asserted that in 'the *transformative* conception, restorative justice is conceived as a way of life we should lead' (Johnstone & Van Ness, 2007, p 15). Johnstone and Van Ness here indicate that individual people are all inextricably connected to each other in complex social networks. They seem to construe *transformative restoration* as an aspiration, as an ideal type of human relation, 'guided by a vision of transformation of people, structures and our very selves' (Johnstone & Van Ness, 2007, p 17). Irrespective of how they are conceived, it is perhaps not surprising that educators have become particularly interested in restorative practices, given they are deemed to be particularly apt for young offenders. But what restorative approaches have been most commonly adopted in education? What, moreover, are the strengths and weaknesses of such approaches?

The nature of restoratives approaches and practices in schools

In educational contexts restorative practices such as mediation and conferencing have been widely advocated in more recent times (Sellman *et al.*, 2013). It is suggested that bringing young persons in conflict together, to enquire more deeply into the conflict, can both support behaviour management in schools and create more inclusive school cultures (Sellman *et al.*, 2013). Proponents of restorative practices claim it is educationally beneficial for students in conflict, to together address questions like what happened, who has been affected, what was I feeling, what might the other person be feeling, how might we repair the harm caused? While there are similarities between restorative justice in the criminal justice system and restorative practices in schools, then, there are also important differences. Morrison explains that schools often adapt the vocabulary employed by the criminal justice system to better reflect the purposes of education. Instead of the terms 'victim', 'crime' and 'offender', schools seem to prefer to speak of 'students who have been harmed or caused harm' (Morrison, 2007). It has similarly been observed that the borrowing of legalistic phrases such as 'victim' and 'perpetrator' should be avoided in schools as they 'may reinforce a discourse that demonises and criminalises young people' (McCluskey *et al.*, 2008, p 204).

Morrison (2007) claims that by far and away the most common restorative model actually employed in schools is a face to face conference, or as Johnstone and Van Ness would put it, an *encounter*. School-based encounters might take the form of community or family conferences, or they may involve less formal peer mediation or problem-solving circles. There are good reasons for thinking that less formal restorative practices might be preferable in many situations though. In the largest evaluation of restorative approaches undertaken in the UK to date, the suitability of formal conferencing for everyday incidents of indiscipline was questioned by staff in local authorities and schools (McCluskey *et al.*, 2008). This evaluation was based on a pilot restorative approaches project carried out in Scottish schools. The review findings suggested that formal conferencing (with parents, teachers, other social services staff, students who have harmed or been harmed) might only be apt for serious indiscipline. Indeed, in Scotland there was a notable tendency to focus more on the training and development of existing staff and pupils and less on external facilitators being parachuted in to attend to incidents where significant harm had occurred (McCluskey et al., 2008).

Significantly, the main success of such ways of working in Scotland was judged to be their capacity to improve relationships in the school community (McCluskey, 2013). Here there are different perceptions about the extent to which restorative approaches are deemed able to improve relationships in the school community. Some (including myself) feel the scope of restorative practices is and should be limited to the resolution of conflict. Others envisage a more expansive role for restorative practices. For example, although secondary school staff in this Scottish-based project tended to perceive restorative approaches as a method for resolving 'particular incidents where relationships had broken down' (Kane et al., 2008, p 102), primary school staff in the same study construed such practices as capable of 'permeating school culture and providing a vehicle for the development of school ethos' (Kane et al., 2008, p 102). Indeed, Morrison notes that many schools are today adopting 'pro-active, as well as reactive restorative measures. The broad aim is to build the social and emotional intelligence and skills within the school community' (2007, p 326). It has similarly been suggested that restorative approaches might prevent harm from arising in the first place via the emotional education of pupils (Cremin, 2013 & McCluskey et al., 2008). McCluskey (2013) also calls for the implementation of a *radical restorative practices* agenda in schools – one that challenges the conservative structures of schooling. What should be made of these claims though? Can restorative practices in education be pro-active and preventative? Can they challenge the conservative structures of schooling?

The illogical language of pro-active and transformative restoration

As I have argued elsewhere (MacAllister, 2013b), once educational practices become focussed on the 'pro-active' prevention of conflict rather than the 'reactive' resolution of conflict they arguably cannot be, at base, 'restorative'. A restoration does after all seem to by definition require effort to make good some already existing harm, damage or deterioration in state. It seems to me that distinctively restorative approaches to education hinge on: 1) some harm having already been caused and 2) attempt being made to repair this harm. Arguably, it makes very good sense to describe educational encounters specifically designed to restore relationships and/or repair harm caused by conflict as 'restorative'. When approaches to dealing with conflict in schools become more pro-active and preventative, however, the term 'restoration' appears to be less apt. This is not to dispute that restorative *practices* might aid the emotion education of pupils or support in the challenging of existing school structures. However, it is to say it is rather perverse to speak of a 'pro-active restoration' as Morrison does. For a 'pro-active restoration' arguably necessitates both the active prevention of deterioration of relationships on the one hand and the actual facilitation or permission of such deterioration on the other.

While a process of restoration may perhaps lead to eventual positive change in a person or relationship over time, I am also inclined to think it mistaken to describe individual restorative encounters as 'transformative' as Johnstone and Van Ness do (2007). Restoration and transformation seem to refer to very different processes. The essence of a restoration involves something being *returned to how it was before,* whereas at its core, a transformation entails something *becoming different and new.* Furthermore, while a 'transformation' suggests a sudden, swift and perhaps radical alteration, restoration implies a more gradual process. Given these differences, it is probable that 'restoration' and 'transformation' are words that cannot be used to describe the same activity or goal without a distortion of the very meaning of these words. Thus, the very idea of a *transformative restoration* arguably hinges on a logical (or at least a linguistic) paradox. On top of these linguistic and conceptual issues there is also evidence to suggest that restorative approaches to discipline may only have challenged existing power dynamics and structures in schools and wider society to a limited extent.

Can restorative approaches challenge conservative school structures?

McCluskey (2013) draws upon the *UK Children's Commissioner Report* to the UN to suggest that contemporary school structures negatively impact upon the life experiences of children in a number of ways. Children feel pressured by the culture of examinations; child mental health has deteriorated in the past 30 years; child poverty is still high; children are too often either demonised by adults and excluded from public spaces on the one hand or treated in an overly protective manner on the other. McCluskey maintains that restorative practices have the capacity to bring about needed change in the overly conservative school structures that perpetuate such issues. Here she stresses that restorative approaches must go beyond a mere rewording of school discipline and behaviour management policies. Indeed, restorative practices need to 'disrupt' and 'unsettle' ineffective school customs (McCluskey, 2013). They need to reject the assumption that schools have a right to expel pupils. However, McCluskey suggests that teacher work continues to be bound and limited by conservative school structures.

Indeed, the conservative structures of schooling are the greatest barrier to more radical restorative practice agendas succeeding (McCluskey *et al.*, 2008b). Vaandering also expresses concern that restorative approaches to school discipline are at risk of being 'co-opted by the power structures that underlie the punitive managerial structures of society' (2014, p 65). In her Canadian-based study Vaandering found that schools only turned to restorative approaches in the first place to reduce suspensions and bullying. There was not any overarching desire to challenge existing, largely authoritarian, school structures. Moreover, when restorative approaches were described in school policy this often reinforced already existing managerial goals of conformity, control and compliance with not enough emphasis on the need for the building of relationships or the repairing of harm. Rules rather than relationships continued to dominate policy in these contexts, allowing the 'explicit legitimating of adult authoritarian power' (Vaandering, 2014, p 69).

However, in spite of these policy formulations, Vaandering (2014) did find that some Canadian educators thought that restorative practices were not just about classroom management, they could also be connected to productive pedagogies. Here teachers did not perceive students as material to be moulded and managed, they were all instead regarded as worthy of honour and respect. What I take from all this is that restorative approaches do have the significant merit of focussing on repairing relationships after a conflict has occurred rather than punishing pupils for being involved in conflict. They do offer a framework for improved communication, care and respect between persons in school when conflict has arisen. However it is notable that Vaandering concludes that restorative justice practices have not yet been able to transform schools into relational rather than rule driven institutions. Too often restorative practices are merely inserted into existing, largely authoritarian, school structures (Vaandering, 2014). Thus, while restorative approaches offer promise of less punitive and conservative school cultures, they have not yet been able to eliminate the culture of excessive management and punishment of students in schools altogether. Indeed, in my view, if they are only used in isolation they will never be able to do so.

Restorative practices cannot by their very definition satisfactorily account for how discipline in schools might become less punitive and more educational beyond situations of conflict. In essence, restorations require effort to make good some already existing harm, damage or deterioration in state. Linguistic paradoxes emerge as soon as restorative practices take on more transformational and radical agendas to challenge existing school structures. I wholeheartedly agree that approaches to discipline need to challenge existing school structures. I just think there are less paradoxical ways of describing such agendas.[7] As we have seen, restoration involves something being *returned to how it was before*. Unfortunately, though, schools have generally in the past been characterised by the very conservative structures that are in need of reform. More radical restorative approaches simultaneously call for a restoration to, and remaking of, conservative school structures. These are two competing agendas that cannot coexist. On top of these linguistic issues, to date restorative approaches to discipline have too often in practice been situated within wider discourses of classroom management.[8] Such associations may well have limited the extent to which they have been able to challenge existing power dynamics and structures in schools and wider society. However, as we shall now see, despite linguistic confusion, restorative approaches do seem capable of contributing to the establishment of more relational and less punitive cultures of discipline in schools.

Restorative approaches to school conflict – A case study

In the spring of 2015 I spent two days in Paddington Primary School in a small town in the northwest of England.[9] Paddington is a large mainstream primary school. Though mainstream, it has developed a reputation for being able to work productively with 'tricky' pupils who had been excluded from other institutions for what was regarded as being unacceptable behaviour. The school has in the last five years adopted restorative approaches to issues of school discipline. In this time, they have also established an emotional well-being team (initially called the behaviour support team) whose task is to provide extra support to particular pupils who may, for whatever reason, be struggling with their learning and behaviour in school. This team is comprised of a social worker, a play therapist and classroom assistants, but it also receives support from the head teacher and other teachers in the school. During my visit I observed lessons, carried out focus groups with pupils and interviews with staff.[10]

From the offset it should be noted that I did not set out to evaluate whether restorative approaches 'worked' in this school or not. Instead I tried to gain a better understanding of pupil and teacher perceptions of the purposes of discipline in the school – of what they thought school discipline *was for* and what they thought it *should be for*. In asking staff and pupils to consider the purposes of school discipline I did though partly hope to understand the extent to which they felt school discipline could challenge rather than reinforce the conservative structures of schooling. I did, however, also ask staff and pupils to reflect upon the actual *practices of discipline* in the school too. I hoped to ascertain which approaches to discipline they felt worked well and which ones they did not feel worked so well – and more importantly why.

Although I did not set out with a research focus on restorative approaches then, upon speaking with staff and pupils in this school and observing lessons there, a clear view emerged that embracing restorative approaches was an important factor in the school moving towards a more relationship-based philosophy of school discipline and a less punitive and rules-based one. Three key themes became visible during my short visit to the school.[11] First, staff at Paddington thought that conventional approaches to discipline in schools may often perpetuate disciplinary problems by focussing too much on rules, rewards and sanctions and not enough on relationships. Second, staff thought it both desirable and possible for school discipline to be educative and relationship-based rather than punitive and rules-based. Third, staff thought that empowering pupils to take responsibility for their learning and conduct through emotion education was at the heart of any successful relationship-based approach to school discipline.

Discipline should be about meeting pupil needs not punishment and reward

During my visit it quickly became clear that staff in the school did not punish pupils for 'bad behaviour'. It also became clear that staff in the school did not punish 'bad' behaviour because they did not think such behaviour *should be punished*. Indeed, they thought that punitive approaches to issues of school discipline might actually perpetuate disciplinary problems rather than ameliorate them. Alison, the head teacher at the school, maintained that the very idea of 'bad' pupil behaviour is problematic.[12] She argued that a focus on bad behaviour obscures the fact that pupils don't generally set out to behave badly when at school. Instead, conduct sometimes construed by school staff as 'bad' may often merely be pupils trying to express (consciously or otherwise) educational needs that are not currently being met. Alison wondered whether schools might unintentionally cause further disciplinary problems when they are not meeting pupil needs and instead punish pupils for what is deemed to be 'bad' behaviour. She expanded upon this view by making a memorable and thought provoking statement that there is no such thing as bad behaviour in schools, only bad teaching.

> There is no such thing as bad behaviour, there is only bad teaching . . . if you meet children's needs they will behave in a way that is appropriate. Often because schools behave inappropriately . . . unwittingly and . . . I don't ever think it's on purpose . . . I think schools behave inappropriately towards children and that causes them to behave inappropriately back.
>
> (Alison, Head Teacher)

Alison was being deliberately provocative here. I don't think she was expressing the view that bad teaching *causes* bad behaviour. This is certainly not my view. As I argued in chapter 1, the causes of 'bad' behaviour are complex and multifaceted rather than singular in nature. Instead, I think Alison was saying that it is 'bad' teaching to call a pupil's behaviour 'bad' without seeking to contextualize it. The point I think Alison is trying to get at here is not that schools should ignore pupil behaviour that falls below what is expected (for all staff and pupils I spoke with were clear that there were very high expectations of pupils at Paddington). Instead her point is that schools fail children and potentially cause further discipline problems when they punish 'bad' behaviour rather than seek to understand it. Her point is that school staff themselves 'behave inappropriately' when they punish pupils instead of listening to them. Another member of staff, Fiona, who is part of the emotional well-being team in the school, gave an example of how they sought to understand rather than punish 'bad' pupil behaviour at Paddington. She explained that in the school they have had a number of restorative conversations where pupils have explained that one of the reasons they were angry was because their parents were splitting up, or because there was an illness or bereavement in the family. Getting such background knowledge helped other staff and pupils understand the underlying context for behaviour that could superficially be regarded as bad. Such conversations and the background knowledge they yield were thought to help the pupils affected be better supported. They were also thought to help other pupils be less judgemental and more understanding of 'bad' behaviour – skills they could take with them into adult life.

> If a child becomes angry in a lot of other schools that can be viewed as quite a negative thing whereas we are saying "right you're expressing something, let us help you, what can we do to help you?"
> (Fiona, member of emotional well-being team)

Listening to pupils and trying to understand where they are coming from seemed to be regarded as vital at Paddington. Vital as background knowledge can help school staff to provide all pupils with the supportive environment they need in order to learn. The other staff interviewed all also stressed that at Paddington Primary, seemingly errant pupil behaviour was regarded as a form of communication with one class teacher, Emma, remarking that 'all behaviour is communication'. The notion that school staff has a *responsibility to understand what pupils might be trying to communicate in their 'bad' behaviour*, is very different to the idea that school staff have *a responsibility to manage pupil behaviour*. Indeed, staff at Paddington Primary seemed acutely aware that the practices adopted in the school deviated considerably from most other state primary schools. They seemed proud of this. Ruth, another teacher in the school, stated she was glad she worked at Paddington precisely because of the successful way in which the school eschewed traditional rewards- and sanctions-based approaches to school discipline. Ruth was clear in her mind that rewards charts were not an effective way of creating a climate of school discipline.

She expressed dissatisfaction with the golden time (the practice of giving pupils who have behaved 'well' during the week free time to choose what they want to do on Fridays) and traffic light (where pupils lose some or all of their golden time if they have more than two incidents of bad behaviour during the week) system of reward and punishment in a previous school she worked at. Ruth remarked that 'I very much felt this isn't working but I don't know what would. I felt very uncomfortable with the punitive system, with teachers in control and a lack of respect'. The other teaching staff I spoke with at Paddington expressed similar disenchantment with reward- and punishment-based systems of school discipline. Alison, the head teacher, explained how Paddington also used to adopt a system of traffic lights and golden time. However, Alison felt that punishing pupils by shouting at them and/or removing their golden time was counter-productive.

Alison put it like so: 'the punitive stuff doesn't work'. Alison felt punitive approaches were especially ineffective for a minority of pupils who routinely fell foul of school rules. When Alison started at the school as deputy head teacher over five years ago, she noticed that by midday on Mondays the same four or five pupils in each class had often already lost all their golden time – this meant they had no incentive to behave well for the remainder of the week. She also commented on the rather draconian disciplinary practice of the previous head teacher who 'would come in and shout at them (pupils who had misbehaved) for half an hour . . . it was just awful.' There was no interest in finding out why pupils might be acting up so the same pupils kept on missing out on golden time and being shouted at. How, though, did staff at Paddington move beyond a punitive and reward-based approach to school discipline? How did staff at Paddington come to realize that relationships might be more important than rules when trying to create a climate of school discipline? Staff attendance at restorative approaches training days seems to have been central to this journey.

Discipline and emotion education: Moving beyond rules, rewards and sanctions

I remain something of a sceptic in respect to the idea that restorative approaches can transform school cultures. However, staff at Paddington Primary that I spoke with did testify to the positive influence that attending restorative approaches training had upon practices in the school. Alison, the head teacher, maintained that restorative training had a 'big impact' on practice in the school. She explained that though we approached the restorative approaches training cynically 'by the end of the three days I was a changed person . . . we decided that was the way we should go'. Ruth, a class teacher, maintained that the restorative training she attended was much more powerful than anything she had received when at university. She explained that 'they did talk to us at university about reward charts, stickers, sanctions but it was . . . two or three lectures . . . it in no way prepared me . . . or gave me knowledge of the different approaches that were available to me . . . when . . . I went to some restorative training . . . it sort of made sense to me, I put it into practice immediately and it was drip fed in the school and is now embedded, everyday practice . . . I saw a massive impact in me as a teacher . . . it enabled me to be the positive teacher that I wanted to be'.

Members of staff at Paddington have embraced restorative approaches because they regard them as a more effective and more educational alternative to the previously existing practices of rules, rewards and sanctions. While some staff became convinced of the merits of restorative approaches straightaway, others took longer to be persuaded. However, after taking time to work through some resistance, now virtually all staff and pupils support the sanction-free approach in the school, as they feel that it works. The head teacher explained that 'we have been sanction free for three and a half or four years . . . using the restorative approach with kids working on what we can do to make this better, really empowering the kids . . . our approach is successful, hugely successful . . . in our context'. It should be acknowledged that one or two teachers have left the school as a result of not agreeing with the new sanction-free ethos. However, Ruth, a class teacher, explained that the biggest obstacle has often come from parents. As she put it: 'the approach we are using isn't quick and it isn't instant and some parents see it as airy fairy. If their child has been hurt, they want to see that the other child is punished . . . we need to communicate to parents why we are doing what we are doing and that can be hard . . . our children are so good at understanding that we are all individuals and all have specific needs – I think our parents struggle with that a bit'. Staff in the school that I spoke with, were clear in their minds that even though the approaches they were adopting were benefitting all pupils (and struggling pupils especially) important work remained in terms of convincing the wider school community of the merits of their focus on understanding rather than punishment.

Like Ruth, Emma, a class teacher also felt that restorative approaches can help staff to deal with issues of discipline in a positive and educational way. She explained that whereas some schools say to pupils 'you have made a mistake now here is your punishment, or look at the reward you have missed out on,' we say to pupils 'you made a mistake – what can we do to make it better?' Whereas behaviour charts on the classroom wall might help staff paper over the cracks of discipline issues in the short term, in the long term Emma and other staff in Paddington realised that they had a responsibility to *educate rather than reward and punish pupils.* Paddington staff educate pupils rather than punish them, by encouraging pupils to progressively take more responsibility for their own learning and conduct. Emma explained that ideally discipline would always come from children in school. However, she recognised that teachers often first need to help pupils acquire the skills they need to discipline and regulate themselves. Emma recognised that a lot of the children who struggle to meet expectations at Paddington School have particular social and emotional needs. Often 'they don't have the emotional literacy to communicate how they are feeling – it is our job to give them that . . . to support them'.

Ruth, a class teacher, also feels that it is the responsibility of staff to help pupils take charge of their learning, emotions and conduct when at school. She feels that restorative principles were extremely helpful here. She commented that 'I was absolutely blown away by the impact of restorative approaches for empowering children, the children . . . are very much in control of their learning and friendships, of their relationships with us, their peers, their parents, themselves'. Like Emma, Ruth also feels that it is her responsibility to support with the emotion education of her pupils and provide them with the vocabulary they need to express how they feel. In her class of young children, they use an invisible bucket analogy to make difficult to grasp concepts like empathy more concrete. 'We talk about everyone having an invisible bucket . . . when you have a full bucket you are ready to learn and ready to love, ready to be a kind friend, ready to learn independently or with a friend'. In contrast to this, when you have an empty bucket you might be cross or sad or a range of other feelings that mean you are not currently ready to learn or love. Ruth explained that staff in the school try to 'give pupils as much language' as they can so that children learn they may 'not just be happy and sad but things in between as well'.

Another educational objective of the bucket analogy is to help children see how their conduct might impact upon others. Staff talk to children about how they should try to avoid taking from the buckets of classmates, when their own one feels empty. Ruth explained that we say to pupils 'when you have an empty bucket you can often dip in other peoples and that does not work . . . we talk to the children about that and they picked it up really quickly and use it all the time, when you ask the children how they are feeling they will often say they have an empty bucket, the next question is what do you need to do to fill it.' When I was at Paddington, I observed Ruth helping two pupils work out what they needed to do to fill their empty buckets. Ruth had a restorative conversation with Bradley and Justin following a minor disagreement they had in the play space.

Justin needed an apology and Bradley a hug. As the hug and apology were offered and received, I felt like I had witnessed a successful restorative conversation. Staff in the school also feel they have been successful in helping pupils to deepen their 'emotional vocabulary' and capacity to see matters from the perspective of others. Alison the head teacher remarked that 'our children have a massive emotional vocabulary . . . we equip them with this'. Fiona, a part of the emotional well-being team, also felt that the approach to discipline issues in the school had helped the pupils to become more empathetic. She stated that 'our children are good at understanding why some pupils might be angry'. Another key step the school has taken to move beyond rewards and sanctions was replacing the behaviour management policy with a relationships policy.

Engaging lessons and good relationships can support personal school discipline

> We have a relationships policy not a behaviour management policy . . . if you get your relationships right you can sort it.
>
> (Alison, Head Teacher)

The stress that staff at Paddington placed on supporting pupils to develop their emotional vocabulary certainly seems to have been influenced by the restorative training staff went on. So, too, does the replacement of a behaviour policy in the school with one that focuses on relationships and emotional well-being. However, Paddington staff members also seem to have adapted and extended some of the ideas they encountered in their restorative training in order to meet the needs of the particular pupils at their school and establish a climate of discipline where all pupils are ready to learn. Sometimes pupils in the school are encouraged, or ask, to move to the class next door if they are having a bad day and this change of environment can often help pupils refocus. In other instances, pupils take some time out of the classroom to work through issues with staff in the emotional well-being team. While good school discipline may sometimes require a change of scene or systematic and personalised support from an adult, for Emma, good discipline almost always needs careful attention to pedagogy and curriculum content too. Emma felt that the importance of the synergy between subject content and pupil discipline was often overlooked.

Emma seemed to agree with Alison's earlier noted point that there may be a connection between 'bad' behaviour and 'bad' teaching. Emma described how if she observes a pupil off task during (for example) a mathematics lesson, she does not regard this as a *behavioural issue*. Instead, she regards this as a *teaching issue*. The pupil may well be struggling with the task and in need of support, or conversely, they may be bored by it. She commented that 'I know that if I did a boring lesson or a lesson that was not well planned to meet their needs, I'd have chaos . . . above anything else if I have got a relationship with pupils . . . if you understand them, you can personalise lessons to stimulate them (pupils)'. Emma thinks it is extremely important to get to know her pupils as persons so that she can then plan interesting lessons for them. She explained that 'we ask our children what they want to learn about, if it (the lesson) is not something they are interested in then that is another barrier to their learning'. If lessons are not interesting to pupils and aptly pitched, then pupils are more likely to go off task. For Emma, getting to know what interests and moves pupils is vital for good discipline. Good discipline requires getting to know pupils as persons for Emma. This is a view shared by the head teacher Alison.

Alison explained that it was not easy moving away from the prior system of rewards and punishment. It takes a lot of hard work and a commitment from all the staff to collectively support pupils when they express a need. Alison thinks that a focus on relationships and getting to know each pupil as a person is the main reason why Paddington have been able to move beyond sanctions and rewards. She explained that 'a massive part of that (move beyond sanctions) is relationships – a massive part of that is giving children the responsibility and actually treating them like people . . . we started talking about having a child centred school and a child centred education . . . it became really obvious really quickly that we couldn't honestly and authentically talk about being child centred with that really punitive' approach. Part of building good relationships with pupils entailed listening to them and supporting them when they expressed a need. Part of it also entailed helping all pupils to feel valued, even when they 'misbehaved'. Emma explained that 'we refuse to label our children as naughty . . . we want our pupils to know that a situation does not define them – we say things like "I know you are having a tough day" or "let's do this together" when things are not going well for someone'. Emma felt it was more important that pupils feel cared for and valued for who they are rather than made to follow rules. Fiona also felt that that fostering good relationships and caring for pupils is at the heart of good school discipline, and much more important than punishment.

> For me discipline is about a child feeling safe, so that they have that safe base so they feel able to learn . . . but also it's about the child knowing what's expected of them . . . expectations come into discipline as well as that safe base and relationships are key . . . Discipline if it is harsh and critical . . . can disempower the child . . . the child loses a voice within that relationship.
>
> (Fiona, emotional well-being team member)

It is notable that there are very few rules at Paddington. Much more focus is placed on establishing clear expectations and safe boundaries for pupils. Emma explained that 'we talk about expectations and occasionally rules' but we stress to children that if there are rules they are there to keep them safe. Emma added that 'the rule doesn't explain why' whereas 'we always try to explain why there is an expectation'. Emma felt that expectations could be more helpfully used to help pupils act differently in the future through phrases such as 'I'm disappointed you did not meet my expectation – you can do better than that, how can we help you to'? There did seem to be widespread acceptance in the school that the few rules that exist are there to keep pupils safe and help pupils learn. Indeed, all the pupils I spoke with felt that the few rules that were there, were there to keep them safe or help them learn. The pupils particularly liked the fact that staff in the school refused to label them as naughty as this would only make misbehaving pupils feel worse. One year 4 pupil, Geoff, remarked that 'we don't call them naughty, we just say they are making the wrong choices . . . it's actually a rule of the teachers not to call children naughty'.

The pupils in the school that I spoke with also appreciated the fact that staff expected them to take responsibility for their behaviour and resolve any conflicts they had themselves as much as possible. One year 6 pupil, Emily, remarked that 'sometimes teachers say to you they don't sort it out, so you have to sort it out'. During this conversation, another pupil, Max, added that normally the teachers expect you to sort it out and when you ask them for help, you need to say that you had tried yourself. However, other pupils in the focus group also stressed that teachers would intervene if anyone was getting hurt or was upset or unsafe. In this respect there was widespread consensus amongst the pupils that staff were really good at helping them to feel valued and cared for. One year 5 pupil stated that 'the teachers here are kind to us whatever we are'. These pupil testimonies help to verify the staff perception that adopting a more personal approach to discipline can be more successful in the long term than the use of rules, rewards and sanctions. In personal approaches to discipline less effort is placed upon rules and incentives. More emphasis is placed on staff and pupils getting to know each other as persons and learning to care for each other as persons. Significant emphasis is also placed on devising engaging lessons for pupils.

Chapter summary

In this chapter I have argued that though restorative approaches do offer a framework for improved communication, care and respect between persons in school when conflict has arisen, they nonetheless cannot, by their very definition, satisfactorily account for how discipline in schools might become less punitive and more educational beyond situations of conflict. I have suggested that claims that restorative practices can positively transform relationships and cultures are paradoxical. Restorations, by their very nature, return things to how they were before – they don't remake and transform them into something new. In this chapter I have also intimated that restorative approaches to discipline have too often been situated within wider discourses of classroom management. Such associations may well limit the extent to which restorative approaches to discipline can challenge existing power dynamics and conservative structures in schools and wider society. Restorative approaches do nonetheless seem capable of contributing to the establishment of more relational and less punitive cultures of discipline in schools.

Indeed, I have in this chapter documented how restorative approaches helped staff in a case study school, Paddington Primary, move towards a more relationship-based philosophy of school discipline and a less punitive and rules-based one. Three key themes emerged from persons I spoke with at Paddington School. First, staff at Paddington thought that conventional approaches to discipline in schools may often (unintentionally) perpetuate disciplinary problems by focussing too much on rules, rewards and sanctions and not enough on relationships. Second, staff thought it both desirable and possible for school discipline to be educative and relationship-based rather than punitive and rules-based. Third, staff thought that empowering pupils to take responsibility for their learning and conduct through emotion education was at the heart of any successful relationship-based approach to school discipline. There are some obvious limits to this case study. This study is small in scale and not generalizable. It is also largely based on staff and pupil perception. A greater number of observations of practice would have been preferable. What this case study nonetheless suggests is that it there is an urgent need for further educational research on the nature and purposes of discipline in education. What it also suggests is that school discipline does not need to be based around rules, rewards and sanctions in order to be successful. School discipline can be done differently. When done differently, discipline can be more educational than it all too often actually is.

If discipline in education is to become significantly less rules-, rewards- and sanction-focussed, then educators will need to reflect not only upon how to restore relationships when they have broken down, but also upon how to foster open, respectful, caring and communicative relationships in the first place. Staff at Paddington seem to have successfully developed such relationships with persons in their school community. Paddington primary school has moved beyond rules, rewards and punishments – but it has moved beyond mere restorative conversations too. Educators there seek to understand 'bad' pupil behaviour rather than punish it. They seek to promote discipline by delivering engaging lessons. They seek get to know their pupils as persons and they try to help pupils learn how to care for each other with a real focus on emotion education. To my mind, their disciplinary practices embody many of the ideas of John Macmurray, ideas explored in depth in the previous chapter. In the next and final chapter, I will summarise and synthesise the main arguments in the book. There I argue that discipline in education should have at least four main purposes.

Notes

1 Vaandering's study (2014) focuses on the Canadian context but begins with the claim that schools across the globe are turning to restorative approaches in the hope of fostering caring and safe school cultures. Sellman *et al.* (2013) provide an excellent overview of how restorative approaches have been developed in schools in the remaining countries identified here.
2 See for example the Scottish government (2013) and the US Department for Education (2014)
3 In suggesting that restorative practices can offer a framework for practice I am not suggesting that they constitute a correct model of 'what works' that can successfully achieve such goals in all contexts. As Sellman *et al.* point out, while restorative practices can point towards a general direction of travel 'there is no pure model that can be seen as ideal or that can simply implemented in any community' (2013, p 3).
4 However, indigenous populations in New Zealand, Canada and Africa have long-established traditional customs that both mirror and significantly precede restorative justice approaches in the criminal justice system. Indeed, Carruthers (2013) notes the irony of how 150 years after British and Europeans abolished the essentially restorative traditional customs and practices of the indigenous Maori population in New Zealand, parliament legislated for the adoption of restorative justice in criminal courts in 1989.
5 Sia (2013) points out that while some proponents of restorative justice maintain there is no role for traditional punishment of perpetrators, others think that restorative processes should and will continue to punish offenders in some ways.
6 For further discussion of various programmes and competing concepts of restorative approaches for young persons and in schools, see Sellman *et al.* (2013).
7 I will explore linguistic and conceptual alternatives to transformative restorative practices in the next chapter.

8 Indeed, it is perhaps telling that the otherwise instructive overview of restorative approaches to conflict in schools, by Sellman *et al.* (2013) includes in its title the idea that restorative approaches are a variety of classroom management.
9 The name of the school has been altered to protect the anonymity of staff, students and parents there.
10 In total I carried out five semi-structured interviews with school staff including the Head teacher, two class teachers, one play therapist and one social worker (the latter two staff are part of the emotional well-being team in the school). I also conducted three focus groups with pupils, one group with years 1–2 pupils, one with year 3–4 pupils and one with pupils in years 5–6. I also carried out three lesson observations as well as the observation of one whole school assembly. All interviews and focus groups were audio-recorded. Selective transcriptions were made of these recordings. I also took field notes from the lesson observations. All participants were informed of their right to withdraw from the study at any time and ethical permission was sought and gained from all participants in the study. Here, parents of pupils who took part in the focus groups gave informed consent on behalf of their children. However, I also sought verbal assurances from all children that they were happy to take part in the study too, prior to speaking with them. These assurances were all given. The research project that led to this case study was also screened and approved by an ethics committee at the University of Stirling.
11 Though these three key themes came to light during my visit to the school, the interviews and focus groups were both structured around gaining a better understanding of staff and pupil perceptions of seven core research questions. These same seven questions were also present in my mind when I was carrying out my observations. The questions were: 1. What does the term discipline mean? 2. What practices of discipline are most 'effective' and why? Which ones are least 'effective' and why? 3. Is there a link between pupils having a voice in and agency over their educational experiences and pupil behaviour in school? 4. Are rules or relationships more important when trying to establish a climate of school discipline? 5. What did participants they think school discipline *is* for? 6. What did they think school discipline ***should be*** for? 7. What education and continuing professional development had staff received in relation to issues of school discipline?
12 All the names of participants in the study have been altered to protect the anonymity of persons involved.

8 Discipline in education
The birth of community

> I think we have got the view of school wrong, as a society. I think we still have a view of school that is outdated and that is not fit for purpose . . . What I think schools should be is somewhere that prepares children for their future whatever that might be . . . That might sound like the view that other people have about school . . . but my view of that is quite different . . . I don't want to homogonise anybody . . . The world needs people that are different . . . My view of school is rather than try and get a massive diverse community and homogonise it in to a blob at the end, we need to be taking our massively diverse community and help them to make it even more diverse. In terms of discipline, actually we need schools to provide a safe place for that process to happen. We need pupils to be safe from physical harm and emotional harm . . . that is where the discipline idea comes from.
>
> (Alison, Head Teacher at Paddington School)

Discipline in education can support the birth of community

There is something very one-sided and faulty with the way many people think about discipline in education. Discipline tends to conjure up negative images and connotations. It is thought to be about grinding students down into a state of conformity. It is thought to be about rules and control, reward and punishment, training and examination. However, as Alison the head teacher from Paddington School suggests – discipline in education need not be about grinding students down into a homogenous blob.[1] Instead, it can be about celebrating, encouraging and developing diversity. It can be about promoting community. For me, the definitive attribute of community is not based upon: geographic boundaries, nationality, ethnicity, historic, legal and economic ties, or shared religious or cultural values. In today's increasingly digital world it is possible to form and sustain meaningful bonds with people physically remote from one's own immediate vicinity and from different cultural contexts. Community membership is thus no longer restricted to actually being permanently located in a specific physical place. Nor must one originally have been brought up in the community of which one is, or seeks to be a member of. With the increased movement of persons today both within and between countries and continents, the boundaries of communities are increasingly more porous and less permanent than in the past. People may enter and leave a number of different communities over the course of their lives as they seek further educational qualifications or work opportunities.

Though communities may often be made up of persons who share certain commonalities, community is not (for me) essentially based upon things people have in common. Indeed, it is probable that communities in good working order are diverse rather than homogenous in character – as Alison suggests. What is community then? To my mind community signifies a very specific set or network of human relationships – relationships where securing the common good is valued above the pursuit of individual goods. Communities begin to emerge when persons prioritise getting to know each other and learning to look out for each other. They become fully fledged when in the getting to know of each other persons end up caring enough about each other that their actions aim at the common good, as opposed to their own. In contrast, communities suffer when persons do not take the time to get to know or care for each other. Communities fail when the majority of persons end up regarding others *not* as persons to be known and cared for but as objects to be used and, if need be, exploited.

Alison suggests that discipline in education can and should be used to foster community. I agree with her. Indeed, I hope this book has helped to show that discipline in education need not only or essentially be about socialisation into existing norms. I also hope this book has helped to show that discipline need not just be something that educational institutions do to students. It can also be something that students do. It can be something for which they take responsibility. It can be something that can lead to the democratic renewal of social norms rather than the mere reproduction of social norms. It can be something that can help students learn – both about bodies of knowledge and about other persons they come into contact with. Discipline should be all of these things and perhaps, more. Discipline conceived of in this broader way is alive with educational possibility and potential. Yet adult and young alike all too often fail to so conceive it. It is certainly quite rare for it to be enacted in this way. But is it not time to stop grinding students down into a state of conformity in the name of education?

Is it not time to stop grinding students down in the name of education?

At the start of this book it was suggested that there is a crisis of discipline in schools. However, I also claimed the crisis is not one of student misbehaviour. Instead, the crisis concerns a fundamental confusion over the purposes that school discipline serves and those it **ought** to serve. I claimed that discipline in education increasingly serves a narrow agenda of training, control, punishment and examination. The remainder of this book has been an attempt to reconsider what discipline in education should be for. The desire to reconsider the nature and purposes of discipline in education led me to review some influential recent policies and practices like zero tolerance, behaviour management and restorative approaches. The same desire also led me to go deeper and explore some accounts that philosophers have given to the role that discipline might or ought to play in education. The same desire also led me to speak with some teachers and students about the nature and purposes of school discipline.

In this, the last chapter, I will attempt to summarise and synthesise conclusions from these different theories, policies, practices and perspectives. I first argue that educational institutions do, or at least ought to have, a variety of purposes. Here I revisit my claim from chapter 2, that much recent policy and practice in respect to discipline in education only supports the narrow end of student socialisation. However, while socialisation is one purpose of education, there are others. Others that are all too often marginalised in current theoretical, policy and practice discourses in respect to discipline in education. These marginalised purposes include the ethical, epistemological and personal development of students and the communities of which they are a part. In this chapter I also consider how discipline might support the development of each of these marginalised educational ends. At this point I stress that **personal discipline** is very different to currently faddish educational ideas like grit and self-discipline. I argue that the work of Duckworth and others on grit and self-discipline does not give sufficient regard to the inherently **reasonable** and **relational** nature of persons.

Grit places the onus on students to rather unthinkingly work harder on specific tasks (like exams), while more or less absolving educators and educational institutions of any responsibility to work towards social and educational reform. Personal discipline by way of contrast stresses that new, revised and improved social orders will only become possible when students, educators, policy makers and other community members collectively think about, value and work towards the common good. I conclude the book with some brief thoughts about how educators, students, policy makers and educational researchers may together reclaim discipline in education. I argue that if discipline is only used in education for the purposes of socialisation, then societies will, as Foucault predicted, increasingly resemble prisons. If discipline in education is instead employed in service of a wider set of purposes including the ethical, epistemological and personal development of students, then communities might yet still be reborn for the better.

Discipline for socialisation

In the first chapter I suggested that a core purpose of educational institutions is to prepare students for meaningful participation in social and economic life. I also suggested that institutional disciplinary mechanisms are central to any such student socialisation. Disciplinary mechanisms such as examinations, school cultures and rules play a key role in passing on ways of acting, being and knowing that are valued while discouraging types of knowing, being and acting that are not. Such forms of discipline do have important social and individual value. Such forms of discipline can also help to create conditions conducive for learning. Schools do need to socialise students and prepare them for life after school. Making students aware of social norms and of the needs and interests of others is an essential function of schooling. School discipline should help make students aware of what conduct is expected in school and in wider society. School discipline can and should help to socialise students. However, it should also do much more than this. Unfortunately, it all too often does not do more than this.

In the second chapter I maintained that behaviour management and zero tolerance discourses have dominated recent policy and practice regarding discipline in the UK and the US. I acknowledged that such approaches may not be without educational value. However, I argued such approaches are ultimately problematic, as they do not encourage school discipline to be for anything beyond socialisation into existing norms. I also claimed such approaches do not support students to take meaningful responsibility for their learning or behaviour in school. Nor do they encourage educators to think about the wider moral educational purposes of school discipline. I suggested zero tolerance approaches are especially worrying as they only seem to have negative long-term effects for individuals and communities, with minority youth being especially 'punished' by zero tolerance. Such approaches probably do not encourage educators to care enough about the long-term destinations and life chances of *all* students. A premium is placed upon training, control, management, examination and punishment to the exclusion of some students and to the exclusion of other possible ways of conceiving and enacting discipline.

Such policies and practices reflect a widespread acceptance that the essential purpose of school discipline is socialisation. However, as I have repeatedly maintained in this book, there are other ways of thinking about the purposes of discipline in education – even if these other ways exist at the margins of educational debate and practice. It is my view that some marginalised ways of thinking about discipline in education need to be brought back into the fold. In this respect the most recent federal policy on discipline in US schools does offer a clear directive for change. As we saw in chapter 2, this guidance specifies that in the future US schools need to do more than punish and exclude 'misbehaving' students. The fact that US schools now need to collect data to help ensure their discipline policies are fair offers hope that a shift away from zero tolerance may actually be possible. Research on the impact of this policy will be necessary. However, the call for discipline to be based upon 1) clearer expectations, 2) less reliance upon the police to resolve minor discipline matters, 3) greater use of restorative practices and 4) tiered support from 'discipline teams' for students not engaged with education is extremely welcome. While the question is not posed directly, such guidance gestures towards a need for re-evaluation of what discipline in education should be for. But if school discipline should be about more than socialisation, as I maintain, for what else should it be for?

Discipline for ethical development

While I may have so far given the impression that I take a rather dim and disdainful view of managerial and behaviourist understandings of school discipline, this does not mean I think the behaviour management literature has nothing of value to say about how discipline might be educational. It is rather to say I do not think such texts go far enough in explicating the links between pupil socialisation on the one hand and the ethical development of pupils on the other. Further consideration of the philosophy of Kant, Durkheim and MacIntyre might help to explain my thinking on this point. As we saw in chapters 3 and 4, Kant thought discipline was inherently negative. It should aim to curb unruliness in students and no more. However, he also thought discipline ought to be regarded as a vital first part of moral education. In particular Kant thought education ought to aim at the future improvement of all of humanity via the cultivation of moral autonomy in persons. Learning to think for one self (autonomy) first entails acquiring discipline and the capacity to follow rules formed by others. Therefore, discipline for socialisation need not be regarded as inherently negative if it helps students become autonomous in the end. If pupils are eventually encouraged to think for themselves, then initiation into the rules and values of a community can be educationally justified. Durkheim followed Kant in trying to articulate an account of how school discipline should be connected to the wider purposes of education. Kant and Durkheim both thought that discipline was a necessary first part of moral education. They also agreed that it was vital that educators initiate students into school rules so as to curb their otherwise limitless desires.

However, in chapters 3 and 4, I also claimed that the thinking of Kant and Durkheim was flawed. They both in different ways supposed that the rules and values of a community (in Kant's case the whole human community) will be the right ones, once they are sufficiently rational. However, in the contemporary educational sphere it would seem abundantly clear that there is not always agreement (rational or otherwise) about what common values are or what rules students should be initiated into or why. Indeed, as MacIntyre points out, any genuine effort to encourage students to think for themselves should involve supporting students to ask difficult questions about current social and economic orders. I am in agreement with MacIntyre here. Educational institutions do not do nearly enough to systematically support students to think about what might be wrong with some of our social norms and values. Too many of us today equate success in life with being where the money is. Too many of us today equate educational success with getting high marks in exams. Educational institutions often socialise students (often unwittingly) to believe these things and these beliefs have become mutually reinforcing.

In this respect, there is a well-established correlation between social class, exam success and prosperous life chances. Economic inequality is high and rising in a number of countries including the US and the UK. It is notable that accessing a high quality university/college education is thought to be an especially vital determinant of later economic success (Jerrim, 2014). Unfortunately, research from the Sutton Trust suggests that in the UK students from the highest social class groups are more than three times as likely to attend an elite university than students from the lowest social class (Lampl, 2012). The picture in the US is only marginally better with the same research suggesting that students from the highest social class will be twice as likely to attend an elite university as those from the lowest social class. Significantly, this research suggests that the varying rates of access to university and college by students from different social class groups are 'explained largely by children's prior school results' (Lampl, 2012, p 2). As we saw in chapter 2, there is also a well-established correlation between student expulsion from school and diminishing life chances, particularly in US schools. It would be naïve to suggest that current examination and discipline arrangements in US and UK schools cause such inequality.[2] However, it would also be naïve to discount the probability that they contribute to it.

It is my view that any genuine attempt at ethical development in education should challenge any social and educational structures that perpetuate inequality of opportunity. Educators should aim to help students learn how to unsettle less than ethical norms, especially when these norms are well ingrained. For if students don't learn how to question questionable social rules and norms in institutions of education, where else are they going to learn how to do this? However, education for ethical development should not just involve students learning to *think for themselves* in this questioning fashion. *Action for the common good* will also be necessary if new and better social orders are to be built. Educators should support students to learn how to think for themselves and act for the common good. Educators should be substantially concerned with the ethical development of their students. Educators and educational institutions should certainly not hinder this process. Yet the currently dominant model of education as examination and discipline as socialisation often needs such ethical development to be ignored. It is my argument that it will take considerable discipline to challenge such entrenched social and educational norms, both discipline in respect to knowledge and discipline in respect to personal relationships.

Discipline for epistemological development

Persons do not learn how to reason and think in a vacuum. Their patterns of thinking are disciplined by the experiences, persons, social structures and bodies of knowledge that they encounter. Unfortunately, a growing number of students, parents and teachers have been patterned into thinking, or at least accepting the thought, that examinations represent the end goal of education. However, as Richard Peters pointed out fifty years ago in his book *Ethics and Education* – the purpose of education is not to arrive, but to travel with an enlarged view. The purpose of education is certainly not just to pass an exam. Education is about engaging in activities that are intrinsically worthwhile for the length of life. Such a perspective may sound quaint or deeply conservative. However, I do not think it is. There is far too much instrumental thinking in respect to the value of education. It is instrumental thinking that justifies the obsession with examinations during certain phases of education. One way in which to challenge the culture of overvaluing exams in education might be to resurrect the old liberal idea of valuing learning for its own sake. The resurrection I have in mind will not work, if valuing learning for its own sake is only used as a slogan. Valuing learning for its own sake needs to be a lived educational practice and it needs to be based upon both disciplines of knowledge and student interests.

This is not to deny that education can often lead to instrumental benefits for students. It can and should. However, there is something wrong with a culture that only values educational experiences in so far as they lead to instrumental gain. Not all educational experiences have been reduced to this, but there does seem to be a clear trend in this direction. However, it does not need to be like this. In chapter 5, I suggested that **epistemic knowledge** is that knowledge which is teachable and pursuable for its own sake (as opposed to for instrumental reasons). In my view student initiation into what a community deems to be valuable knowledge must always be a key purpose of education. In this respect, liberal educationists such as Peters and Oakeshott explained that pupils are far from passive when pursuing knowledge in any meaningful sort of way. Indeed, for both thinkers, the pursuit of valuable knowledge requires significant student discipline and agency. Indeed, in chapter 5, I suggested it is educationally important for students to be *disciplined by knowledge*.

Following MacIntyre, I also suggested there is an educational need for disciplines of knowledge and wider social orders to be continually questioned, and where necessary, remade. MacIntyre stresses that traditions of knowledge are most educationally valuable when they support students and communities to become more socially just. Furthermore, unlike Foucault, MacIntyre considers how **disciplinary arrangements** in educational institutions like universities and schools might become less 'punitive'. In suggesting that the preoccupation with examinations in education needs to be scaled back and replaced with a focus on encouraging students to think for themselves and ask questions of unjust dominant social orders, MacIntyre at least gives suggestions as to how such important educational challenges might be faced. This is more than Foucault did. In chapter 4, I acknowledged that Foucault's later work on the care for the self might offer some suggestions about how the disciplinary mechanisms in educational institutions can be opposed. However, such opposition to disciplinary power seems to be much more a matter of *care for the self than discipline. Disciplinary power* is generally presented in a negative light by Foucault. It classifies students according to their productive capacities – it normalises, but it does not develop their *political capacities*. In chapter 5, I also documented the views of Pat Wilson and Dewey. Wilson was especially critical of the liberal educational idea that pupils should be initiated into disciplines of knowledge. Instead, their interests should form the cornerstone of the curriculum.

Wilson and Dewey showed that discipline need not be thought about as either the imposition of rules or knowledge into pupils. While Hirst, Peters, Pat Wilson and Dewey may not have agreed on the content or ways toward significant learning, all these thinkers nonetheless shared a view that discipline becomes educational for students when they *persist in the pursuit of significant learning*. Wilson and Dewey make especially clear that discipline entails a capacity to work toward valuable goals and overcome obstacles in the process. For them discipline is a positive quality of learners because of the agency they exercise over their own learning and conduct. While genuinely educational discipline may well often require that learning begins from immediate pupil interests and experiences, Peters and Hirst also bring home how it is educationally valuable for student interest and effort to be disciplined within and by wider traditions of knowledge too. Whether epistemological development begins from student interest (Dewey and Wilson) or teacher knowledge (Peters and Hirst), there is general philosophical consensus that students should be supported to engage in the disciplined pursuit of valued interests and knowledge. It is doubtful that such learning happens enough in today's schools, colleges and universities. This is not to say that educators and educational institutions don't help students to pursue learning for its own sake. They do. I myself am grateful to some of my own teachers for helping me to learn to value inquiry for its own sake at least at times. I have no doubt many other persons are grateful to their teachers for helping them to learn how to do this too.

However, currently dominant modes of discipline in education certainly do not help this process. The two ends may not be mutually exclusive, but there is often a world of difference between teaching students to prepare for a test and teaching students to love learning. Unfortunately, far too many educators, students, parents and policy makers have caught exam fever. Fortunately, fevers can pass. Indeed, President Obama's recent call for US schools to spend no more than 2% of teaching time on testing, suggests it ought always remain a live possibility for students to be disciplined by experiences and bodies of knowledge valued for their own sake.[3] Passing an exam can be part of a person's epistemic development. However, there is more to rounded epistemic development than passing an exam. Much more. What is more, discipline can greatly contribute to the rounded epistemic development of students. The acquisition and development of valuable knowledge is rarely easy. This is part of the reason why discipline is so important in education.

It is often extremely difficult to learn to think for oneself, especially when that means learning how to question generally taken for granted social and economic norms. A deep knowledge of morality, politics, economics and social justice issues might greatly help here. It takes epistemic discipline to develop such deep knowledge.

Education not examination

There is so much more to education than examination, yet a generation is being disciplined to think that the end of education *is* examination. What might be forgotten in such conditions is that students can be positively disciplined via the pursuit of specific bodies of knowledge for their own sake. Such disciplined engagement with knowledge might help students learn how to love learning for the length of life if teaching and learning are arranged more often with this end in mind. Such disciplined engagement with knowledge might also help students to develop the critical reasoning powers and political nous necessary for questioning unjust social and economic arrangements. Many educators, students and parents will no doubt need to recalibrate their focus here if these more radical educational ends are to be pursued. Many education policy makers will need to recalibrate their focus too.

In many contexts of contemporary learning there may be a need to focus a little less educational attention on exams and a little more educational attention on what students find exciting about a subject discipline. Many educators are brilliant at inspiring students, at capturing their imagination, at passing on knowledge in an engaging way, but many educators probably could do this better and more often. There may often also be a need for students and teachers to be more involved in the development of context sensitive curricula and lessons that help particular students learn about what they are interested in learning about and not just what they need to know to pass an exam. Educators are not helped by current education policy trends here. League tables and related education policy at national and international levels place huge pressure on educators to get as many students to pass exams as possible. This desire is understandable but it is also short sighted. The lifeblood is taken out of education during phases of exam fever. When timetables are crammed full and exams are looming, ideals like learning to think for oneself or learning to love learning may well sound like luxuries. But they are only luxuries if the end game is preserving the status quo. They are necessities if the end game is change.

Discipline for personal development

However, all the knowledge in the world will not lead to social and educational reform unless there is collective will for it. Educational institutions should not then just focus on passing on the knowledge students might need to pass an exam. Nor should they only focus on helping students to learn to love learning, nor only on supporting them to question social orders. Educational institutions ought to systematically encourage students to develop a genuine concern for the well-being of other persons too. In chapter 6, the views of Dewey and Macmurray were explored. Contrary to Foucault, Dewey and Macmurray maintained that discipline was needed in education if community is to be established and better social orders built. Dewey suggested that too often approaches to discipline in schools encourage students to take on the role of disembodied, passive spectator rather than participative, embodied agent. Dewey thought greater student agency was needed in education. He maintained that on-going disciplined communication of interests and purposes was necessary in education if community was to emerge and society become more democratic.

Macmurray in turn emphasised the primacy of fostering disciplined relationships. Discipline should for Macmurray focus the attention of persons less upon intellectual matters, abstract ideas and the study of books and knowledge. It should instead promote the fostering of personal relationships and the overcoming of the human tendency towards egocentricity. While Kant thought discipline in education should repress feeling, Macmurray felt education needs must develop out from feeling. Macmurray held that human emotions are far from unruly self-centred passions. They are not states that need to be supressed before education can begin. Rather, they are the foundations upon which discipline and education must be built. Personal discipline is needed in education if social orders are to be questioned, interrupted when needed and eventually remade for the better. Personal discipline, with an onus on persevering in the face of difficulty, may sound a bit like a currently faddish educational idea – grit. However, it could not be more different.

Personal discipline is preferable to grit and self-discipline

'Grit' has become very fashionable in educational circles of late. Duckworth *et al.* (2007) define the concept as trait level perseverance and passion for long-term goals. Duckworth and her colleagues make some very bold claims about the value of grit. They maintain that grit is possessed by the 'most prominent leaders in every field' (Duckworth et al., 2007, p 1087). They argue that grit is essential for high achievement. They posit that it is, as good, if not a better, predictor of academic success than IQ. Duckworth and Seligman (2005) have also carried out similar research that suggests that 'self-discipline' can predict academic success better than IQ tests. Here they suggest that self-disciplined students are different from students who lack self-discipline. They are less impulsive, more self-controlled, better at ignoring distractions like TV when doing their homework, better at delaying gratification and better at making good monetary choices. Duckworth and her colleagues suggest that if gritty, self-disciplined students are more likely to succeed in exams, then grit is a quality that is worth measuring more – and worth educating. Grit and self-discipline so construed would seem to be dispositions well worth educating. However, I have some significant reservations.

First, grit and self-discipline are usually measured by self-report or by reports on student behaviour from parents and educators. However, such reports are notoriously subjective and unreliable – as Duckworth *et al.* (2007), Duckworth and Quinn (2009) and Duckworth and Seligman (2005) concede. For example, there would be nothing stopping a student from saying (in a grit scale questionnaire) that they never get distracted when pursuing a goal when actually they often do. Moreover, emerging evidence in the UK suggests grit is no better at predicting academic outcomes than already existing psychological measures of personality (Rimfeld et al., 2016). Furthermore, Gutman and Schoon (2013) conclude that: 1) there is no robust evidence establishing causal links between non-cognitive dispositions such as grit and academic attainment and, 2) relatively little is known about how possible it is to develop a person's non-cognitive dispositions via intervention. Bearing these findings in mind, there is good reason to be very sceptical about some of the bold claims being made on behalf of grit and other non-cognitive dispositions.

There are though much more substantial reasons for doubting the educational value of grit and self-discipline. Duckworth and her colleagues maintain that grit is a *non-cognitive disposition*. Though Duckworth acknowledges the oddity of describing grit and other traits like conscientiousness, self-control and growth mind-set as non-cognitive, the label continues to be used.[4] However, I think it is deeply mistaken to conceive of perseverance as unthinking, especially so in educational settings. Such constructions of perseverance make it much easier to justify encouraging students to focus on goals that reinforce rather than interrupt current social and educational arrangements. Goals like exam success. Proponents of grit don't seriously consider the possibility that there might be more to education than exam success. Nor do they seem very interested in the idea that discipline might actually require the exercise of intelligence, agency, morality and cognition. The trouble with grit is that it places all the responsibility on students to work harder, be more controlled, less impulsive.

The work of Duckworth and her colleagues on grit and self-discipline does not give sufficient regard to the inherently **reasonable** and **relational** nature of persons.[5] Gritty persons could in theory be extremely selfish, money grabbing, self-promoting, immoral and narcissistic achievement fiends. There is nothing in the grit scale that suggests gritty persons need to do anything other than persevere in service of their *own* (often academic) goals. There is no need to think about the needs of others. There is no need to think about injustice. In fact, there is no need to think at all if you are gritty! Grit places the onus on students to unthinkingly work harder on specific tasks (like exams), while more or less absolving educators and educational institutions of any responsibility to work towards social and educational reform. Of course, grit and other non-cognitive dispositions might help some students to better themselves, but I strongly suspect not all students will benefit from the agenda to promote non-cognitive dispositions such as grit.[6]

In this respect, my desire to draw a clear distinction between grit, self-discipline and personal discipline is not based on an arbitrary whim. The US Department for Education has recently published a report recommending educational adoption of policies and practices that cultivate non-cognitive dispositions like grit, tenacity and perseverance (Shechtman et al., 2013). The merits of grit and other non-cognitive dispositions have also recently been highlighted in educational debate in the UK (Gutman & Schoon, 2013). However, I think Dewey's work on discipline can help to reveal the danger of portraying perseverance as non-cognitive and unthinking. In Dewey's terms, gritty persons are *obstinate* rather than *disciplined*.[7] Disciplined persons set their own goals with awareness and care for the needs and interests of others. Obstinate ones instead pursue their own goals with little thought or care for others. Grit and personal discipline place very different demands on educators. Personal discipline is underpinned by the view that students are necessarily thoughtful, reasonable and relational in nature. Unlike grit and self-discipline, personal discipline stresses that new, revised and improved social orders will only become possible when students, educators, policy makers and other community members collectively think about, value and work towards the common good. It is therefore my view that educators ought to aim to promote personal discipline ahead of grit or self-discipline.

Four purposes of discipline in education

I do not think it is helpful to think that unthinking conduct should be encouraged in education. Grit and related non-cognitive traits only seem to have potential to socialise students into already existing norms, much like behaviour managerial approaches. They don't seem well placed to shake them up. I therefore do not think educational institutions should aim to foster grit, self-discipline or any other non-cognitive trait. Instead, personal discipline is preferable. For me, educational institutions need to socialise students less, through discipline, and instead focus on a more rounded set of disciplinary arrangements and goals. Discipline should socialise, but it should also support the epistemic, ethical and personal development of students and the communities of which they are part. Indeed, in my view discipline in education should be employed in service of at least four goals. Disciplinary processes should first initiate students into existing community norms, rules, values and knowledge (socialisation).

However, community norms, knowledge and values are not always the right ones – they could often benefit from revision. Second, discipline in education should support students to learn how to question and if necessary to remake the norms, rules, values and knowledge of their community (ethical development). Students may well resist such norms themselves without any encouragement – this can often be educational and ethical. Such behaviour should not always be punished. Indeed, an important part of learning to be ethical may well involve transgressing social norms. As Freire puts it, persons can only learn to be 'ethical' if they also have the possibility of transgressing norms and being 'unethical' (2001, pp 100–101). Such transgressions, such updating of norms, knowledge and values as needed, will rarely be easy. It will take discipline. It will require a balance between the freedom of the student and the authority of the teacher – neither too much freedom on the one hand nor authority on the other.

Moreover, discipline in education should also support students to love some aspect of learning for its own sake and preferably for the length of life. Students should not be disciplined to equate education with examination. They should be disciplined by a love of knowledge; they should be disciplined by their interests and curiosities, at least at times.

Third, discipline in education should contribute to the rounded epistemic development of students (epistemic development). Finally, discipline in education should also be about helping students become a little less self-absorbed. A no doubt important aspect of personal development involves learning how to set goals for oneself and see them through even in the face of challenge and difficulty. However, an equally important aspect of personal development involves learning from and with other persons. Students should be supported to develop a sense of responsibility and care for other persons. Learning how to care for other persons is rarely easy, it takes discipline. Here, school staff should not leave students to develop personal discipline by themselves. Instead they may well need to focus on forging relationships in schools that transcend the managerial. School staff will arguably need to *understand* rather than *manage* student 'misbehaviour' if genuinely personal relationships are to be developed and maintained. School staff should certainly not practice discipline with zero tolerance if they intend to foster the personal development of all students. Fourth, educational processes should support students to be disciplined by their own unique needs, interests and life goals as well as those of other persons (personal development).

As I try to show in Figure 1, ideally students would experience a balance of each of these different types of discipline over the course of their education. In some phases of learning socialisation may be paramount, in others ethical development, in others still epistemic or personal development. Particular lessons could also involve more than one aspect of discipline. Unfortunately, as shown in Figure 2, I fear that all too often students only really experience discipline as a socialising force. Too often there is not enough opportunity for students to exercise agency over their own learning and conduct in schools. Too often they are told what they need to know, do and be. Too often they are not given enough encouragement to explore what they want to know and do and be. However, to call for greater student agency in education is manifestly not to say that students should be left to

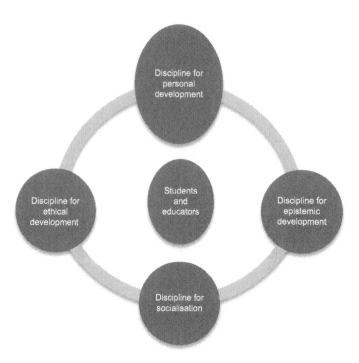

Figure 1 The four purposes of discipline

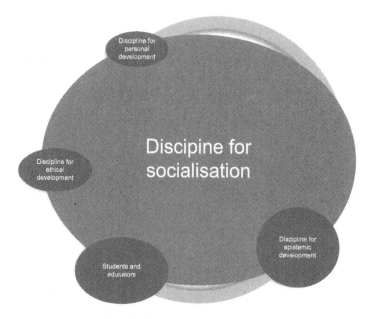

Figure 2 The domination of discipline for socialisation

their own devices. School structures and pedagogies may need altering at times and in places so that student agency can flourish more. A balance needs to be found.

The four purposes of discipline in education that I have outlined should not be thought of as conflicting with each other. They can and should complement each other. For example, very often we can only learn to question social orders once we have experience and knowledge of them. Similarly, having knowledge about injustices probably only matters if students have also learned how to care for others and act for the common good. The four purposes that I have outlined are not intended to represent an exhaustive list – clearly, there are other possible ways of thinking about the purposes of discipline in education. Nor are they intended to offer definitive or specific guidance to educators about how they should seek to arrange discipline in their teaching spaces – far from it. Educators probably need to work out for themselves how best to promote discipline in their classrooms, schools and university buildings. Some forms of discipline will no doubt seem more natural than others to particular educators, but some sort of balance should be sought.[8] If discipline is only about socialisation, substantial *educational* opportunities will be lost.

Escape from Aramanth

I began this book with a fictitious example of discipline in education. I will end it with one too. However, this fiction is not of my own making. It is taken from William Nicholson's novel *The Wind Singer*. The story begins in the walled city of Aramanth. Examinations are carried out endlessly in Aramanth. Adults and young alike are disciplined by exams. They are socialised into feeling shame when they fail an exam and they are enculturated to believe that doing better in exams is the only way to improve one's lot in life. Everyone accepts that this is the way things are. No one questions it. Until a young girl, Kestrel, does question it. She defies her teacher and refuses to participate in the regimented culture of examination. Under peril from the authorities, she leaves the city. Upon leaving Aramanth, Kestrel encounters a variety of unusual persons, creatures and communities. She is wholly enriched by her experiences. She learns with others and from others who are different to her. Above all else, she learns that life does not have to be wholly determined by exam success. Kestrel eventually returns to Aramanth. With the help of the Wind Singer, an ancient and mythical statue, she is able to save the city from the examination fever which it has been bedevilled by.

I recall this narrative now as I think certain parallels can be drawn between it and the current state of many Western education systems. Happily, I don't know of any actual cities or education systems so driven by examinations as Aramanth. However, as Foucault has shown us, examinations in education are increasingly disciplining all of us in troubling ways. This book has aimed to take this crisis of discipline in education seriously. Unlike Foucault, I have maintained that discipline in education need not be part of the problem. Indeed, I have argued that we need *more* discipline in education if the current fixation with examination is to be overcome. Just discipline of a different sort. Discipline that focusses on the ethical, epistemic and personal development of students and the communities of which they are part as well as the more usual goal of socialisation. This book does not aim to tell educators how to discipline. However, it does aim to encourage educators, policy makers, parents and students to think about the purposes that discipline in education serves and those it *ought* to serve. I hope that the philosophies explored in the book will encourage further thought, debate and research amongst researchers, educators, students, parents and education policy makers about the distinctively educational purposes that school discipline is put to.

I also hope this book has shown that no one philosophy, concept or approach to discipline in education will ever be perfect or work in all circumstances. Kant, Durkheim, Foucault, Dewey, Macmurray and Peters all developed ideas about discipline that had commendable and questionable aspects. I also hope my book has shown there are better and worse educational policies in respect to discipline in education. But educators should not be too critical of education policy makers if their policies continue to be flawed. If some of the finest scholars in the history of educational theory have some questionable ideas about discipline in education, policy makers with less time to reflect on the matter should certainly be cut some slack. But this does not mean educators should implement discipline policies or educational research uncritically. Instead, educators have a responsibility to ensure that practices of discipline meet the long-term needs of the schools and the communities they serve.

In this respect there would seem to be a need for policy makers to help practitioners move away from behaviour managerial language. Such vocabulary encourages the view that schools and educators need to manage students who would otherwise be out of control. Such vocabulary does not encourage students to take appropriate responsibility for their own learning or actions. I would instead urge policy makers and educators to use the language of discipline. While this may seem like a trivial shift, I do not think it is. The vocabulary educators use influences what students do, think and feel. If educators use language that sends a message that students cannot be trusted to behave and that someone else needs to manage them, then many might start to believe this is what teachers really think about them. If educators instead consistently say to students that all persons in schools are responsible for establishing a climate of discipline, that discipline is something to be done together – then students may be more inclined to believe their teachers want them to take ownership over their learning and conduct. If teachers also stress to students that discipline requires constant communication about rules, knowledge and the needs and interests of self and others, then students may find it easier to believe that teachers and schools are genuinely interested in their development as persons. If teachers say to students we might not always get discipline right but we need you to help us, then students might learn to be disciplined in ways beyond socialisation.

Of course, discipline in education is perhaps more a matter of practice than language but language still matters. Language is a vital part of social practices. As such, it is my view that the language of discipline is preferable to the language of behaviour management, or for that matter zero tolerance or grit. Unfortunately, the language of behaviour management continues to animate education policy in England and Wales. In this respect, a Department for Education working group chaired by Tom Bennett (whose views were explored in chapter 2) has recently recommended that sustained behaviour management training become a mandatory element of teacher education (Bennett, 2016). The report stresses a need to focus on observation, practice and evaluation with more 'abstract and complex material' (Bennett, 2016, p 5) only being introduced, if it is at all, after behaviour management skills are already in place. Having structured practical sessions where student teachers get the chance to develop their authority and skills in discipline seems like a good idea. In fact, I wholly agree that there should be more of a focus in teacher education in supporting students to develop the practical skills they need to establish climates of discipline in their classrooms.

However, I do not agree that more 'abstract' material should only be introduced after behaviour management skills have been learned. Engagement with academic research and theories about discipline from the start in teacher education might actually help new teachers to critically evaluate the short and long term strengths and weaknesses of the practical skills they are developing. It is after all often harder to think critically about something once it has become ingrained habit. Nor do I agree that 'behaviour management training' is the *necessary* starting point for the development of teacher authority and discipline skills. Especially if teachers want to do more than socialise their students through discipline. Indeed, there really is something very peculiar and regrettable in the latter-day policy trend that encourages teachers to first and foremost manage student behaviour. If new teachers think the first and most important thing they need to learn is behaviour management skills, then a host of more educational ways of doing discipline get side-lined. The recommendations in the report also encourage the view that discipline in education is not part of learning but something that needs to be established prior to learning. This is a woefully incomplete view.

Behaviour managerial approaches prioritise the short term need for order over the long term needs of all students. Indeed, as I have tried to show in this book, behaviour management approaches give teachers too little incentive to care about the long term destinations and life chances of their students. Teachers should first and foremost act as educators not managers. To think otherwise is to pervert the process of education.

Behaviour management skills may not be devoid of value, but surely it makes more sense to start from the premise that educators should plan engaging lessons that capture student attention and help them to be disciplined through the learning itself? Surely it makes more sense to prioritise fostering open, honest relationships with students rather than managerial and manipulative ones? Like the staff at Paddington, surely teachers should also primarily seek to understand 'bad' behaviour rather than just manage, judge and punish it? Teachers should not then in my view begin thinking about issues of discipline with a managerial mentality.

First and foremost, when it comes to the matter and manner of school discipline, I think teachers should ask a set of questions of themselves that focus on educational rather than managerial or punitive ends. Instead of asking: "what strategies can I learn to better manage my students", I think teachers should instead ask "how might discipline in my class and/or school be educational?" While not wanting to restrict possible ways of thinking about discipline to the specific literatures and notions explored in this book, further questions geared toward unpacking how discipline may become educational could include: (1) what knowledge and skills are worth passing on to my particular students and what knowledge and skills are my students interested in learning about – and how can I help them acquire such knowledge and skills in a disciplined way; (2) how can I help students become disciplined by and acquainted with social rules and norms but in a way that also encourages critical questioning and debate about social norms and rules; and (3) how can I help students to persevere in pursuit of the needs, interests and goals of both themselves and others. While these questions are admittedly very general, they nonetheless open up debate about the wider aims of school discipline in a way that managerial discourses tend not to do. While behaviour management strategies are not necessarily without practical value, their practical value is probably limited to pupil socialisation rather than any wider ethical, epistemic or personal development.

However, it is not just teachers and policy makers who are responsible for school discipline – far from it. Teacher educators arguably also need to do more to encourage new and beginning teachers to think about the long-term purposes of school discipline as well as the short-term need to establish classroom order. This might mean designing and implementing courses in teacher education with more of a focus on: 1) critical reflection about the long term purposes of discipline in education, 2) supporting student teachers to better understand the complex causes of student 'misbehaviour' in school, 3) supporting student teachers to develop behaviour management type skills (though I would prefer to call them skills of teacher authority and discipline) as well as the capacity to think critically about possible limitations of such skills. Educational researchers have responsibilities too. It is the responsibility of educational researchers to not just critique education policy and practice and reveal what is problematic and inadequate in it. Instead, they should also work with policy makers and practitioners to try to improve things. This might also mean researching and documenting practices in schools which are able to move beyond managerial or socialising approaches. This is what I have tried to do in this book, especially in chapter 7. There I tried to show that there are educators out there who believe discipline can be done differently and more *educationally*. In chapter 7 we saw that staff at Paddington School firmly believed that discipline policy and practice should focus on relationships rather than rules or behaviour management. Staff at Paddington also felt it vital that they try to understand what pupils might be trying to communicate when they are 'misbehaving'. Paddington staff also felt that behaviour managerial and rules-based approaches to discipline may actually perpetuate poor behaviour and further alienate students from education. However, substantially more empirical research is needed about the nature and purposes of discipline in education.

All too often discipline in education merely socialises students and prepares them for exams. With inequality rising and employment and education opportunities increasingly hard to come by, personal, epistemic and ethical discipline are arguably needed more than ever. I fear we will continue to edge closer to the prison-type societies Foucault foretold unless and until we do discipline in education differently. I don't think waiting for another Kestrel and Wind Singer to come along is our best bet though. I rather think that students, educators, parents, policy makers and other persons in communities besides these, together need to use discipline in education for more than socialisation. If discipline in education is instead employed in service of a wider set of purposes, including the ethical, epistemological and personal development of students, then communities might yet still be reborn for the better. Discipline in education needs to be reconsidered and reclaimed. Communities don't ever need to become like Aramanth. Discipline in education should be employed to ensure that this particular fiction never comes to pass.

Notes

1 There is a case study in the previous chapter that outlines different perspectives on discipline from students and staff at Paddington School.
2 Perhaps especially so given that a quarter of the differences between students from different social class grouping who access elite universities is not thought to be explained by academic ability (Jerrim, 2014).
3 See Walters (2015) for discussion of Obama's stance.
4 See West *et al.* (2016). For an interesting philosophical discussion of grit and other non-cognitive dispositions in education see Peterson (2015).
5 It is not clear to me if Duckworth and Seligman (2005) imagine 'self-discipline' to be non-cognitive or not. However, it is clear that they regard self-discipline to be largely a matter of self-control and gratification delay. Such a concept of discipline is radically different to Dewey's and Macmurray's. Self-discipline focusses on controlling the impulses of the *self* – Deweyian and Macmurryian discipline is about persevering for the sake of the long-term prospering of ***both self and other***.
6 I do not appear to be alone with my concerns here. Mendick *et al.* (2015) suggest that we should not blindly celebrate hard work in education. While hard work might open up possibilities for previously marginalised groups, it may also reinforce and reproduce neo-liberal class and gender distinctions.
7 For further discussion of the distinction between discipline and obstinacy, see chapter 5.
8 I should acknowledge that my thinking about the purposes of discipline education has been greatly influenced by the work of Biesta (2010). However, I also think the purposes of discipline in education discussed here are different from the purposes of education articulated by Biesta. For further discussion of differences between my thinking and that of Biesta regarding the purposes of education, see MacAllister (2016).

Bibliography

Allan, J & Harwood, V (2013) Medicus interruptus in the behaviour of children in disadvantaged contexts in Scotland, *British Journal of Sociology of Education*, 35 (3), 413–431.
Arendt, H (2006) *Between Past and Future: Eight Exercises in Political Thought* (London, Penguin).
Aristotle (1981) *The Politics* (London, Penguin).
Aristotle (2004) *The Nichomachean Ethics* (London, Penguin, 3rd Edition).
Ball, S ed. (1990) *Foucault and Education: Disciplines and Knowledge* (London, Routledge).
Ball, S (1999) School management – Myth: Good management makes goods schools (pp 88–106), chapter 5 in *Modern Educational Myths: The Future of Democratic Comprehensive Education*, ed. O'Hagan, B (London, Kogan-Page).
Ball, S (2003) The teachers' soul and the terrors of performativity, *Journal of Education Policy*, 18 (2), 215–228.
Ball, S (2009) Privatising education, privatising education policy, privatising educational research: Network governance and the 'competition state', *Journal of Education Policy*, 24 (1), 83–99.
Ball, S (2013) *Foucault, Power and Education* (Abingdon, Routledge).
Barrow, R (2007) *Plato* (London, Continuum Library of Educational Thought).
Bartky, S (1996) The pedagogy of shame (pp 225–242), in *Feminism and Pedagogies of Everyday Life*, ed. Luke, C (Albany, State University of New York Press).
Bennett, T (2010) *The Behaviour Guru: Behaviour Management Solutions for Teachers* (London, Continuum).
Bennett, T (2016) *Developing behaviour management content for initial teacher training* (London, Crown Copyright).
Biesta, G (2006a) *Beyond Learning: Democratic Education for a Human Future* (London, Paradigm).
Biesta, G (2006b) Of all affairs communication is the most wonderful: The communicative turn in Dewey's democracy and education (pp 23–38), chapter 2 in *John Dewey and Our Educational Prospect: A Critical Engagement with Dewey's Democracy and Education*, ed. Hansen, D (Albany, State University of New York Press).
Biesta, G (2008) Encountering Foucault in lifelong learning (pp 193–205), chapter 15 in *Foucault and Lifelong Learning: Governing the Subject*, eds. Fejes, A & Nicol, K (London, Routledge).
Biesta, G (2009) Good education in an age of measurement: On the need to reconnect with the question of purpose in education, *Educational Assessment, Evaluation and Accountability*, 21 (1), 33–46.

Biesta, G (2010) *Good Education in an Age of Measurement: Ethics, Politics, Democracy* (London, Paradigm).
Boler, M (1997) Disciplined emotions: Philosophies of educated feelings, *Educational Theory*, 47 (2), 203–227.
Cambridge Dictionary (2016) *Cambridge Dictionaries Online*. Accessed on 15.02.2016: http://dictionary.cambridge.org/dictionary/english/discipline
Carr, D (1991) *Educating the Virtues: An Essay on the Philosophical Psychology of Moral Development and Education* (London, Routledge).
Carruthers, D (2013) The journal from criminal justice to education: Utilising restorative justice practices in schools in England (pp 23–31), chapter 3 in *Restorative Approaches to Conflict in Schools: Interdisciplinary Perspectives on Whole School Approaches to Managing Relationships*, eds. Selman, E, Cremin, H & McCluskey, G (Abingdon, Routledge).
Cladis, M ed. (1999) *Durkheim and Foucault: Perspectives on Education and Punishment* (London, Durkheim Press).
Clark, C (1998) Discipline in schools, *British Journal of Educational Studies*, 46, 289–301.
Cremin, H (2013) Critical perspectives on restorative justice/restorative approaches in educational settings (pp 111–122), chapter 11 in *Restorative Approaches to Conflict in Schools: Interdisciplinary Perspectives on Whole School Approaches to Managing Relationships*, eds. Selman, E, Cremin, H & McCluskey, G (Abingdon, Routledge).
Costello, J (2002) *John MacMurray: A Biography* (Bristol, Floris Books).
Cowley, S (2010) *Getting the Buggers to Behave* (London, Continuum, 4th Edition).
Cunningham, P (2012) John Macmurray's learning to live and the new media, 1931–1949: Learning for labour or leisure? *Oxford Review of Education*, 38 (6), 693–708.
Curren, R (2000) *Aristotle on the Necessity of Public Education* (Oxford, Rowan & Littlefield).
Darling, J (1986) Child-centred, Gender-centred: A criticism of progressive curriculum theory from Rousseau to Plowden, *Oxford Review of Education*, 12 (1), 31–40.
Darling, J (1993) Rousseau as progressive instrumentalist, *Journal of Philosophy of Education*, 27 (1), 27–38.
Department for Education (2010) *The Importance of Teaching: Schools White Paper* (London, Department for Education).
Department for Education (2012a) *Behaviour and Discipline in Schools: A Guide to Head Teachers and School Staff* (London, Department for Education).
Department for Education (2012b) *A Profile of Pupil Exclusions in England* (London, Department for Education).
Department for Education (2014) *Behaviour and Discipline in Schools: Advice for Head Teachers and School Staff* (London, Department for Education).
Dewey, J (1997) *Experience and Education* (New York, Touchstone, First published 1938).
Dewey, J (2007) *Democracy and Education* (Middlesex, Echo library).
Dill, J (2007) Durkheim and Dewey and the challenge of contemporary moral education, *Journal of Moral Education*, 36 (2), 221–237.
Dixon, T (2012) Educating the emotions from Gradgrind to Goleman, *Research Papers in Education*, 27 (4), 481–485.

Duckworth, A L, Peterson, C, Matthews, M D & Kelly, D R (2007) Grit: Perseverance and passion for long-term goals, *Journal of Personality and Social Psychology*, 92 (6), 1087–1101.

Duckworth, A L & Quinn, P D (2009) Development and validation of the short grit scale (Grit-S), *Journal of Personality Assessment*, 91 (2), 166–174.

Duckworth, A L & Seligman, M E P (2005) Self-discipline outdoes IQ in predicting academic performance of adolescents, *Psychological Science*, 16 (12), 939–944.

Dunlop, F (1984) *The Education of Feeling and Emotion* (London, Allen & Unwin).

Dupper, D (2010) *A New Model of School Discipline: Engaging Students and Preventing Behavior Problems* (New York, Oxford University Press).

Durkheim, E (1951) *Sociology and Philosophy* (London, Cohen and West Ltd).

Durkheim, E (1961) *Moral Education; A Study in the Theory and Application of the Sociology of Education* (New York, Macmillan).

Durkheim, E (1972) *Emile Durkheim: Selected Writings*, edited, translated and with an introduction by A Giddens (Cambridge, Cambridge University Press).

Ecclestone, K (2011) Emotionally vulnerable subjects and new inequalities: The educational implications of an 'epistemology of the emotions', *International Studies in Sociology of Education*, 21 (2), 91–113.

Ecclestone, K & Hayes, D (2009) Changing the subject: The educational implications of developing emotional wellbeing, *Oxford Review of Education*, 35 (3), 371–389.

Edwards, R (2008) Actively seeking subjects? (pp 21–33), chapter 2 in *Foucault and Lifelong Learning: Governing the Subject*, eds. Fejes, A & Nicol, K (London, Routledge).

English, A (2009) Transformation and education: The voice of the learner in Peters concept of the teaching, *Journal of Philosophy of Education*, 43 (s1), 75–95.

Facer, K (2012) Personal, relational and beautiful: Education, technologies and John Macmurray's philosophy, *Oxford Review of Education*, 38 (6), 709–725.

Fejes, A & Nicol, K eds. (2008) *Foucault and Lifelong Learning: Governing the Subject* (London, Routledge).

Fenstermacher, G (2006) Rediscovering the student in democracy and education (pp 97–112), chapter 6 in *John Dewey and Our Educational Prospect: A Critical Engagement with Dewey's Democracy and Education*, ed. Hansen, D (Albany, State University of New York Press).

Fergusson, D (2002) The contours of MacMurray's philosophy (pp 35–51), in *John MacMurray: Critical Perspectives*, eds. Fergusson, D & Dower, N (New York, Peter Lang).

Fielding, M (1999) Communities of learners – Myth: Schools are communities (pp 67–87), chapter 4 in *Modern Educational Myths: The Future of Democratic Comprehensive Education*, ed. O'Hagan, B (London, Kogan-Page).

Fielding, M (2006) Leadership, radical student engagement and the necessity of person-centred education, *International Journal of Leadership in Education*, 9 (4), 299–313.

Fielding, M (2007a) On the necessity of radical state education: Democracy and the common school, *Journal of Philosophy of Education*, 41 (4), 549–557.

Fielding, M (2007b) The human cost and intellectual poverty of high performance schooling: Radical philosophy, John Macmurray and the remaking of person-centred education, *Journal of Education Policy*, 22 (4), 383–409.

Fielding, M (2012) Education as if people matter: John MacMurray, community and the struggle for democracy, *Oxford Review of Education*, 38 (6), 675–692.

Fielding, M & Moss, P (2011) *Radical Education and the Common School: A Democratic Alternative* (London, Routledge).

Fordham, M (2015) Teachers and the academic disciplines, *Journal of Philosophy of Education*, forthcoming, doi:10.1111/1467–9752.12145

Foucault, M (1987) The ethic of care for the self as a practice of freedom: An interview with Michel Foucault on January 20th 1984, conducted by Fornet-Betancourt R, Becker H and Gomez-Muller A, *Philosophy and Social Criticism*, 12, 112–131.

Foucault, M (1991) *Discipline and Punish: The Birth of the Prison* (London, Penguin).

Foucault, M (2007) What is critique? (pp 41–81), in *The Politics of Truth*, ed. Lotringer, S translated by Hochroth, L & Porter, C (Los Angeles, Semiotext(e)).

Freire, P (2001) *Pedagogy of Freedom: Ethics, Democracy, and Civic Courage* (Oxford, Rowman & Littlefield).

Gaita, R (2012) Love and teaching: Renewing a common world, *Oxford Review of Education*, 38 (6), 761–769.

Garland, D (1999) Durkheim's sociology of punishment and punishment today (pp 19–38), chapter 2 in *Durkheim and Foucault: Perspectives on Education and Punishment*, ed. Cladis, M (London, Durkheim Press).

Gephart, W (1999) The realm of normativity in Durkheim and Foucault (pp 59–70), chapter 4 in *Durkheim and Foucault: Perspectives on Education and Punishment*, ed. Cladis, M (London, Durkheim Press).

Goldie, P (2000) *The Emotions: A Philosophical Exploration* (Oxford, Clarendon).

Goldman, D (1996) *Emotional Intelligence* (London, Bloomsbury).

Goodman, J (2006) School discipline in moral disarray, *Journal of Moral Education*, 35 (2), 213–230.

Goodman, J (2007) School discipline, buy-in and belief, *Ethics and Education*, 2 (1), 3–23.

GTCS (2012) *The Standards for Registration: The Mandatory Standards Required for Registration with the General Teaching Council for Scotland* (Edinburgh, GTCS).

Gutman, L & Schoon, S (2013) *The Impact of Non-cognitive Skills on Outcomes for Young People: Literature Review* (London, The Institute of Education).

Hansen, D (2006) *John Dewey and Our Educational Prospect: A Critical Engagement with Dewey's Democracy and Education*, ed. Hansen, D (Albany, State University of New York Press).

Hassard, J & Rowlinson, M (2002) Researching Foucault's research: Organisation and control in Joseph Lancaster's monitorial schools, *Organization*, 9 (4), 615–639.

Haydn, T (2014) To what extent is behaviour a problem in English Schools? Exploring the scale and prevalence of deficits in classroom climate, *Review of Education*, 2 (1), 31–64.

Hickman, L (2006) Socialization, social efficiency and social control: Putting pragmatism to work (pp 67–80), chapter 4 in *John Dewey and Our Educational Prospect: A Critical Engagement with Dewey's Democracy and Education*, ed. Hansen, D (Albany, State University of New York Press).

Hirst, P (1968) Liberal education and the nature of knowledge (pp 113–138), in *Philosophical Analysis and Education*, ed. Archambault, R (London, Routledge & Kegan Paul).

Hirst, P (1973) Forms of knowledge – A reply to Elizabeth Hindness, *Journal of the Philosophy of Education*, 7 (2), 260–271.

Hirst, P (1997) Education, knowledge and practices (pp 184–199), chapter 10 in *Beyond Liberal Education: Essays in Honour of Paul H Hirst*, eds. Barrow, R & White, W (London, Routledge).

Hirst, P & Peters, R (1975) *The Logic of Education* (London, Routledge & Kegan Paul, First published 1970).

Hoskin, K (1990) Foucault under examination: The crypto-educationalist unmasked (pp 29–53), chapter 3 in *Foucault and Education: Disciplines and Knowledge*, ed. Ball, S (London, Routledge).

Hunter, I (1994) *Rethinking the School: Subjectivity, Bureaucracy, Criticism* (St. Leonards, Allen & Unwin).

Jackson, C (2006) *Lads and Ladettes in School: Gender and a Fear of Failure* (Maidenhead, Open University Press).

Jerrim, J (2014) *Family Background and Access to 'High Status' Universities* (London, The Sutton Trust).

Johnstone, J & Van Ness, D (2007) The meaning of restorative justice (pp 5–23), in *The Handbook of Restorative Justice*, eds. Johnstone, G & Van Ness, D (Devon, William Publishing).

Kafka, J (2011) *The History of "Zero Tolerance" in American Public Schooling* (New York, Palgrave MacMillan).

Kamens, D (2013) Globalization and the emergence of an audit culture: PISA and the search for 'best practices' and magic bullets (pp 117–140), chapter 5 in *PISA, POWER and POLICY: The Emergence of Global Education Governance*, eds. Heinz-Dieter, M & Aaron, B (Southampton: Symposium).

Kane, J, McCluskey, G, Riddell, S, Lloyd, G, Stead, J & Weedon, E (2008) Collaborative evaluation: Balancing rigour and relevance in a research study of restorative approaches in schools in Scotland, *International Journal of Research & Method in Education*, 31 (2), 99–111.

Kant, I (2003) *On Education* (New York, Dover Publications).

Kant, I (2007) *The Moral Law; Groundwork of the Metaphysics of Morals* (London, Routledge Classics, 3rd Edition).

Kemp, A (2014) Classrooms in crisis: Violent incidents and discipline problems plague Oklahoma's largest school district, *The Oklahoman*, 2nd June 2014. Accessed on 26.2.2016: http://newsok.com/article/4869670

Kim, C, Losen, D & Hewitt, D (2011) *The School-to-Prison Pipeline: Structuring Legal Reform* (New York, New York University Press).

Kohn, A (1999) *Punished by Rewards: The Trouble with Gold Stars, Incentive Plans, A's, Praise, and Other Bribes* (Boston, Houghton Mifflin).

Kristjánsson, K (2007) *Aristotle, Emotions, and Education* (Aldershot, Ashgate).

Lampl, P (2012) *Social Mobility and Education Gaps in the Four Major Anglophone Countries: Research Findings for the Social Mobility Summit, London* (London, The Sutton Trust).

MacAllister, J (2012) Virtue epistemology and the philosophy of education, *Journal of Philosophy of Education*, 46 (2), 251–270.

MacAllister, J (2013a) School discipline, educational interest and pupil wisdom, *Educational Philosophy and Theory*, 45 (1), 20–35.

MacAllister, J (2013b) Restoration, transformation or education: A philosophical critique of restorative approaches in schools (pp 97–110), chapter 10 in *Restorative Approaches to Conflict in Schools: Interdisciplinary Perspectives on Whole School Approaches to Managing Relationships*, eds. Selman, E, Cremin, H & McCluskey, G (Abingdon, Routledge).

MacAllister, J (2014a) Why discipline needs to be reclaimed as an educational concept, *Educational Studies*, 40 (4), 438–451.

MacAllister, J (2014b) Education for personal life: John MacMurray on why learning to be human requires emotional discipline, *Journal of Philosophy of Education*, 48 (1), 118–136.

MacAllister, J (2015) MacIntyre's revolutionary Aristotelian philosophy and his idea of an educated public revisited, *Journal of Philosophy of Education*, doi:10.1111/1467-752.12151

MacAllister, J (2016) What should educational institutions be for? *British Journal of Educational Studies*, doi:10.1080/00071005.2015.1131811

MacIntyre, A (1984) *After Virtue: A Study in Moral Theory* (Notre Dame, University of Notre Dame).

MacIntyre, A (1987) The idea of an educated public (pp 15–36), in *Education and Values: The Richard Peters Lectures*, ed. Haydon, G (London, Institute of Education).

MacIntyre, A (1988) *Whose Justice? Which Rationality?* (London, Duckworth).

MacIntyre, A (1990) *Three Rival Versions of Moral Inquiry: Encyclopaedia, Geneaology and Tradition* (Notre Dame, University of Notre Dame).

MacIntyre, A (1991) *How to Seem to Be Virtuous without Actually Being So* (Lancaster, Lancaster University).

MacIntyre, A (1999) *Dependent Rational Animals* (Chicago, Open Court).

MacIntyre, A (2009) The very idea of a university: Aristotle, Newman, and us, *British Journal of Educational Studies*, 57 (4), 347–362.

MacIntyre, A (2009a) Notes from the Moral Wilderness (pp 45–68), in *Alasdair MacIntyre's Engagement with Marxism*, eds. Blackledge, P & Davidson, N (Chicago, Haymarket Books).

MacIntyre, A (2009b) What is Marxist theory for? (pp 95–104), in *Alasdair MacIntyre's Engagement with Marxism*, eds. Blackledge, P & Davidson, N (Chicago, Haymarket Books).

MacIntyre, A (2009c) 1958, 1965, 1995, three perspectives (pp 411–425), in *Alasdair MacIntyre's Engagement with Marxism*, eds. Blackledge, P & Davidson, N (Chicago, Haymarket Books).

MacIntyre, A (2011) *God, Philosophy and Universities: A Selective History of the Catholic Philosophical Tradition* (Plymouth, Rowman and Littlefield).

MacIntyre, A (2013) Where we were, where we are, where we need to be, in *Virtue and Politics: Alasdair MacIntyre's Revolutionary Aristotelianism*, eds. Blackledge, P & Knight, K (Indiana, University of Notre Dame Press) pp 307–334.

MacIntyre, A & Dunne, J (2002) Alasdair MacIntyre on education: In dialogue with Joseph Dunne, *Journal of Philosophy of Education*, 36 (1), 1–19.

Macleod, G, MacAllister, J & Pirrie, A (2012) Towards a broader understanding of authority in student teacher relationships, *Oxford Review of Education*, 38 (4), 493–508.

Macmurray, J (1956) *The Self as Agent* (London, Faber and Faber).

Macmurray, J (1961a) *Reason and Emotion* (London, Faber and Faber).

MacMurray, J (1961b) *Persons in Relation* (London, Faber and Faber).

Macmurray, J (1964) Teachers and pupils, *The Educational Forum*, 39 (1), 17–24.
Macmurray, J (2012) Learning to be human, *Oxford Review of Education*, 38 (6), 661–674.
Marshall, J (1990) Foucault and educational research (pp 11–28), chapter 2 in *Foucault and Education: Disciplines and Knowledge*, ed. Ball, S (London, Routledge).
Martinez, S (2009) A system gone Beserk: How are zero-tolerance policies really affecting schools? *Preventing School Failure: Alternative Education for Children and Youth*, 53 (3), 153–158.
McCluskey, G (2013) Challenges to education: Restorative practice as a radical demand on conservative structures of schooling (pp 132–141), chapter 13 in *Restorative Approaches to Conflict in Schools: Interdisciplinary Perspectives on Whole School Approaches to Managing Relationships*, eds. Sellman, E, Cremin, H & McCluskey, G (Abingdon, Routledge).
McCluskey, G, Lloyd, G, Kane, J, Riddell, S, Stead, J & Weedon, E (2008b) Can restorative practices in schools make a difference? *Educational Review*, 60 (4), 405–417.
McCluskey, G, Lloyd, G, Stead, J, Kane, J, Riddell, S & Weedon, E (2008) 'I was dead restorative today': From restorative justice to restorative approaches in school, *Cambridge Journal of Education*, 38 (2), 199–216.
McIntosh, E (2002) Educating the emotions (pp 133–141), in *John MacMurray: Critical Perspectives*, eds. Fergusson, D & Dower, N (New York, Peter Lang).
McIntosh, E (2015) Why we need the arts: John Macmurray on education and the emotions, *Educational Philosophy and Theory*, 47 (1), 47–60.
McLaughlin, T & Halstead, J (2000) John Wilson on moral education, *Journal of Moral Education*, 29 (3), 247–268.
Mendick, H, Allen, L & Harvey, L (2015) 'We can get everything we want if we try hard': Young people, celebrity, hard work, *British Journal of Educational Studies*, 63 (2), 161–178.
Merrett, F & Wheldell, K (1993) How do teachers learn to manage classroom behaviour? A study of teachers' opinions about their initial training with special reference to classroom behaviour management, *Educational Studies*, 19 (1), 91–106.
Millei, Z, Griffiths, T & Parkes, R (2010) *Re-theorizing Discipline in Education: Problems, Politics and Possibilities* (New York, Peter Lang).
Mintz, A (2012) The happy and suffering student? Rousseau's Emile and the path not taken in progressive educational thought, *Educational Theory*, 62 (3), 249–265.
Moran, K (2009) Can Kant have an account of moral education? *Journal of Philosophy of Education*, 43 (4), 471–484.
Morrison, B (2007) Schools and restorative justice (pp 325–350), in *The Handbook of Restorative Justice*, eds. Johnstone, G & Van Ness, D (Devon, William Publishing).
National Association of School Psychologists, NASP (2008) *Zero Tolerance and Alternative Strategies: A Fact Sheet for Educators and Policymakers* (Bethesda, National Association of School Psychologists). Accessed on 23.02.2016: http://www.naspcenter.org/factsheets/zt_fs.html
Nicholson, W (2000) *The Wind Singer* (London, Mammoth).
Noddings, N (2012) The caring relation in teaching, *Oxford Review of Education*, 38 (6), 771–781.

Noguera, P (2003) Schools, prisons and social implications of punishment: Rethinking disciplinary practices, *Theory into Practice*, 42 (4), 341–350.

Nussbaum, M (1997) *Cultivating Humanity: A Classical Defense of Reform in Liberal Education* (London, Harvard).

Oakeshott, M (1972) Education: The engagement and its frustration (pp 19–50), in *Education and the Development of Reason*, eds. Dearden, R R, Hirst, P H & Peters, R S (London, Routledge & Kegan Paul).

Ofsted (2014) *The Framework for School Inspection* (London, Ofsted).

Ofsted (2015) *Unannounced Behaviour Inspections: Guidance for Inspectors* (Manchester, Ofsted).

Perryman, J (2006) Panoptic performativity and school inspection regimes: Disciplinary mechanisms and life under special measures, *Journal of Education Policy*, 21 (2), 147–161.

Peters, R S (1967) Authority (pp 83–96), in *Political Philosophy*, ed. Quinton, A (Oxford, Oxford University Press).

Peters, R S (1968) Education as initiation (pp 87–111), in *Philosophical Analysis and Education*, ed. Archambault, R D (London, Routledge & Kegan Paul).

Peters, R S (1970) *Ethics & Education* (London, George Allen & Unwin, First published 1966).

Peters, R S (1972) Education and the educated man (pp 3–18), in *Education and the Development of Reason*, ed. Dearden, R, Hirst, P & Peters, R (London, Routledge & Kegan Paul).

Peters, R S (1973) *Authority, Responsibility and Education* (London, Unwin University Books, First published 1959).

Peters, R (1981) *Essays on Educators* (London, George Allen & Unwin).

Peterson, D (2015) Putting measurement first: Understanding 'Grit' in education policy and practice, *Journal of Philosophy of Education*, 49 (4), 571–589.

Pickering, W (1999) The administration of punishment in schools (pp 39–58), chapter 3 in *Durkheim and Foucault: Perspectives on Education and Punishment*, ed. Cladis, M (London, Durkheim Press).

Plamenatz, J (1972) Rousseau: The education of Emile, *Journal of Philosophy of Education*, 16, 176–192.

Plato (1987) *The Republic* (London, Penguin Books).

Pring, R (2007) *John Dewey: A Philosopher of Education for Our Time?* (London, Continuum).

Pring, R (2012) Putting persons back into education, *Oxford Review of Education*, 38 (6), 747–760.

Pugmire, D (1998) *Rediscovering Emotion* (Edinburgh, Edinburgh University Press).

Ramp, W (1999) Durkheim and Foucault on the genesis of the disciplinary society (pp 71–103), chapter 5 in *Durkheim and Foucault: Perspectives on Education and Punishment*, ed. Cladis, M (London, Durkheim Press).

Ransom, J (1997) *Foucault's Discipline: The Politics of Subjectivity* (Durham, Duke University Press).

Reid, K & Morgan, N (2012) *Tackling Behaviour in Your Primary School: A Practical Handbook for Teachers* (London, Routledge).

Rimfeld, K, Kovas, Y, Dale, P S & Plomin, R (2016, February 11) True grit and genetics: Predicting academic achievement from personality, *Journal of Personality and Social Psychology.* Advance online publication, http://dx.doi.org/10.1037/pspp0000089

Rogers, B (1998) *'You Know the Fair Rule and Much More': Strategies for Making the Hard Job of Discipline and Behavior Management in School Easier* (Melbourne, ACER Press).

Rogers, B (2011) *Behaviour Management: A Whole School Approach* (London, Paul Chapman, 2nd Edition).

Roth, K & Surprenant, K eds. (2012) *Kant and Education: Interpretations and Commentary* (London, Routledge).

Rousseau, J (1993) *Emile* (Vermont, Everyman).

Ryan, R & Deci, E (2000) Intrinsic and extrinsic motivations: Classic definitions and new directions. *Contemporary Educational Psychology*, 25, 54–67.

Saito, N (2006) Growth and perfectionism? Dewey after Emerson and Cavell (pp 81–98), chapter 5 in *John Dewey and Our Educational Prospect: A Critical Engagement with Dewey's Democracy and Education*, ed. Hansen, D (Albany, State University of New York Press).

Scottish Government (2013) *Better Relationships, Better Learning, Better Behavior* (Edinburgh, Scottish Government).

Sellman, E, Cremin, H & McCluskey, G eds. (2013) *Restorative Approaches to Conflict in Schools: Interdisciplinary Perspectives on Whole School Approaches to Managing Relationships* (Abingdon, Routledge).

Shechtman, N, DeBarger, A H, Dornsife, C, Rosier, S & Yarnall, L (2013) *Promoting Grit, Tenacity, and Perseverance: Critical Factors for Success in the 21st Century* (Washington, DC, US. Department of Education, Office of Educational Technology, Center for Technology in Learning, SRI International). Available online at: http://www.ed.gov/edblogs/technology/files/2013/02/OET-Draft-Grit-Report-2-17-13.pdf

Sia, L (2013) Restorative justice: An international perspective (pp 11–22), chapter 2 in *Restorative Approaches to Conflict in Schools: Interdisciplinary Perspectives on Whole School Approaches to Managing Relationships*, eds. Sellman, E, Cremin, H & McCluskey, G (Abingdon, Routledge).

Skiba, R, Reynolds, C, Graham, S, Sheras, P, Conoley, J & Garcia-Vazquez, E (2008) Are zero tolerance policies effective in the schools? An evidentiary review and recommendations, *American Psychologist*, 63 (9), 852–862.

Slee, R (1995) *Changing Theories and Practices of Discipline* (London, The Falmer Press).

Smith, R (1985) *Freedom and Discipline* (London, George Allen & Unwin).

Stern, J (2012) The personal world of schooling: John Macmurray and schools as households, *Oxford Review of Education*, 38 (6), 727–745.

Steutel, J & Spiecker, B (2000) Authority in educational relationships, *Journal of Moral Education*, 29 (3), 323–337.

Straughan, R (2000) Revisiting Wilson's moral components, *Journal of Moral Education*, 29 (3), 367–370.

Tait, G (2010) *Philosophy, Behaviour Disorders and the School* (Rotterdam, Sense Publishers).

Townsend, M (2013) Massive rise in disruptive behaviour, *The Guardian*. Available online at: http://www.theguardian.com/education/2013/mar/24/schools-disruptive-behaviour

UK Children's Commissioner (2008) *UK Children's Commissioner Report to the United Nations Committee on the Rights of the Child* (London, UK Children's commissioner).

UN Handbook on Restorative Justice Programmes (2006) Criminal Justice Handbook Series (New York, UN).

U.S. Department of Education (2014) *Guiding Principles: A Resource Guide for Improving School Climate and Discipline* (Washington, U.S. Department of Education).

Vaandering, D (2014) Implementing restorative justice practice in schools: What pedagogy reveals, *Journal of Peace Education*, 11 (1), 64–80.

Van Ness, D (2013) Restorative justice as world view (pp 32–39), chapter 4 in *Restorative Approaches to Conflict in Schools: Interdisciplinary Perspectives on Whole School Approaches to Managing Relationships*, eds. Sellman, E, Cremin, H & McCluskey, G (Abingdon, Routledge).

Walters, J (2015) Obama calls for cuts to schools standardized testing regimens, *The Guardian*, 24th October 2015. Accessed online on 26.02.2016: http://www.theguardian.com/education/2015/oct/24/obama-education-standardized-testing-limits

Way, S (2011) School discipline and disruptive classroom behavior: The moderating effects of student perception, *The Sociological Quarterly*, 52, 346–375.

West, M, Kraft, M, Finn, S, Martin, E, Duckworth, A L, Gabrieli, C F O & Gabriele, J D E (2016) Promise and paradox: Measuring students' non-cognitive skills and the impact of schooling, *Educational Evaluation and Policy Analysis*, 28 (1), 148–170.

Wheldall, K, Merrett, F & Borg, M (1985) The behavioral approach to teaching package (BATPACK): An experimental evaluation, *British Journal of Educational Psychology*, 55 (1), 65–75.

Whitehead, A (1967) *The Aims of Education and Other Essays* (New York, The Free Press).

Whitty, G (1997) Education policy and the sociology of education, *International Studies in Sociology of Education*, 7 (2), 121–135.

Whitty, G (2006) Education(al) research and education policy making: Is conflict inevitable? *British Educational Research Journal*, 32 (2), 159–176.

Wilson, J (1981) *Discipline and Moral Education: A Survey of Public Opinion and Understanding* (Windsor, NFER-Nelson).

Wilson, J (2000) A response, *Journal of Moral Education*, 29 (3), 371–375.

Wilson, P S (1971) *Interest and Discipline in Education* (London, Routledge).

Wilson, P S (1974) Interests and educational values, *Journal of Philosophy of Education*, 8, 181–199.

Woods, R (2008) When rewards and sanctions fail: A case study of a primary school rule-breaker, *International Journal of Qualitative Studies in Education*, 21 (2), 181–196.

Woolcock, N (2015) Teaching in crisis because heads 'fail over discipline', *The Times*, 22nd June 2015. Accessed online on 26.02.2016: http://www.thetimes.co.uk/tto/education/article4476413.ece

Young, M (2009) What are schools for? (pp 10–18), in *Knowledge, Values and Educational Policy*, eds. Daniels, H, Lauder, H & Porter, J (London, Routledge).

Young, M, Lambert, D, Roberts, C & Roberts, M (2014) *Knowledge and the Future School: Curriculum and Social Justice* (London, Bloomsbury).

Young, M & Muller, J (2010) Three educational scenarios for the future: Lessons from the sociology of knowledge, *European Journal of Education*, 45 (1), 11–27.

Zembylas, M (2005) Discursive practices, genealogies, and emotional rules: A post-structuralist view on emotion and identity in teaching, *Teaching and Teacher Education*, 21, 935–948.

Index

accountability 13–14, 19
Aramanth 139, 143
Aristotle 17, 69–70, 84n3, 105n20
authority 25, 40–4, 51–3, 71–2, 99–103, 141–2

Ball, Stephen 29n1–3, n5, 62, 65n7, 66n20, n22
The behaviour guru (Tom Bennett) 16
behaviour managerial approaches 21, 29, 136
Bennett, Tom 4, 16–17, 20–1, 44, 88, 141
Biesta, Gert x, 62, 104
birth of community 125

canonical texts 74, 75
communication and community 88
compulsion 79
conservative school structures 104, 112–13
controlling 4, 14, 16–17, 80, 143n5
crisis 2–3, 11n2, 43, 126, 140

Dewey, John 8–9, 87–94, 101, 103–4, 144, 146
discipline and punish ix, 7, 47, 54–7, 60–4, 105n14
discipline and punishment 4–5, 7, 49, 67, 80
disciplined interests 68, 79
discipline for epistemological development 130
discipline for ethical development 129, *138*
discipline for personal development 133, *138*
discipline for socialisation 127, 129, *138*

Duckworth, Angela-Lee 11, 127, 134–5, 143n5
Durkheim, Emile 7, 8, 19, 32–3, 39–42, 44–8

education of the emotions 95, 97, 99
egocentricity 9, 96–7, 104, 134
emotional reason 97–8

Foucault, Michel ix, 54, 147
four purposes of discipline 136, 138–9
Freire, Paolo 137

good education 34–5
grit 11, 127, 134–6, 141

Hirst, Paul 8–9, 68–72, 77, 83–5, 132

Kafka, Judith 22–6, 30
Kant, Immanuel 32–40, 42–50, 60–1, 63–6, 87–9
knowledge disciplines 72–3, 85n11

league tables 15, 61, 133
learning to be human 94–5, 97–8, 101–2, 105n15
liberal education 70–3, 80, 84, 93, 101, 131–2
love of knowledge 11, 137

MacIntyre, Alasdair 8, 68–9, 73–7, 84–6, 129, 131
Macmurray, John 9, 87–8, 94–103, 123, 134, 140
maxims 36–8, 46, 47n4
measurement 13–14, 29n5, n6, 61, 75–6
mutual improvement school 59

normalization 66n13

obedience 37, 42–3, 61–2, 69
obstinate 82, 136

Panopticon 57–9
personal discipline 11, 99–101, 109, 127, 134, 136–7
Peters, Richard 5, 68–72, 131–12
positive reinforcement 19–20
power to punish 57–8, 63, 65n9
progressive education 78, 90
punishment in schools 50–1, 53–4, 60, 64, 65n1

restorative approaches to school discipline 9, 27, 107–8, 112
restraining 4, 7–8, 35, 68, 72, 83
rewards and sanctions 10, 16, 20, 108, 114–19, 122–3
Rogers, Bill 4, 11n3, 17–21, 30n19–21, 104n1

school rules 7, 32–3, 40–2, 45–7, 49–53, 63, 69, 72, 117, 129
school to prison pipeline 23, 31n34, 63
self-discipline 11, 43, 72, 127, 134–6, 143n5
Smith, Richard 12n8, 30n23, 43, 80
spectatorship 91
student agency 9, 68, 82, 88, 91, 134
surveillance 55–62, 64–5, 67n28

universities 3, 6, 33, 61, 69, 73–5, 84, 131–2, 143n2

visible 57–8, 60, 85n4, 114, 119

Wilson, John 7–9, 32–3, 42–6, 48n14
Wilson, Pat 68–9, 77–84, 92, 101, 132

zero tolerance 6–8, 22–31, 44–8, 68, 108, 127–8